A Book of Numbers

By the same author

A DIRECTORY OF DISCARDED IDEAS
THE DIRECTORY OF POSSIBILITIES (edited, with Colin Wilson)
THE BOOK OF TIME (edited, with Colin Wilson)
ARIES 1 (edited)
and others

JOHN GRANT

A Book of Numbers

ASHGROVE PRESS, BATH

Published in Great Britain by
ASHGROVE PRESS LTD
26 Gay Street,
Bath, Avon BA1 2PD

ISBN 0 906798 19 1

First published 1982

DEDICATION
To Donald and Margaret Stewart, with much love and affection

Phototypeset in 10/11½ pt Palatino by
Wyvern Typesetting Ltd, Bristol

Printed by Hillman Printers
(Frome) Limited

Contents

Acknowledgements

Many people have contributed information or support to this book – far too many to be mentioned. Here, in no particular order, are those who come to mind: Anna Beadel; Douglas Mounce of "Morning Sou'West"; David Langford; V. I. Maund, of the National Westminster Bank, Newton Abbot (who for the most part has been sympathetic to my impoverished squeals); John Hayes and Edward Driver of British Telecom; Southwood's Typewriters, Exeter; the staff of Exeter Central Library and Exeter Central Reference Library (particular mention must be made of Ruth Chapman, who went far beyond the call of duty in finding for me obscure books); Carole Pengelly and Tony Mulliken of Carole Pengelly Publicity; Robin Campbell of Ashgrove Press for constant encouragement and support, and for putting up with my various neurotic antics; the authors of all the books, articles and radio and TV broadcasts which have started me off along one line or another; the editors of the following journals who have allowed me to air my views: *Common Ground* (Kevin McClure), *Drilkjis* (David Langford and Kevin Smith), *Extro* (Paul Campbell), *The Indexer* (Hazel Bell) and *Knave* (Ian Pemble); and especially Keith Barnett, who has gone out of his way to find information for me, and whose several conversations with me have done much to shape this book.

And, as always, where would I have been without Jane Barnett, whose school peg-number is 26, and Catherine Barnett, whose school-number, a good while ago, was 130? ($4\pi + 0$.)

Introduction

> The proof of self-evident propositions may seem, to the uninitiated, a somewhat frivolous occupation. To this we might reply that it is often by no means self-evident that one obvious proposition follows from another obvious proposition; so that we are really discovering new truths when we prove what is evident by a method which is not evident. But a more interesting retort is, that since people have tried to prove obvious propositions, they have found that many of them are false. Self-evidence is often a mere will-o'-the-wisp, which is sure to lead us astray if we take it as our guide. For instance, nothing is plainer than that a whole always has more terms than a part, or that a number is increased by adding one to it. But these propositions are now known to be usually false. Most numbers are infinite, and if a number is infinite you may add ones to it as long as you like without disturbing it in the least. One of the merits of a proof is that it instils a certain doubt as to the result proved; and when what is obvious can be proved in some cases, but not in others, it becomes possible to suppose that in these cases it is false.
>
> – Bertrand Russell, *Mysticism and Logic*, 1963

This is *not* a book for mathematicians; it is a book of numerically arranged information.

I say this immediately because I am only too conscious of the fact that many of us are frightened of mathematics. That this should be so is, of course, extremely strange; after all, mathematics is, like English, merely a language – and, in so far as it is a language constructed upon strictly logical foundations, it is in many ways an easier language to understand than is English. In fact, the relationship between the two languages is much closer than one might at first think: a piece of prose written according to mathematical syntax is considerably easier to understand than one written without regard to logic at all – an assertion whose proof can be established simply by comparing the works of Edgar Rice Burroughs with those of William Burroughs.

Nevertheless, most of us are frightened of mathematics; I think this is true even of some mathematicians. But almost all of us seem to be fascinated by numbers. For example, in the 1894 edition of that most curious of reference books, Brewer's *Dictionary of Phrase and Fable*, we find the following information under the heading "Bible Statistics":

The number of authors is 50.

About 30 books are mentioned in the Bible, but not included in the canon.

	In the Old Testament	*In the New Testament*	*Total*
Books	30	27	66
Chapters	929	260	1,189
Verses	23,214	7,959	31,173
Words	592,439	181,253	773,692
Letters	2,728,800	838,380	3,567,180

And so on, and on – until we discover such intriguing bits of information as that the word "and" turns up in the Old Testament 35,543 times and in the New 10,684 times! All of this information is, of course, quite useless: it is going to help not one single student in his or her appreciation of the Bible. And yet it is strangely fascinating; and it must have been more than that to the person who sat down and *counted* the number of letters in the Old and New Testaments.

Consider, again, the oddly precise estimate made by the Bishop of Jerusalem in 1273 of the number of fallen angels: 133,306,668 (266,613,336 remained behind in Heaven, we are told). His estimate is in at least one sense reassuring: while you have only about a 1 in 15 chance of having a guardian angel (or, at least, exclusive access to one), these odds are nevertheless only half those against your being the sole object of the attentions of a "guardian devil". Leaving that aside, one can do little other than marvel at the precision of the Bishop of Jerusalem's statement – in the same way that one is staggered by the accuracy of Archbishop James Ussher's calculation from the 1650s that the Earth was created in 4004BC on October 21st at 9.00 in the morning. In both cases, we see people to whom numbers manifestly mean little striving towards a precision that can only be expressed numerically.

We find a similar ascription of odd properties to numbers in everyday life. I know several people who find that, in their mind's eye, the numbers from 1 to 9 are inseparably linked with colours: for example, they might think of 3 as being red. I know myself that some of the single-digit numbers are in my mind linked with letters: if sleepy, I tend to type "R" instead of "3", and so forth. We shall return in a moment to ideas of numbers being at the heart of far more fundamental everyday activities.

A very persistent and apparently worldwide tradition has it that odd numbers are male and even numbers female. The sexual natures of numbers are possibly underconsidered – which is not to say that I am looking forward to the publication of the bestselling *The Curvaceous 6* (although see the discussion of *3's luckiness and/or unluckiness). Similarly, few studies seem to have been carried out on the way in which we visualize numbers, or the images which individual numbers conjure up in us – or even on the way in which we *feel* when we think of a particular number. While engaged upon the research involved in the writing of this book, I spoke at length on several occasions with my brother, who is a practising mathematician (and a good one). More than once, we chatted about possible reasons why numbers like *7 and *13 are supposed to have "mystical powers", and at one point he remarked: "Yes, I can see that in some strange way 13 is emotive – as opposed to a number like 21, which nobody could give two hoots about." Oddly enough, he'd hit upon one of my "favourite" numbers . . . and so we laughed together about my general idiocy. Later, of course, I realized that 21 is the product of mystic 7 and mystic *3, so perhaps I'm not such a fool after all. (But only perhaps.)

In the same way, my brother couldn't understand why I have no difficulty in remembering his birthday each year (it is the 27th of September) but have great difficulty in remembering that of my mother, the 28th of March: each year I have to check to make sure it's the 28th rather than the 26th. Until recently, *I* had no idea why there was this disparity – and I was very annoyed to find, Smirnoff-style, that 27 is one of the "sacred" numbers (presumably because it is mystic 9 times mystic 3). The numbers 26 and 28, on the other hand, are, so far as my *feelings* about them are concerned, indistinguishable.

These are very personal matters – but I'm quite sure that

everybody has similar feelings about certain numbers.† The first hypothesis that springs to mind is that the "favourite" numbers simply *look* nice: are they, then, merely a result of the fact that we count to the base 10? Ask yourself, is the decimal 13 more or less dreadful than the binary equivalent 1101?

Curiously, there *is* an idea that 13 is unlucky because it is 1 more than the "ideal" and "complete" number 12, which in binary notation is 1100; certainly, in a complacent sort of a way, 1100 is a more satisfying number than is its "excess", 1101. One can take this further – with some surprising results. 7, which is possibly the most important number of all to the mystically inclined, is in binary notation the supremely satisfying 111. Another "important" number, 365, produces in binary notation the elegant palindrome 101101101. All seems well – perhaps numbers really *do* have an emotional appeal outside their mere forms – until we look at such numbers as binary 1000 (8), 1111 (15), 11111 (31) and 1111111 (127), whose decimal equivalents are not emotive in the sense that 13 certainly is. Even the great number 666, the Number of the Beast, produces in binary only the rather featureless 1010011010.

It would seem, therefore, that the reasons why certain numbers have gained their reputations are not susceptible to simple analysis: in some cases it may be the number itself, in others it is the way the number features in the decimal system. The mystique of certain numbers is due, I would suggest, less to the numbers themselves and more to the mind of Man.

Before we plunge into a fuller discussion of this matter, let's look back to the words of Bertrand Russell, quoted at the head of this introduction. Russell points to the fact that most numbers are infinity – but leaves the matter there. We can go one further – and, indeed, we have to if the following discussion it to make much sense. First of all, we have to recognize that there are several infinities. The simplest is the one that you never reach if you start counting 1, 2, 3 . . . and so on. But in the very act of

† I suppose that one must, with reluctance, exclude from this discussion the innumerate cultures. Until quite recently, the numbering system of the Tasmanians (a race extinct since about 1876) was the simplest I'd come across: in translation it went roughly "1, 2, lots". However, a few years ago I came across references to the number system used by a certain New Guinea tribe, which outdoes even this. The system goes "1, lots". And only the other day I learnt of a Brazilian tribe which has no words to do with numbers at all except a word meaning "to resemble", which, I suppose, implies a knowledge of the number 2.

counting there is inherent a much greater infinity: it is easy enough to count up to 10, and in so doing you use 10 numbers in a strict order; but think of the number of different ways in which you could *order* 10 things – it is 3,628,800, or $10 \times 9 \times 8 \times 7 \times 6 \times 5 \times 4 \times 3 \times 2 \times 1$. In other words, you could in theory count up to infinity and get a result, but as soon as you start to think about the order in which you could place all those numbers you've thought of you find yourself with another, and far larger, infinity. Here we find ourselves looking, as if by accident, at two different classes of numbers: the cardinal numbers, which tell us *how many* things are in the group under discussion (e.g., 10 numbers) and the ordinal numbers, which tell us the *position* of each of the things in the group (3 has the 3rd position in the numbers counted straightforwardly from 1 to 10).

There are other infinities greater than the one reached by counting from 1 to ∞. Obviously, one can reckon in all the fractions; or one can consider the points on a line – however close together two points are, you can always put another in between them. To return to numbers, as soon as you've counted up to infinity in a positive direction, including all the fractions, you can suddenly double the number of numbers in your count by putting a minus sign in front of each (and remembering zero). But there are numbers such as π which can't be expressed as fractions, so one should bring them into consideration, too. *Then* consider the number of different orders in which you can place the numbers on your list . . .

Discussions of different infinities clearly lead us into the realm of the mathematician; yet I repeat that this is not a book merely for mathematicians. However, I think that if we are to gain some understanding as to *why* numbers have such a curious appeal to the human mind we are going to have to look in a little more detail at the ideas of one of them: Pythagoras.

It is notoriously hard to separate the notions of Pythagoras of Samos (*c*560–*c*480BC) from those of his followers, and this has led to a general linguistic mix-up, with the name "Pythagoras" frequently used when one is in fact talking of the Pythagoreans. I have done my best to avoid this confusion in the following discussion, but I am only too well aware that the fog of the centuries makes such a task impossible.

To the Pythagoreans, the importance of numbers was absolutely fundamental – even in terms of the life of the soul or spirit.

They believed that philosophy – which, for our purposes, we can define as the study of the Universe and all that is in it – was the highroad to the soul's salvation. Since the nature of the Universe is manifestly one of diversity amidst an overall unity, it was clear to the Pythagoreans that the Universe is essentially of a numerical character: numbers were, then, the key to the physical and, more importantly, hence the divine aspects of the cosmos.

Wherever the Pythagoreans looked there was confirmation of this. There was a harmony throughout all parts of the Universe, the most accessible manifestation of which was to be found in music . . . and examination of the "consonant intervals" showed that there are indeed straightforward numerical relationships between them (to look at the simplest example, if you half the length of a vibrating string you get the octave of the original note: the relationship is 1:2). Moreover, these relationships involve only the numbers 1 to 4 – i.e., the ratio 1:2 represents the octave, 4:3 the 4th and 3:2 the 5th – and the numbers 1, 2, 3 and 4 give, when added together, the number 10, which was to the Pythagoreans a sacred number, being as it is the base of the decimal system by which we count. If these numerical relationships were present in music then, necessarily, they were fundamental to the rest of the Universe, too.

From this simple – one is tempted to say simplistic – notion sprang that of the Music of the Spheres, the musical harmony created by the planets in their orbits. Indeed, Pythagoras himself may originally have considered only three spheres, those of the Sun, Moon and stars (both fixed and unfixed stars – i.e., the planets as well as the stars), in order to stay in accord with the discoveries of the relationships of the octave, 4th and 5th. This tends to disguise the essential Pythagorean idea that the relationships between the orbits of the planets could be expressed in simple numerical terms. A long, long time later such notions were to reach the peak of their explication in Bode's Law and Kepler's Laws.

Bode's Law, formulated in the late 18th century, gave good approximations for the distances of the known planets from the Sun. If you take the sequence 0, 3, 6, 12, 24, 48, 96, 192 . . . and add 4 to each term, you get the result 4, 7, 10, 28, 52, 100, 196 and so on. Divide each of the terms of this new sequence by 10 and you get a reasonable set of values for the mean distances from the Sun, expressed in astronomical units (for our purposes, 1 astronomical unit is the distance from the Earth to the Sun), of Mercury, Venus, Earth, Mars, Ceres (the first asteroid to be discovered, in 1801, as a result of the search for a planet in the orbit indicated by the Bode's Law sequence), Jupiter, Saturn and Uranus (discovered in 1781). After Uranus the Law breaks down: the orbits of Neptune and Pluto simply do not obey it. However, there is evidence that something peculiar happened a long time ago in the outer reaches of the Solar System, so perhaps the orbits of those two planets, and any others which may be out there, did obey Bode's Law once upon a time. (A vastly more complicated "resonance" can be calculated to which all the known planets conform.)

Kepler's Laws, published in 1609, stated: (1) that planetary orbits about the Sun are elliptical; (2) that the line "joining" a planet to the Sun sweeps out equal areas of space in a given time (i.e., that the planet moves faster when closer to the Sun than it does when further away); and (3), most important from the Pythagorean viewpoint, that the square of the time a planet takes to orbit the Sun is proportional to the cube of its mean distance from the Sun.

These 4 laws were, of course, empirical: they were derived from observation of the reality, and in themselves explained nothing. However, there is a difference worth noting: Bode's Law retains its empirical status (and may be no more than a coincidence – although it seems a jolly odd coincidence to me), while the 3 laws of Kepler proved to be confirmable by mathematical physics – a task performed, in short order, by Isaac Newton. In other words, Kepler's Laws really do reflect a fundamental truth about the behaviour of bodies in the Universe – in the case of his 3rd law, this is a matter for celebration amongst any latter-day Pythagoreans who care to think about it.

But let us return to the numbers 1 to 4. These turn up again as fundamental to the Universe if we consider the dimensions. 1 point is simply a point, 2 points define a line, 3 points define a triangle (the "minimum" plane figure) and 4 points define a tetrahedron (a pyramid with a triangular base, the "minimum" 3-dimensional figure). Since we find it difficult to think of a "minimum" 4-dimensional figure defined by 5 points, clearly the numbers 1 to 4 were in some way magic.

There were other peculiar numbers, the primes. These are numbers which can't be divided by whole numbers; 7 is probably the one which is most familiar to us. There are rather a lot of prime numbers, some of them very large. The largest which I know of is the one discovered in 1979 which can be expressed in the form $2^{44,497}-1$; this number is of the order of $8.5 \times 10^{13,394}$, and would fill six or seven pages if I wrote it out in full. Enthusiasts who seek other prime numbers are referred to Appendix III, page 240.

The Pythagoreans were perfectly satisfied with all this but ran into problems when they came to examine some of the numbers which simply did not obey the rules. For example, there is the number which expresses the relation between the diameter of a circle and its circumference: π. (This number is the only non-integral number given a separate entry in this book.) There is no way in which π can be expressed as a fraction – in other words, as a ratio between two integers. And closer to the Pythagorean home, there were others. To take a very simple example, if, by the famous Pythagorean theorem the square on the hypotenuse of a right-angled triangle is equal to the sum of the squares on the other two sides, then there is the problem of the isoceles right-angled triangle, the one formed by drawing the diagonal of a square. If the "other two sides" are by definition of length 1, then the hypotenuse is by definition of length $\sqrt{(1^2 + 1^2)} = \sqrt{2}$, and $\sqrt{2}$ cannot be expressed as a fraction – it's about 1.414213562. (The argument is unaffected if one uses a different scale: if the sides of the triangle are 6 units long one has the situation that the length of the hypotenuse is $\sqrt{(6^2 + 6^2)} = \sqrt{(2 \times 6^2)} = 6\sqrt{2}$.)

Of course, to the Pythagoreans it was a major shock to find that such a triangle did not have sides whose lengths could be expressed in terms of the ratios between whole numbers. How could they cope with numbers like $\sqrt{2}$ and π? In order to dodge the issue they developed the idea of "fluxions". This notion implies that the difference between two numbers can be infinitely subdivided so that, *eventually*, after a colossal number of subdivisions, numbers like π and $\sqrt{2}$ could indeed be expressed as a ratio between two integers. While this theory was misleading (the irrational numbers simply cannot be expressed as fractions), the notion of infinite subdivision, of continuous change, foreshadowed in a very woolly way the calculus developed independently in the 1680s by Leibniz and Newton (Newton actually called calculus "fluxions").

Leaving such problems aside, the Pythagoreans' main thrust – that the essence of the Universe could be expressed in terms of whole numbers – was further bolstered by the fact that there exist right-angled triangles with integral sides (that is, triangles in which the ratios between the lengths of the sides can be expressed easily in terms of whole numbers). For example, there's the triangle whose sides are 3, 4 and 5 units long; others are the 5, 12, 13 triangle and the 7, 24, 25 triangle. The relationships between these numbers can be set out as follows:

$$3^2 + 4^2 = 5^2,$$
$$5^2 + 12^2 = 13^2,$$
$$7^2 + 24^2 = 25^2.$$

These relationships can be expressed as, in general, $a^2 + b^2 = c^2$. And in this equation we find yet another numerical puzzle – one which probably did not occur to the Pythagoreans. If there are values of a, b and c such that $a^2 + b^2 = c^2$, then surely one might reasonably expect that there ought to be values of a, b and c such that $a^n + b^n = c^n$. Unfortunately, this just isn't the case. One of the most famous issues in mathematics is that of "Fermat's Last Theorem". Pierre de Fermat (1601–1665) was one of the finest mathematicians of all time, and thus it was particularly infuriating for later researchers to discover, scribbled in Fermat's hand in the margin of a maths textbook, the following words: "Where n is a number larger than 2, there are no whole numbers a, b, c such that $a^n + b^n = c^n$, and of this I have found a most marvellous proof, but this margin is too small to contain it." (See *100.) Ever since, mathematicians have been trying to find the "most marvellous proof", but without success.

There were other types of numbers which interested the Pythagoreans. For example, there were the so-called "amicable numbers", pairs of numbers in which the factors of one of the pair add up to the other – a concept that may seem difficult until we take the example of 220 and 284. The factors (whole-number divisors) of 220 are 1, 2, 4, 5, 10, 11, 20, 22, 44, 55 and 110, and when these are added up they come to 284; similarly, the factors of 284 (1, 2, 4, 71, 142) when added together equal 220.

Taking the matter of factors a stage further, there is the idea of numbers being abundant or deficient: an "abundant" number is one whose factors add up to a greater number than the original (for example, 18 is abundant because $1 + 2 + 3 + 6 + 9 = 21$) and a "deficient" number is one whose factors add up to less than the original (15 is deficient because $1 + 3 + 5 = 9$). Naturally, the Pythagoreans were led to speculate about numbers whose factors, when added up, *equalled* the original number – and sure enough they found some of these "perfect numbers".

Perfect numbers are rare creatures – to date only 26 have been discovered. The Pythagoreans almost certainly knew of the first four – 6, 28, 496, 8128 – but the 26th was certainly beyond their ken; this number, $(2^{44497}-1) \times 2^{44496}$, was discovered only in 1979. (See *26 for further discussion.) The Pythagoreans considered in addition a furthur "perfect number", of a different type from the others: 10. 10 was out on its own (I'm tempted to say that it was out on a limb) because it was the basis of our decimal system of counting and because, as we've already seen, it was the sum of 1, 2, 3 and 4.

They were probably aware, too, of the "golden ratio", 1:0.618 (approximately). Artists have known since the dawn of time that this ratio is a particularly satisfying one to the eye, but without realizing why. The "why" is still a problem: one can explain the occurrence of the ratio, but one cannot explain why its graphic representation induces such a feeling of content in the spectator. The ratio turns up if you divide a straight line, AB, in such a way that the relations between the lengths AB, AC (C being the point at which you've cut the line) and BC obey the very simple rule that

$$\frac{AC}{AB} = \frac{BC}{AC}.$$

Both fractions work out at about 0.6180339885. The "golden rectangle" which artists discovered by experiment is one in which the shorter sides are of length 1 and the longer sides of length 1.6180339885.

That the golden ratio has a meaning in numbers as well as in geometry emerged in the work of Leonardo Fibonacci (or Leonardo of Pisa; *c*1180–*c*1240); he it was who discovered the famous "Fibonacci Sequence", which has first terms of 0 and 1 and, thereafter, terms which are devised by adding the previous two terms together. This all sounds complicated until you look at the first few terms of the sequence: 0, 1, 1, 2, 3, 5, 8, 13, 21, 34, 55, 89, 144 . . . The sequence turns up in nature; but what is especially intriguing about it is that the relationship between succeeding terms becomes progressively closer to the golden ratio. For example, 144 divided by 89 is about 1.6179775, and 233 (the next term) divided by 144 gives 1.6180556 or so. That a simply derived sequence should produce something aesthetically satisfying supports the Pythagorean contention that numbers lie at the root of all!

(The "golden ratio" should not be confused with the "golden numbers" of the Christian Church. The golden number of a particular year is the number which it has in the Metonic lunar cycle of 19 years (see *235 for explanation). The golden number of the year n is easily enough found: it is the remainder left over in the division $(n + 1)/19$. Thus the golden number of the year 1982 can be found from (1982 + 1)/19, which equals 104 remainder 7; in other words, 1982's golden number is 7.)

While there is no reason to believe that the Pythagoreans discovered the Fibonacci Sequence, they certainly did do some early work on sequences – although it is quite likely that they had little or no understanding of the tiger they'd caught by the tail. They were interested in what one might call "shape numbers", such as the "triangular numbers" 1, 3, 6, 10, 15 and so on. If this sequence seems obscure, just look at this simple diagram:

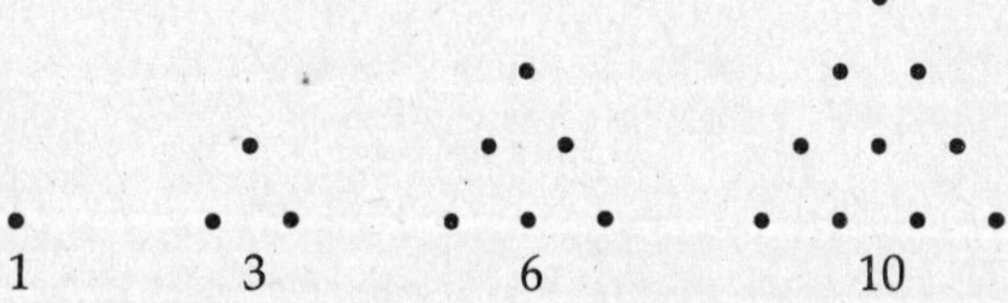

An obvious development from here was to move into three dimensions, to the "pyramidal numbers" with a triangular base. By considering piles of triangles, one gets the sequence 1, 4 (= 3 + 1), 10 (= 6 + 3 + 1), 20 (= 10 + 6 + 3 + 1), and so forth.

Returning to plane figures, the Pythagoreans had the "square numbers" 1, 4, 9, 16, 25 . . . and even such delights as the "pentagonal numbers" 1, 5, 12, 22, 35 . . . ; the "square numbers" were of especial importance to them because of the Pythagorean theorem, that the square on the hypotenuse of a right-angled triangle is equal to the sum of the squares on the other two sides. That the numbers were called "square numbers" is easily explained – just look at another simple diagram:

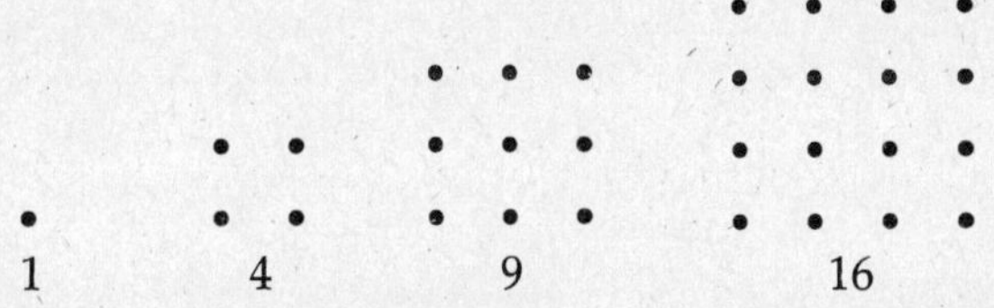

To the modern student of numbers, all of these are interesting sequences, some of them of fundamental importance, but it seems that the Pythagoreans regarded them in a rather different way. In a sense, while they were as an article of faith fundamental to the nature of the Universe, they were at the same time merely curios, deriving any importance which they might have from their magical/mystical properties rather than from their mathematical significance. This is a prominent example of the knack which the ancient Greeks had of missing the point of their discoveries – like Hero of Alexandria (*fl.* AD62), who invented the steam engine but did nothing more with it than build executive toys.

There were other, more physical, ways in which the integral numbers could be shown to be basic to the state of Nature: one was to be found in the crystals. Naturally occurring crystals could be (and still can be!) found in the forms of the regular solids. Most of us are familiar with the cubic crystals of sodium chloride (common salt), but other more complicated examples exist – e.g., the dodecahedronal (with 12 pentagonal faces) crystals of iron pyrites. Indeed, modern crystallographical classification systems rely for their working upon the resolution of all naturally occurring crystal shapes into combinations of up to 7 fairly simple solid shapes. And, of course, the human body itself displays examples of the smaller integers: we have 1 nose, 2 eyes, 3 joints to each finger, 4 limbs, 5 digits to each hand, 6 orifices in the head (counting the nose as 1), and so on.

From the foregoing discussion it might seem as if the Pythagoreans viewed the numbers merely as tags – important tags, but tags nonetheless. However, their vision of the rôle of numbers went much further than that. We've noticed that they saw numbers as fundamental – boil the whole cosmos down and you'd be left with a pile of numbers – but also they believed in what one might think of as nonquantitative, or ordinal, numbers: it was not merely the character of a thing which could be expressed in numerical terms, it was also the thing's *form* (or, to use a word that makes more sense in modern English, its essence). This idea of *form* is akin to the alchemists' "spirit" of later centuries: physical objects are made up of mixtures of matter and "spirit", with God being the purely spiritual stuff; matter without "spirit" would have no form (rather like neutron soup, the stuff of which neutron stars, pulsars, are made). Thus, if one could establish the underlying numerical *form* of someone or something, one could work out the details of all the rest of the whole – in much the same way that a chemist can work out the properties of a compound just by knowing its formula. With their customary zeal the Pythagoreans took this notion to ridiculous extremes: not only did they attempt to establish the numerical essences of each other, they tried to do the same for their pets and their horses (perhaps some racehorse punters still do). This was, of course, to be the basis for the modern pseudoscience of numerology.

We've mentioned in passing that some numbers are sacred: 3, 7, 9, 10, 12, 13, 27, 40, 63, 70, 100, 666 and 888 are examples. The reasons for their being sacred (by which term I do not mean holy) are not always easy to establish. 7 seems to be a mystic number in all cultures, even those which do not know of the 7 classical planets and do not count 7 days to the week. The sacred nature of 3 dates back long before the idea of the Trinity.

This power of numbers in the essentially innumerate mind can be demonstrated by the tale of an 84-year-old Neapolitan butcher who in 1972 "died", only to come back to life again a few hours later. The news of this astonishing "resurrection" spread swiftly – and clearly the numbers involved in the incident had to have something to do with the ones which were going to be lucky in the state lottery! Betting was, therefore, heavy on 84, since the butcher was 84 years old, and even more so on that number's "reflection", 48, which in lottery lore traditionally stands for death; other popular numbers were 49, representing laughter, 90, fear, and even – in what seems to me a rather desperate attempt to drag *any* numbers into one's superstition – 4, for the number of candles arranged around the butcher's "deathbed".

Of course, the superstitions involved here are much the same as those surrounding the idea of "lucky numbers", promoted so zealously in the "Your Stars" sections of some of our murkier newspapers. Similar superstitions play their part in the "numbers racket", a gambling game which is illegal in the US but nevertheless widely practised there. The principle of the game is that the punter selects a number between 1 and 999, and bets that that number will "come up". The winning number is selected by use of some indicator independent of the promoters (so that, in theory at least, there can be no cheating), such as a bank's financial statement published on a given day. Since the winning punter is usually paid 540 times his stake, with the "runner" receiving a further 60 times the stake, and since the odds against winning are a healthy 998 to 1, it can be clearly seen that there are substantial profits to be made out of running a numbers game. Since all numbers are equally likely to "come up", the wise punter consistently backs his "lucky number"; should he or she make a killing, then this is proof that "lucky numbers" really *are* lucky.

Numeracy and intelligence do not seem necessarily to go hand in hand: even people who are otherwise perfectly intelligent have superstitions – if that is the right word – about numbers, usually large numbers. The tale is told of an Iowan schoolboy whose teacher said to him that it was impossible to count up to 1,000,000 (a feat which, as a child, I several times performed for myself – just for the sheer pointless hell of it). The boy's mother, Mrs Marva Drew, was so justifiably furious about the teacher's idiocy that she not only counted up to 1,000,000, she typed all the numbers out to provide tangible proof of the feasibility of the exercise. She may not have initially realized quite what she was letting herself in for, of course: the resulting document required 5 reams of typing paper!

Such superstitions are taken to the *n*th degree in numerology. It's worth pointing out, to start with, that there are really two "schools" of numerology which, while in many cases they overlap, are really quite distinct. The lesser but older of these two is the "Hebrew school" which relies upon the fact that in Hebrew the symbols for the consonants are used to represent numbers; thus, by the judicious insertion of appropriate vowels, one can convert a number into a word and, conversely, a word can be given a numerical value. You can therefore quite simply convert the letters of your name into a number – and away you go.

The other school comprises almost all of the numerological systems in popular use today, all of which have to cope with the fact that one cannot convert the letters of the English language directly into numbers: one has to establish a convention for the conversion. In the course of compiling this book I have made use of several numerological texts (although, as you will have noticed while riffling through the pages, this is no more a book of numerology than it is one of mathematics); the various systems differ, not only in terms of the meaning attached to each number but also in terms of the technique of converting a name to a number (i.e., the convention used). For the sake of simplicity I've selected a single system, that outlined in Austin Coates' *Numerology* (1974), for discussion here.

Think of the numbers from 1 to 9 laid out in the following grid:

3	6	9
2	5	8
1	4	7

We find (says Coates) that the first horizontal row gives the numbers of the head, the second those of the heart, and the third those of the stomach. Moreover, the first vertical column contains the numbers associated with thought and the Aristotelian element air, the second those associated with activity and earth, and the third those to do with power and water (those numbers which the schoolboy in me is tempted to call the "hydroelectric numbers"). Returning to the horizontal rows, we can interpret them also in terms of a country scene, with the sunny sky at the top, the crops in the middle, and the soil at the bottom.

Thus each of the nine numbers has four ideas associated with it, two because of its horizontal position and a further two as a result of its vertical position. For example, to quote Coates: "In SEVEN the earthy stomach lies conjoined with watery power, a situation liable to end in mud. This is the number of agriculture: human power applied to the soil." Personally, I find this and most other numerological qualities rather opaque; I'll settle for the mud.

Converting the letters of one's name to numbers is child's play – here's the necessary chart:

1	*2*	*3*	*4*	*5*	*6*	*7*	*8*	*9*
A	B	C	D	E	F	G	H	I
J	K	L	M	N	O	P	Q	R
S	T	U	V	W	X	Y	Z	

(Other systems have different charts.) So the name "John Grant" can be expressed numerologically as 1, 6, 8, 5, 7, 9, 1, 5, 2; adding these digits together, we get the result 44; adding 4 + 4 we get the digit 8, which is my "name number". To look at this in most simplistic terms, my name number, 8, implies that I should be a sober, steady fellow in something productive but plodding like banking, shipping or insurance – not writing books at all.†

Naturally, the system is quite a lot more complicated than this. Although the name "John Grant", taken all together, has a value of 8, it is important to note also that "John" has the value 2 and "Grant" the value 6; the numbers 2 and 6 "qualify" my full name number, 8 – as does the result of adding up my date of birth, 22nd November 1949. 2 + 2 = 4, 1 + 1 = 2 (November being the 11th month, you see), and 1 + 9 + 4 + 9 = 23 = 2 + 3 = 5 . . . so the whole of my birth-date number is 4 + 2 + 5 = 11 = 1 + 1 = 2. Add this 2 to my name number, 8, and you get a "balancer" (Coates' term) of 10 = 1 + 0 = 1.

† To be fair, "John Grant" is actually a *nom de plume*: my real name gives a value of 4, which implies that I should work only within a strictly defined sphere, churning over the same material again and again. Since this has been an extremely difficult book to write – this is my third draft of the Introduction – I am beginning to be unnerved by the chilling accuracy of this evaluation of myself.

So, all told, I'm a named 8 and a born 2, with a balancer of 1. The two components of my name testify to my qualities of 2-ishness and 6-ishness, while the three components of my birth-date demonstrate the 4-ish, 2-ish and 5-ish elements of my nature. There are a lot of 2s about, and 2 is the number of imagination, emotion and desire – indicating, I suppose, that I'm imaginative, emotional and (I like to tell myself) desirable. However, these qualities are tempered, courtesy of my other numbers, by inventiveness, unproductive ploddishness, organizational industry (there must be some mistake here), commercial and entrepreneurial flair, and productive ploddishness. (To be fair, Coates' system goes far further than this, but to explain it in full would take up several pages.)

These qualities might seem, taken all together, to comprise a fairly complete character sketch – and, indeed, I recognize something of myself in it. But wait a moment! Don't *you* recognize something of *your*self in it – and you, and you?

And this is the difficulty shared by all numerological systems, even those as sophisticated and plausible as Coates' one: in the final reckoning, the results of your calculations are almost always so woolly, in dramatic contrast to the precision of the calculated number itself, that they could be applied to *anyone*. Even if all of a person's essential numbers come out to be, for example, 7, the picture is not much better: this tremendously strongly 7-ish person should really be a farmer, but if he or she happens instead to be by vocation a graphic designer, and a good one at that, there is absolutely nothing the numerologist can do about it except blush and start making excuses. ("Er, I haven't counted in your telephone number," can be a useful one, depending on circumstances.)

It is tempting, then, to dismiss numerology and the whole idea of numbers having "properties" or "powers" as just so much nonsense (the Pythagoreans did not have a monopoly among the Greek philosophers for producing nonsense). However, it's not quite as easy as this. While compiling this book I discovered to my rationalist horror that certain numbers *did* seem to attract certain types of information. For example, the sacred number *27 seems to have some very bizarre connotations. (And can it be a coincidence that when I first typed the preceding sentence the word "sacred" came out as "scared"? Probably.) I'm not trying to make a case for numbers being in some way paranormal – any statistician will point out that it would be rather surprising if there were *no* examples of specific types of information grouping themselves around certain numbers – but numbers, some numbers, *do* have a certain power simply as a result of the fact that we *think* they have.

The Pythagoreans thought that the cosmos was fundamentally of a numerical nature, and they found evidence in favour of their belief; the devotee of numerology looks at a hazy character-description and recognizes therein an uncannily accurate portrayal of him- or herself; the average person on the street has "favourite" numbers, which perhaps he or she regards as "lucky" numbers, and certainly finds it easier to remember some numbers than others. The Pythagorean legacy to us was, therefore, not the "truth" that numbers lie at the heart of everything, but the *belief* in that truth – a belief which has become so integral a part of our cultural heritage (if you'll excuse the pun) that we all subscribe to it, even if we've never consciously thought about it.

Which leads me, in a roundabout way, to this book. In most of our established reference sources the numbers are neglected: I have checked every encyclopaedia in the nearest reference library and not one carries entries on numbers (the odd one has an entry on 7 or 666). If you think about it, this neglect is astonishing – it's on the same scale as omitting mention of sex. Even books which one might at first sight conceive to be packed with numerical information (e.g., the *Guinness Book of Records*) are concerned with the numbers almost exclusively as quantities only – so and so lost 148 *pounds* in 12 *months*, and so forth.

In this book I've tried to steer clear of such unit-oriented information (please forgive the ghastly compound adjective) because it is not absolute: there is nothing particularly interesting about a ship (say) being 328 feet long, because one could equally well talk about it being 109⅓ yards long or, more importantly, 100 metres long (students of coincidence, or something, will be intrigued to discover that "magic" 328, for which this conversion works so excitingly well, was my school number, many years ago). Nevertheless, I confess that I have included the odd bit of such information, especially if it is particularly fascinating and/or if the unit involved is a natural one, such as the day or the year.

This book is divided into two parts, covering on the one hand the integral numbers from 0 to 100, about which there is generally quite a lot of information, and on the other the whole numbers from 101 to 500 – a finishing point which is, of course, arbitrary.

(Appendix I deals with 666 and ∞.) While not every integer in the range 0 to 500 is covered, this should be regarded as a matter of selection rather than as one of omission: it would be stupidity to lose some of the interesting information about, say, *7 for the sake of inserting a few boring lines vaguely linked to the number 467. That said, for a while the apparent "gaps" nevertheless nagged away at the back of my mind – by nature I'm a completist – until it struck me that an alphabetical dictionary or encyclopaedia does not contain entries under every possible combination of letters from aaaaaa to zzzzzz – and a good thing too, because if only the six-letter keywords of such a compilation were *listed* they would fill about 120,000 pages like this one. I was reassured, too, by the fact that in many specialist or shorter alphabetical works of reference there are no keywords beginning with "Q" or "X".

My criteria for inclusion of information are not easily explained. Some of the material is very firmly tied to its numerical content (some is concerned with the numbers themselves; 467, mentioned as boring, is in fact a prime number), and I've tried to include such information at least in brief form, even if it is otherwise not of especial interest. But in most cases information is included simply because it is fascinating, whether or not its numerical nature is the most important thing about it. This is not to say that I've desperately dragged in interesting material which happens to have some tenuous connection with a number; similarly, it doesn't mean that I've chucked in lots of dull stuff that happens to be numerically oriented. I have, in short, tried to strike a balance; I believe that most readers will find most of the information in this book in some way fascinating . . . if for no other reason than that numbers are fascinating in themselves.

The compilation of this book has involved casting a very wide net; not only the more obvious reference sources but also some of the extremely unorthodox ones have had to be sieved. Wherever possible, I've checked information in divers sources before including it, but I am nevertheless conscious of the fundamental Law of nonfiction writing: there are some mistakes lurking in there, somewhere. (A pseudo-corollary of the Law runs roughly thus: "And those mistakes will all lie within the specialist field of knowledge of the reviewer.") In this light, if you spot some howler or other, I'd be grateful if you could write and tell me about it so that I can make a deft alteration in time for the next reprint.

That said, I take heart from the fact that in researching this book I've found so many howlers in other reference works that I could hardly begin to list them. In one I came across the golden suggestion that, since Emma Hamilton in her youth worked for a while as an attendant to London's "Electric Bed", Nelson was probably the first admiral to have a working knowledge of electrics. (Presumably Emma is supposed to have murmured Ohm's Law into his passionate ear.) Now, it can hardly be expected to be common knowledge that the "Electric Bed" was one of the greatest triumphs of quack technology – its "electricity" had roughly the same status as Mesmer's animal "magnetism" – but it is possible to note that Emma Hamilton's liaison with Nelson began in the 1790s while the realization that there is such a thing as an electric current didn't happen until about 1800, with Volta's invention of the voltaic pile (known to us as the battery). I am only too conscious of the fact that there may lie, within these pages, similar howlers; once again can I ask you to tell me about them.

As I have already mentioned, this has been a difficult book to research and write – if for no other reason than that there have been no other similar compilations. Nevertheless, it has been tremendous fun, and I for one have learnt a lot. I hope that you, too, as you browse through this book, find plenty to divert, entertain and delight you. If so, thank *numbers*, the unacknowledged basis – *pace* the Pythagoreans – of so much of our thinking.

PART ONE

Zero to One Hundred

In which we learn how many characters in *No Orchids For Miss Blandish* get "bumped off", how many whiskies Dylan Thomas claimed to have drunk the night before his last coma, how many times the number 7 appears in *The Book of Revelation*, the length of the shortest reign of any pope, some of the theories about the unluckiness of 13, the number of lives lost in the Great Fire of London, the number of grains of sand in the Universe (as calculated by Aristotle), and much else besides.

Preamble

In this first part of *A Book of Numbers*, each of the whole numbers between 0 and 100 is treated in a certain amount of detail. In addition I have included a short piece on one number which is not merely a fraction but actually irrational. That number is π, the ratio between the circumference of a circle and its diameter. I've made this exception not just because π is as familiar a number to that mythical being, "every schoolchild", as are many of the integers but also because of its uniqueness and importance.

Readers of a mathematical bent will be quick to point out that I could have included other important numbers as well. The obvious example is the exponential, or Euler's number, *e* (2.71828183 . . .), the base of the natural logarithms. Granted, this is an important number to the scientists, but for some inexplicable reason it has failed to catch hold of the public imagination . . . and so I've omitted it.

One of the people mentioned on the Acknowledgements page

asked me if I planned to include another of the fundamentally important numbers in mathematics, the square root of -1, the imaginary number *i*. I said I did not. When he protested loudly about the omission I pointed out that it was difficult to know where in the order to put *i* . . .

For reasons which are quite beyond my control, there might at first seem to be a certain bias towards religion in this first part of the book. This is because all religions and mythologies contain considerable quantities of covert or overt numerological information and symbolism. In terms of size, the Christian religion is the most important religion in our Western culture (with the possible exception of atheism, another doctrine born of faith) and is certainly the most easily accessible to a product of that culture, such as myself. I feel certain that, had I written this book a few thousand years ago in Greece, or today in Japan, the balance between religious/mythological and secular/temporal information would have been much the same – although the information itself would, of course, have been rather different.

Most of the information in this section derives from the cardinal numbers of things – Heinz's 57 varieties, for example, or Luther's 95 Theses – but I have paid some attention to the ordinal numbers, too. This is why you'll find that I've followed through some of the lists of numbered things or individuals – in particular the popes, the elements, and the presidents of the USA.

Enough of this. Let me just say that I hope you enjoy sailing at the whim of the winds across this sea of serendipitously acquired data. *Bon voyage!*

Zero

The idea that 0 is a number in its own right is a startlingly recent one. Certainly 0 had been "invented" in the East by AD600 (although not *long* before this date); curiously, the discovery of this concept came at least 3 centuries later than the bringing into use there of the negative numbers.

In the backward West the first rigorous examination of 0 as a number – with properties at least analogous to those of all the other numbers – seems to have been by the great Italian mathematician Leonardo Fibonacci (*c*1180–*c*1240). His work was probably a direct result of the introduction into the West of the work of an Arab mathematician called Al-Khwārizmi (*c*780–*c*850) who had, in his turn, borrowed something from the East. This "something" was the Hindu system of numerals, which included 0, which he naturally preferred to the cumbersome occidental systems (have you ever thought about trying to do long-division using Roman numerals?). Slowly the West came to adopt the so-called "Arabic" numerals, and under their cover 0 crept into Western mathematics.

It seems likely that the symbol, 0 became as it is today – an upright ellipse or a circle – for reasons very closely related to the practice whereby I, while proofreading this book, circled any full stop which I wished the typesetter to insert. It seems that, for a while at least, the symbol for 0 – the "blank" entry in the columns of units, tens, hundreds, thousands, etc. – was a dot; in this way, for example, 101 would be shown "1.1". Because a reader could easily fail to notice the dot, and probably also because it was quite easy fraudulently to remove the dot (handy for reducing debts), it became the custom to encircle it. In this way, the guiding circle came itself to be the symbol for 0.

Here is a certainly incomplete list of synonyms for 0, to which you are invited to add: aught, cipher, damn all (and other less printable variations), duck, duck egg, goose egg, love, naught, nihil, nihility, nil, nix, nothing, nothing at all, nothingness, nothing on Earth, nothing under the Sun, nothing whatsoever, nought, nowt, null, nullity, ought, owt, scratch, void, zero, zilch.

Some of these words are sporting terms, of course. For example, to an outsider the cricketing term "a duck", meaning a zero score, may seem obscure in origin. That origin supplies us with an interesting example of punnery at work. The fact that 0 is clearly egg-shaped gave rise to the public-school pun that a youngster who won his 1st school prize was "breaking his duck's egg". His *dux* egg – hilarious.

The expression made its way onto the playing fields of Eton and elsewhere, with a batsman scoring his 1st run of the innings being described as "breaking his duck's egg". This became "breaking his duck"; and eventually, by back-derivation, the word "duck" came to mean 0.

The word "love" in tennis and other games seems to have had its origins in gambling. You could be playing, say, cards either in order to gamble or simply because you enjoyed the game – that is, for money or for love. Thus "love" came to mean "zero stakes" or "nothing", and it was in the sense of "nothing" that it found its way into tennis.

One

According to a prediction of the numerologist Vincent Lopez, World War II should have been over within 1 day.

Charles Dickens made exactly 1 submission to *Punch,* the famous satirical magazine founded in 1841. The piece was promptly rejected, and so Dickens never bothered with the magazine again.

The biblical books *Obadiah, Philemon, 2 John, 3 John* (see *294) and *Jude* each have only 1 chapter.

The element of atomic number 1 is hydrogen (H), a colourless, odourless gas which makes up about 92.7% of the Universe. Almost all the other elements of our bodies and surroundings were formed from hydrogen by nuclear fusion in the great pressure-cookers of the stars (it is possible that some elementary nuclei were created in the even more severe conditions shortly after the Big Bang). These new elements were released to the rest of the Universe when the stars exploded as supernovae.

It's rather alarming to think that much of this book, and of your fingers holding it, started off in the heart of an exploding star.

Since Spring 1982 the island of Sark in the English Channel has had a police force numbering a grand total of 1. Before that, it made do with a couple of part-time reserves and an officer "borrowed" from nearby Guernsey for 5 months of the year.

The 1st bishop of Rome, and therefore by definition the 1st pope, was of course Simon Peter, commissioned by Christ himself to be "shepherd of the flock". As might be expected, little is known of Peter, and almost nothing about his pontificate, beyond the perhaps not entirely reliable accounts given in the New Testament. He died in about AD64 or AD67, and there is a strong if unsubstantiated tradition that he suffered martyrdom in Rome, under the persecution of Nero.

The Eleatic 1 is the proposition put forward by Parmenides of Elea (*fl*500BC) that Being is 1, unique; that it is indivisible and continuous; and that it is all that there ever has been, is, or ever shall be. By "Being" Parmenides was referring to the material substance of the Universe; and it followed as a consequence of his proposition that, since there could be no such thing as "Not-Being" (i.e., empty space), motion and change of any kind were impossible, and must be merely illusions of the senses.

Surprisingly, for several hundred years this proposition was taken seriously.

A python can survive quite happily on only 1 good meal per annum.

In a 1973 election to the Machars Community Council in Aberdeen, Scotland, only 1 vote was cast. Its recipient, the new Councillor George Kindness, confessed that he hadn't in fact voted for himself: he'd thought voting would be a waste of time.

And in the January 1961 general election in Zanzibar the Afro-Shirazi party won power by 1 seat; moreover, it had won the Chake-Chake constituency by only 1 vote.

On 7th December, 1787, Delaware ratified the US Constitution, thereby becoming the 1st state of the Union.

In numerological terms, 1 is the number of the Creator and Prime Mover, and hence of the unity of all things (even the Trinity, while it shows that 1 has a three-ness, shows also that *3 can be unity). Again because of its equation with God, 1 can be taken to symbolize such attributes as creativity, industry and drive. Perhaps less respectably, there is a tradition that 1 is a male symbol because of its overt phallicity; as you might expect, it has to be united with the female number 2 in order to give either 3 or 12, both of which are often regarded as numbers of completeness and perfection.

The 1st president of the United States was George Washington (1732–1799), who held office from 30th April, 1789, until 3rd March, 1797. Although he was elected unopposed, his presidency was not unmarred by controversy – e.g., the Whiskey Rebellion of 1794, concerning the imposition of federal excise tax on whiskey (the rebels, naturally enough, were mainly Scots and Irish settlers) – especially during his 2nd term of office. Nonetheless, he was offered a 3rd term, which he refused.

The cherry-tree story is apocryphal, a later addition to the Washingtonian mythology.

Sir Winston Churchill wrote, oddly enough for one otherwise so prolific, only 1 novel: *Savrola*, published in 1900. This political tale was not a total financial flop, although it was generally agreed to be a poor, shoddy and amateurish book. Churchill decided to turn his talents to war reporting . . . and eventually to history and politics.

Two

Only 2 English novels feature in the *Index Librorum Prohibitorum* – the Vatican's list of banned books. These 2 dangerously pornographic works are Richardson's *Pamela* (1740–41) and Sterne's *A Sentimental Journey Through France and Italy* (1768).

Hysterectomy, the surgical excision of the uterus, is the 2nd most frequently performed operation in the USA. In 1977, 705,000 hysterectomies were performed. According to a roughly contemporaneous survey, 30% – i.e., some 200,000 – of these operations were quite unnecessary.

However, all is not gloom on the hysterectomy front. Mrs Len Trott, who underwent the operation in March, 1978, was 18 months later able to give birth to a baby boy, Martin.

The 2nd Pope is thought to have been called Linus and to have held office from perhaps AD67 to perhaps AD79. Nothing is known about him except his name – although it was at one time believed that a piece of his tombstone had been discovered during the 17th century at St Peter's. If he existed, he may have been the Linus mentioned at the end of Paul's 2nd letter to Timothy: "Greetings to you from Eubulus, Pudens, Linus, Claudia and all the brothers."

The 2nd president of the United States was John Adams (1735–1826), earlier Vice-President under Washington. He defeated Jefferson to take office on 4th March, 1797; he held it for only 1 term, until 3rd March, 1801. A deeply unpopular president at the time – although, with hindsight, we can see that he saved his country from an expensive war with France – he was the 1st to live in the White House.

At his birth, in 1638, Louis XIV – the Sun King – was distinguished by the fact that he already had 2 teeth.

The element of atomic number 2 is helium (He), one of the inert gases; it makes up about 7.2% of all the matter in the Universe. (Since a further 92.7% is made up of hydrogen, one can calculate how much of the Universe is made up of all the other elements put together.) Within 2.8 C° of the Absolute Zero of cold, liquid helium-4 displays the interesting property of superfluidity: it flows without any trace of friction at all. It thus has a nasty habit of flowing up and over the sides of any container into which it's put – like the last pint of beer before closing-time.

There is a tradition that the number 2 symbolizes evil because, in the *Genesis* account of the Creation, only on the 2nd day is there a failure to mention that God saw that his work was good. The work done on that day was the making of the vault to separate the waters above from the waters below – the making of the vault called Heaven.

Uniting this with the ubiquitous tradition that 2 is a female number may explain why, later in the Bible, the figure of the woman is widely used as a synonym for corruption and evil. In other words, some of the apparently appalling remarks made about women may contain nothing of offence to the female sex at all, but be merely numerological. It would be startling to find that our culture's repression of women is based on nothing more than a numerological misunderstanding.

On the 12th of December, 1787, Pennsylvania ratified the US Constitution, thereby becoming the 2nd state of the Union.

The Book of Revelation, like *Genesis*, is crowded with numerical and numerological references (as consultation of the index to this book will show). In *xi* 3–4 we find mention of the 2 witnesses who, we are told, represent the 2 olive trees and the 2 lamps that stand before the Lord of all the world. Later we encounter a servant to the Great Beast (see Appendix I); this "Lesser Beast" has 2 horns, like a lamb, yet it roars like a dragon (*xiii* 11).

According to an old Chinese proverb, there are only 2 good types of person: the dead and the unborn. The plucky American pioneers later simplified this proverb in their application of it to the Red Indian.

Three

There's a well known spell which you can use to make 3 members of the opposite sex appear in your bedroom. First of all you have to shun wickedness for a full 3 days; then you have to clean your room thoroughly and take down everything in it that hangs (e.g., pictures, curtains). After supper you have to go to your room and set out a clean tablecloth, 3 white wheaten rolls and 3 glasses of water; then put 3 chairs around the table and another at the side of the bed.

Open the window and then go to bed saying: "*Besticitum consolatio veni ad me vertat Creon, Creon, Creon, cantor laudem omnipotentis et non commentur. Stat superior carta bient laudem omviestra principiem da montem et inimicos meos o prostantis vobis et mihi dantes quo passium fieri sincisibus.*"

As noted, the reward for all this complicated preparation will be the appearance in your bedroom of 3 members of the opposite sex. They may be nurses.

In some cultures 3 is a number implying sexuality: where *1

signifies the male and *2 the female principle, their sum clearly signifies sexual union – as well as reconciliation, perfection and the making-complete of things.

Another reason for 3's importance in the mystical scheme was the realization by ancient geometers (geometry, remember, was then a mystical art) that the simplest geometrical figure of all is the one with 3 straight sides – i.e., the triangle.

As one might expect, the numerological importance of 3 is reflected in the Bible, where it appears a virtually uncountable number of times. The best known examples are probably those of the 3 Magi, who brought their gifts to the infant Christ, and the 3 days which passed between the crucifixion and the resurrection.

You may be wondering why I haven't included the Trinity as by far the most famous of such examples. Well, the idea of the Trinity is probably a lot more recent than most of us think – perhaps newer, even, than the New Testament. For example, it seems likely from his writings that Paul was quite unaware of the notion, and the mentions of it in *Matthew* and *John* are almost certainly later interpolations. Not until the 3rd century did the idea become popular, and it was not to be officially incorporated into the main body of Christian teachings until 381.

In *Revelation*, a mystical book full of numerological symbolism, we encounter 3 fairly frequently – although not generally as itself. There is reference to 3 rations of barley as payment of a day's wages in *vi* 6; 3 foul spirits appear in *xvi* 13; and in *xvi* 19 we are told of the Great City being sundered into 3 parts.

More significantly there is a preoccupation with 3's inverse, $\frac{1}{3}$ – especially in the passage in *viii* where the 1st 4 angels of the *7 blow their trumpets. At the 1st blast $\frac{1}{3}$ of the earth and $\frac{1}{3}$ of all trees are burnt up; at the 2nd, $\frac{1}{3}$ of the sea turns to blood, $\frac{1}{3}$ of all sea-creatures perish and $\frac{1}{3}$ of all ships are destroyed; at the 3rd blast the star called "Wormwood" descends (to the delight of Velikovsky fans), turning $\frac{1}{3}$ of the world's waters to wormwood, the drinking of which causes great loss of life; and at the 4th blast $\frac{1}{3}$ of the Sun, $\frac{1}{3}$ of the Moon and $\frac{1}{3}$ of the stars disappear, so that $\frac{1}{3}$ of both the day and night are lightless. Later (*ix* 17–18) the 3 plagues of fire, smoke and sulphur kill $\frac{1}{3}$ of the human race.

$3\frac{1}{2}$ makes its appearance in *Revelation*, too, in its role as $\frac{1}{2}$ of the mystically important number 7. For $3\frac{1}{2}$ days ($\frac{1}{2}$ a week) the Lord's 2 witnesses shall lie dead before they are resurrected (*xi* 9, 11); and the woman is protected from the Beast for 3½ years (½ a "week of years"; *xii* 14). (See *42 for more on this.)

It's curious that 3 can be either a lucky or an unlucky number, depending upon which system you choose to follow. Most of the systems which declare 3 to be lucky rest their belief on the obvious fact that, as noted above, there are 3 involved in the act of procreation – mother, father and child – so that 3 represents the positive life-force, the bringer of fertility and plenty. In other systems 3 is unlucky; for example, there is a Christian tradition that 3 is unlucky because of Peter's 3 denials of Christ. This may or may not explain why, in numerological terms, 3 is rather under-represented in *Revelation*. On the other hand, in light of what the book's author(s) managed to do with its inverse, ⅓, this may be a good thing.

An interesting property of the number 3 is that, if you add up the digits of any of its multiples, you get a number which is also divisible by 3. Multiplying the unpromising-looking number 1,698,724 (selected by random stabbing at the buttons of my calculator) by 3 we get 5,096,172, which if anything looks even less promising. However, if we add the digits we find 5 + 0 + 9 + 6 + 1 + 7 + 2 = 30, which is of course divisible by 3.

Towards the end of the last century Menelik II, Emperor of Abyssinia, determined to order 3 of these new-fangled electric chairs everyone was talking about as a part of his attempts to boost his country firmly into the approaching 20th century. It was only when the chairs arrived from the USA that he realized that, in order to use them to kill people, you had to have an electricity supply – and Abyssinia did not. A cost-conscious ruler, Menelik put one of the chairs to use as his new imperial throne.

According to derogatory English proverbs from earlier centuries, the 3 Ps of Italy are Poison, Pride and Piles; while those of the city of York are Pretty, Poor and Proud.

The element of atomic number 3 is lithium (Li), a white metal which is the lightest element to be a solid at room temperatures. Its main mineral, spodumene, has an interesting property called pleochroism: the colour of the mineral changes according to the direction from which you look at it.

The isotope lithium-5 is the least stable of any, having a halflife of 0.000 000 000 000 000 000 000 44 seconds.

New Jersey became the 3rd state of the Union when it ratified the US Constitution on 18th December, 1787.

In Chinese history the Period of the 3 Kingdoms lasted from 220 until 263–4. After the Han dynasty had collapsed, the country was divided into 3 states or kingdoms: Wei in the north, Shu Han in the southwest, and Wu in the southeast. In 263–4 Wei conquered Shu Han; in 265 the Wei throne was usurped by the founder of the new Tsin dynasty. In 280 this dynasty conquered Wu, and China was reunited. However, the Tsin dynasty collapsed shortly afterwards and so it was back to chaos again.

In Korean history, too, there was a Period of 3 Kingdoms. It lasted substantially longer, from about 60BC until AD668; the kingdoms into which the country was divided were called Koguryo, Paekche and Silla.

Flush, Elizabeth Browning's cocker spaniel, was kidnapped and bought back for ransom no fewer than 3 times.

The 3 "borrowed days" of February are the 12th, 13th and 14th, supposedly borrowed from January: bad weather on these days indicates the weather for the rest of the year will be clement, and *vice versa*. March 29th, 30th and 31st are borrowed from April.

And now the dizzying plunge into Greek mythology:

The 3 Graces, Aglaia, Euphrosyne and Thalia, were born from the union of Zeus with one of the daughters of Oceanus and Tethys, Eurynome. (In a few accounts the number and parentage of the Graces vary, but these are in the minority.) Closely associated with the Muses (see *9), with whom they were bosom friends, these nature deities were linked also to the Sun and hence to Apollo: Aglaia was the "brilliant", Euphrosyne "she who makes the heart rejoice" and Thalia the "flower-bringer". Apart from their other chores, they served as handmaidens to Aphrodite, attending to her make-up and general appearance when she had set her heart upon seducing somebody. Generally naked, these 3 young girls brought joy and sweetness to the hearts of all.

And then there were the 3 Furies – Alecto, the implacable, Megaera, the disputatious, and Tisiphone, the avenger of blood. They owed their birth to the cruel action of Cronus, the youngest son of Uranus and Gaea, who had hacked off his father's genitalia with a sickle and thrown the grisly bundle into the sea. From Uranus' wound poured blood which seeped into the ground, commingled with it, and gave birth to the Furies.

Uranus, indeed, must have cursed the number 3, for he and Gaea gave birth to (apart from the *12 Titans, of whom Cronus was one), the 3 Cyclopes (Arges, Brontes, and Steropes) and the 3 Hecatoncheires, hideous monsters each with 100 arms and 50 heads (Briaraeus, Cottus and Gyges). Naturally enough, as each of his ghastly children appeared, Uranus despatched them forthwith to a subterranean tomb. It was in revenge for these acts that Cronus put into practice his rather drastic contraceptive technique – at the instigation, let it be noted, of his mother, Gaea.

During the reign of Cronus, after the emasculation of Uranus, there came into the world the 3 Fates, or Moerae, the daughters of Night. They were: Clotho, who held the distaff of life; Lachesis, who span the thread of life; and Atropos, who daintily cut the thread at the end of life. Otherwise expressed, Clotho symbolized the thread of life, Lachesis the element of good luck which we're all entitled to expect during life, and Atropos the inescapable fate which awaits us all.

The 3rd president of the United States was Thomas Jefferson (1743–1826) of the Democratic-Republican Party (later to become the Democratic Party). In the election of 1800 he tied with Aaron Burr but, thanks to the influence of Alexander Hamilton, was chosen by Congress as president; a few years later, in 1804, Burr slew Hamilton in a duel. Jefferson took office on 4th March, 1801, and retired after his 2nd term on 3rd March, 1809. In later years he founded the University of Virginia.

The expression "3-time loser" dates from the enactment in 1926 in New York State of the "Baumes Laws" (Caleb H. Baumes chaired the NY State Commission), one of which imposed mandatory life imprisonment on any felon convicted for the 4th time. Macho tough, but what of the poor fellow caught committing 4 *minor* felonies . . . ?

This law system, which carefully omitted to remove any of the *causes* of crime, was tremendously admired and much imitated by other states.

Julius Caesar remarked in his *de Bello Gallico*: "*Gallia est omnis divisa in partes tres*." ("All Gaul is divided into 3 parts.") Any Asterix fan could have told Caesar that, of course, he was wrong.

According to Thomas Carlyle (1795–1881), in an essay on German literature, there are 3 great elements of modern civilization – "Gunpowder, Printing and the Protestant Religion".

One of the most intriguing problems in mathematical physics is the famous 3-body problem, whose concern is the behaviour of 3 objects (for the sake of argument, two stars and a planet) moving freely in space under no other influences than their gravitational effects upon each other. No general solution to the problem is known – nor, indeed, is any thought possible – although, in the case where one of the bodies is of negligibly small mass (as with a space colony in the Earth-Moon system), solutions do exist. In the coming decades, those solutions may prove to be very important ones.

To Plato and to the mediaeval writers who found their inspiration in his works there was not merely 1 world (for "world" read "Universe") but 3. These 3 were: (1) the suprasensible world, which could not in any way be appreciated by the senses, where God and his angels (or their analogues, depending upon your beliefs) dwelt; (2) the intelligible world, which in some aspects could be appreciated by the senses while in others it could not (mathematics was a part of the intelligible world); and (3) the world of the senses.

This hierarchy obviously comprises an intelligent way of rationalizing, of ordering, the Universe which we see about us. Unfortunately, it was taken literally.

The 3 Holy Children were the 3 people cast by Nebuchadnezzar (a possible candidate for the *real* Great Beast – see Appendix I) into the furnace, then to be saved from the flames by an angel (*Daniel iii*). They were called Abednego, Meshach and Shadrach.

Despite popular rumour to the contrary – despite, too, what your kids are probably being taught in school – the Mississippi-Missouri river is *not* the longest in the world. At 5970 km (3710 mi) it is only the 3rd longest: way ahead of it are the Nile, at 6630 km (4120 mi), and the Amazon, at 6450 km (4008 mi).

St Nicholas – better known to most of us as Santa Claus – has a legend attached to him which depends heavily upon the number 3. In its most prevalent form, it tells of how he saved from prostitution 3 women by creeping up to their window at night and hurling through it 3 bags of gold for them to use as dowries; he gained thus the emblem of 3 golden balls. Because the balls became confused with heads, variant forms of the legend emerged; he had saved 3 innocents from execution; he had saved 3 sailors from drowning; he had brought to life 3 murdered children. Confusing the last of these legends with the most likely one, you can understand how he gained the reputation of going around tossing goodies through children's windows. Unfortunately, owing to continuing doubts as to his existence, he has been recently "de-sainted".

Pi

The number π, the ratio of the circumference of a circle to its diameter, is an irrational number – which is to say that, no matter how many decimal places you might take it to, your answer is still not quite right. A reasonable approximation for most purposes is 3.1415926536.

The irrational nature of π did not stop the General Assembly of Indiana from declaring in 1897 that in future the value of π was to be regarded as 4. Of course, this tale, related gleefully in Stephen Pile's *The Book of Heroic Failures* (1979), may be apocryphal. In 1981 Chris Morgan and David Langford, in their *Facts and Fallacies*, noted that the nearest to this story which they could trace for certain was that in 1897 the Indiana State Legislature missed by only 2 crucial votes coming to the decision that hereafter π was to be regarded as having the value of 3.2 exactly.

Two French mathematicians, Martine Bouyer and Jean Guilloud, in 1973 calculated the value of π to 1 million significant figures. Their achievement was published in book form, and was over 400 pages long. Sales were disappointing.

Since π is a universal constant – after all, it doesn't matter where you draw your circle (so long as it's on a flat surface, of course), the ratio between its circumference and its diameter is still going to be the same – it has often been suggested that a sensible way of attracting the attention of any extraterrestrial civilizations to ourselves might be to broadcast the value of π out into space in all directions. In *The Earth Watchers* (1973) Brian Ford casts scorn upon such an idea – because the aliens might not count using the decimal system, and so would not recognize 3.1415926536 . . .

Oh dear! (I'm sure that's what the bank means when it puts "O/D" on my statement.) First of all, π is a ratio, so it doesn't matter to what base you count: the value is still the same. Secondly, the broadcast would anyway be of necessity in the binary rather than the decimal system (π would look rather like 11.00100100001111 . . .). A more important point, of course, is that the aliens might not think circles, spheres and so on as important as we do: the line of approach used in much of our physics does, after all, date back to Greek preoccupation with the circle and the sphere as "perfect" shapes, and this may be rather arbitrary. In other words, the aliens might not recognize π simply because, to them, it is a relatively unimportant ratio. But I should stress that this is extremely unlikely.

In 1873 the mathematician William Shanks willed that the value of π, which he had calculated to no less than 707 decimal places, be engraved upon his tombstone. His last wishes were executed. However, and very unfortunately, he'd got the last 200 decimal places or so wrong.

In 1761 the German mathematician Johann Heinrich Lambert (1728–1777), who is of interest also because he was the first to suggest that our Galaxy might be only one of countless others, proved π to be an irrational number – one which cannot be expressed in terms of the ratio between any two integers. A century or so later, in 1882, another German mathematician, Ferdinand Lindemann (1852–1939), went one further to show that π is also a *transcendental* number; that is to say, there is no algebraic equation whose coefficients are rational numbers which can have a solution π.

This may seem a fairly obscure point, of interest only to mathematicians; but Lindemann's proof, translated into geometrical terms, implies that it is impossible to construct a line of length π using the tools of the classical geometer, the straight-edge and compass, alone. He thus put an end to a quest which had been under way for 2 millennia: the ancient geometric problem of constructing a square equal in area to a given circle – the "squaring of the circle" so often referred to in curious contexts by modern politicians.

The reason is easy enough to see, assuming one screws up one's eyes in preparation for what might at first appear a little complicated. A circle of radius r has an area of πr^2, and so a square of the same area would have to have sides of length $r\sqrt{\pi}$ (because the area of a square is given by multiplying the length of 1 side by itself). Now, if π is transcendental, then $\sqrt{\pi}$ must be every bit as transcendental . . . which means that you can't construct a square of area equal to that of a given circle!

Since many of the most perplexing problems in mathematics are those concerned with proving that something is impossible, Lindemann had done a great service. This has not prevented countless amateur mathematicians, myself among them, from wasting the occasional futile hour or two manipulating ruler and compasses . . . just in case.

It is interesting if irrelevant to notice that Lindemann's proof used, among other things, an equation "coined" by the prolific Swiss mathematician Leonhard Euler (1707–1783), which reads:

$$e^{i\pi} + 1 = 0$$

(*e* is another transcendental number, the base of the natural logarithms, and has a value of 2.71828183 . . . ; *i* is an imaginary number, the square root of −1). The interesting thing about this equation is that it includes the 5 most important numbers in mathematics – and none other.

Four

4 record companies managed to turn down the Beatles before they were finally taken on by Parlophone. The 4 were Columbia, Decca, HMV and Pye, of which Decca must be the most famous for its remark about the "Fab 4" to their manager, Brian Epstein: "These boys won't make it. Four-groups are out. Go back to Liverpool, Mr Epstein: you have a good business there."

Hot-cross buns date, perhaps surprisingly, from long before Christianity. The 4 quarters of the bun symbolize the 4 phases of the Moon.

The 4th president of the United States was James Madison (1751–1836), like Jefferson before him a Democratic-Republican; he served from 4th March, 1809, until 3rd March, 1817. His trade embargo against the British during the Napoleonic Wars, at the request of the French, led to the War of 1812 between Britain and the USA, with the resultant sacking of Washington and the burning of the White House.

The press is often popularly referred to as "the 4th Estate of the Realm" – the other 3 are the Lords Spiritual, the Lords Temporal, and the Commons (often incorrectly rendered as the Sovereign, the Lords and the Commons). The press's inclusion in the list is probably traceable to a remark made by Macaulay: "The gallery [in Parliament] in which the reporters sit has become a fourth estate of the realm."

The British Parliament has passed 4 acts of union in all: England and Wales were united in 1536; Scotland was added in 1707; and

Ireland was added in 1801. The 4th UK Act of Union, passed in 1840, united Upper and Lower Canada.

The 4 fingers of the hand are the index (1st) finger, the middle (2nd) finger, the ring (or medical, 3rd) finger, and the ear (little) finger. The 3rd finger gets its 2 names from the ancient idea that there was a direct connection between it and the heart. Obviously this made it a good site for the betrothal and wedding rings; but also it made it the preferred finger for stirring medicines and applying salves, in the belief that, were there something wrong with the medicine, the heart would give a swift, sharp warning. (Cholesterol worriers please note: use one of the other fingers.)

With a practicality curious in traditions of this sort, the ear finger got its name because, being smaller than the others, it's much better at digging out wax when no one's looking. Odd it isn't called the nose finger, really . . .

The element of atomic number 4 is beryllium (Be), a grey metal whose principal mineral is of course beryl, of which emerald and aquamarine are both types.

While in occidental numerological tradition 4 is a fairly innocuous number, in oriental superstition it is extremely unlucky, owing to an association between it and death.

The English coin called the groat, or silver penny, first issued in 1351–2 during the reign of Edward III, was equal in value to 4 penny pieces. The coin ceased to be issued in 1662, although a modern equivalent was in circulation between 1835 and 1887.

The 4th pope was Clement I; he may have been the Clement mentioned by Paul in *Philippians*: "These women were a help to me when I was fighting to defend the Good News – and so, at the same time, were Clement and the others who worked with me."

Clement is thought to have held office from *c*92 until *c*101. His epistle to the Corinthians is important; his so-called 2nd epistle to them is by another hand. The tradition that he was martyred at the behest of Trajan by being thrown into the sea with an anchor tied around his neck is a 5th-century fantasy. Nevertheless, the anchor remains Clement's symbol.

On 2nd January, 1788, Georgia ratified the US Constitution and thereby became the 4th state of the Union.

According to Aristotle (384–322BC), there were only 4 elements involved in the substance of the Universe: earth, air, fire and water. That statement is something of a simplification, and modern minds are likely seriously to misunderstand it. For Aristotle conceived that all matter was actually made of the same "stuff", but that that stuff could take various forms depending on the amount of earthiness, airiness, wateriness or fieriness the particular object had; the "elements" of Aristotle were thus what we might call "properties".

Because matter was all made of the same stuff, it seemed obvious that matter of one kind could be transformed into matter of another simply by fiddling around with its "forms". Thus started the centuries-long irrelevancy of alchemy.

Aristotle's idea of the elements gave rise to the persistent medical belief in the 4 bodily humours, which matched the 4 elements: earth was analogous to black bile or melancholia; air to choler or yellow bile; fire to blood; and water to phlegm. The notion has left its mark in our language, with words such as "choleric", "sanguine", "bilious", "phlegmatic" and "melancholic".

There are 4 states of matter, according to modern physics; and 3 of them are familiar to us. The 4 are: gas, liquid, solid, plasma. The unfamiliar one is, obviously, plasma: although plasmas are found in stellar atmospheres, electron discharge tubes, etc., they don't really accord with the "commonsense" encountered in highschool physics. Suffice it to say, more or less accurately, that a plasma is a gas in which all the atoms are ionized.

The Koran tells us that there are 4 archangels: Azrael (angel of death), Azrafil (who will sound the Judgement trumpet), Gabriel (angel of revelations), and Michael (champion of faith).

There are 4 corners to the Earth, according to *Isaiah* ("He will bring back the scattered people of Judah from the four corners of the Earth") and *Revelation* (see below). But in their *Facts and Fallacies* (1981) Chris Morgan and David Langford have pointed out that a 4-cornered Earth need not be a flat rectangle, as so often assumed by fundamentalists: it could equally well be a tetrahedron (a triangle-based pyramid). In fact, this theory has a lot more going for it than the idea that the Earth is a flat rectangle, because in mystic terms part of 4's importance is that the tetrahedron, the simplest of the solids, has 4 sides and 4 corners.

4 was certainly an important number to the author(s) of *Revelation*: 4 animals surround God's throne (*iv* 6 and elsewhere); there are 4 Horsemen of the Apocalypse (*vi* 2–8); there are 4 angels (*vii* 1 and elsewhere) at the 4 corners of the Earth (*vii* 1) holding back the 4 winds of the world (*vii* 1); there are 4 horns to the golden altar of God (*ix* 13), and 4 angels chained by the Euphrates (*ix* 14–15); and there is mention, too, of the 4 quarters of the Earth (*xx* 8).

Tradition has it that 4 sorts of wood were used in the making of Christ's cross: the woods represented the 4 quarters of the Earth, or possibly its 4 corners. They were cedar, cypress, olive and palm. (Will the person who pointed out that only 2 pieces of wood were needed to build the cross please leave the room?)

In his 1st sermon at the Deer Park near Benares the Buddha proclaimed the "4 Noble Truths". These are: (1) being is suffering; (2) there's a cause for this suffering; (3) this cause can be pushed down and extinguished; (4) this can be achieved by way of the *tao* of the 8-Fold Path.

Farthings ("4th-ings") seem to have come into existence because the Normans impressed the penny coin with such a deep cross that it could easily be broken into 4 parts.

One of the most interesting problems in mathematics has always been the famous 4-colour problem. In essence this can be stated as follows: how many colours do you need in order to colour a (flat) map – *any* map – so that no two adjoining areas are the same colour? (No, no, not one of those complicated Ordnance Survey jobs – just a plain political map.) It was known from experiment that 3 colours were not enough and that 5 colours would always be too many; but *proving* that 4 colours would always be enough wasn't easy.

It is claimed that, for the first time, the problem has been solved – ignoring the optimistic cries of untold thousands of amateur mathematicians (to whom let us pay tribute: in my futile jottings I've never even come within sight of a solution to the problem) – in 1976, by a set of workers at Illinois University. They required more than 1000 hours of computer time, and their proof fills several hundred pages. Their proof is, basically, one of exploring every conceivable avenue to find that 4 colours will suffice for any map. My own feeling is that 2 possibilities exist: (1) there is a much simpler proof, a genuinely mathematical one; or (2) that the team hasn't covered *every* possibility.

In January 1941 Franklin Roosevelt put forward his plan for "4 Freedoms". These were: (1) freedom of expression; (2) freedom of worship; (3) freedom from want; (4) freedom from fear. In 1942 the UN signed the Atlantic Charter, based largely on the 4 Freedoms, but since then . . .

The Scots' pride in their educational system is to a great extent justified – at least if history tells no lies. From 1583 until 1832 the situation was that Scotland had 4 universities (St Andrews, Glasgow, Aberdeen, Edinburgh – from 1593 Aberdeen actually had 2 universities) while England had only the 2 (Oxford and Cambridge). Sadly, the balance has now changed a little: Scotland has 8 universities while England has 33.

Five

$5 per word was the rate at which Rudyard Kipling was paid – or so thought one autograph hunter who, after having written several times imploring Kipling for an autograph, finally sent the writer $5 and a request for "just 1 word". Kipling's written reply was "Thanks".

The 5 "alls" are: (1) the sovereign, who rules all; (2) the bishop, who prays for all; (3) the lawyer, who pleads for all; (4) the soldier, who fights for all; (5) the labourer, who pays for all. Things haven't changed much since the time of the old proverbs.

According to tradition, we are possessed of 5 senses: smell, taste, hearing, touch and sight. The 6th, available only to a few, should more properly be called the 7th, since the *true* 6th sense is proprioception, the sense which tells you how the various parts of your body – legs, arms, etc. – are disposed relative to each other.

If you and your circle of friends enjoy watching old westerns and superciliously counting the number of bullets the cowboys fire between each loading of their guns, it's worth noting, if only for the sake of one-upmanship, that to a real cowboy a 6-shooter was fully loaded when it had only 5 bullets in it: just imagine wandering around with your gun in its holster, a bullet already in the chamber, and the hammer resting on that bullet . . .

Although Noah's wife is mentioned 5 times in *Genesis*, nowhere in the Bible is her name given. Since she played a large part in saving the human race from total annihilation, this seems to be an early example of male chauvinism at work.

According to the pundits, the results of the 1982 Glasgow Hillhead by-election were a tragedy for everybody. They were a disaster for the Labour Party, which came 3rd instead of 2nd; for the Conservative Party, which lost the seat; for the Scottish Nationalists, who lost their deposit; and even for the victorious Social Democrats – who didn't win the seat by as big a margin as they "ought" to have. But for one candidate the results were a triumph. Lieutenant-Commander William Boakes, running his 24th campaign in 31 years, standing on the Public Safety, Democratic Monarchist and White Resident ticket, polled 5 votes. He thereby set a UK record low since the declaration of Universal Suffrage.

The element of atomic number 5 is boron (B), a nonmetal whose principal minerals include borax. Boron was first isolated on 21st June, 1808, by the French chemists Joseph Louis Gay-Lussac and Louis Jacques Thénard – to the delight of Napoleon, who had been concerned that France was falling behind in the prestigious matter of isolating elements. French delight was intensified when it was discovered that they had beaten the British Humphry Davy, their principal bugbear in matters scientific, by a mere 9 days: he isolated boron on 30th June.

☆

In the Prologue to the *Canterbury Tales* we discover that the lusty Wife of Bath had had 5 husbands – not to mention "other companye in youth".

☆

Only 5 regular convex polyhedra (or Pythagorean solids, or Platonic solids – i.e., 3-dimensional geometric figures all of whose sides are identical) can be constructed. They are: the tetrahedron (or triangle-based pyramid; 4 triangular faces), the cube (6 square faces), the octahedron (8 triangular faces), the dodecahedron (12 pentagonal faces), and the icosahedron (20 triangular faces).

Kepler, whose 3 laws of planetary motion were to put astronomy on the map and, in due course (thanks to Newton), bring physics kicking and struggling into the realms of the rational, used the 5 regular solids to construct a very silly model of the Solar System, in which polyhedra lay between the spheres of each of the planets. Working outwards from the Sun, the order was as follows: sphere of Mercury, octahedron, sphere of Venus, icosahedron, sphere of Earth, dodecahedron, sphere of Mars, tetrahedron, sphere of Jupiter, cube, sphere of Saturn. (Of course, Uranus, Neptune, Pluto and any further planets were unknown in Kepler's time.)

One of the most infuriating things about this totally irrational model is that it works quite well.

☆

5 represents in some systems the divine incarnate, since it can be thought of as the union of 1 (representing God) and 4 (representing matter).

But it has other meanings. Those pictures of the human body fitted neatly into a pentagon are symbolic representations of the correspondence between the microcosm (the individual human being) and the macrocosm (the Universe at large). Continuing in the train of 5-ish geometrical figures, 5 possibly owes its magical properties (think of the pentagram and pentacle), according to some systems, to the fact that it is the sum of the powerful numbers 2 and 3, the first even and (excluding 1) odd numbers.

The 5th president of the United States was James Monroe (1758–1831); he served from 4th March, 1817, until 3rd March, 1825. A one-time law student of Jefferson, and co-founder with Jefferson and Madison of the Democratic-Republican Party, his early political career was marred by several periods as the USA's minister abroad, at which his record can most charitably be described as patchy. His presidency (he served 2 terms) is best known for the Monroe Doctrine (1823).

Akin to the *4 Aristotelian elements, the Chinese had the 5 elements earth, fire, metal, water and wood.

The number 5 is mentioned only once in *Revelation* (except, of course, in contexts like "the 5th of the *7 angels"), which is slightly surprising. In *ix* 3–6 locusts fall from the skies to sting those who have not been saved so that for 5 months they suffer the agony of a scorpion's sting and thus learn to long for death.

The general equation of the 5th degree (that is, an equation in which the unknown or unknowns are raised to the 5th power; e.g., x^5 or x^2y^3) cannot be solved by the use of algebra, as was proven in 1824 by the Norwegian mathematician Niels Henrik Abel.

In 17th-century England there arose a fanatical sect known as the 5th-Monarchy Men. Their belief was that Christ's return to Earth was imminent, and that it was their duty to prepare for His coming. Christ's return would establish the 5th Universal Monarchy, the previous 4 being the Assyrian, Persian, Macedonian and Roman empires. Initially supporters but later opponents of Cromwell, the sect attempted coups in 1657 and 1661. After each of these failures the leaders of the sect were executed; since there hadn't been all that many 5th-Monarchy Men in the first place, the sect gradually disappeared.

Connecticut became the 5th state of the Union on 9th January, 1788, when it ratified the US Constitution.

The group of composers known as "The 5" determined to create a distinctively Russian school of music. The group's members were: Mily Balakirev (1837–1910), Alexander Borodin (1833–1887), César Cui (1835–1918), Modest Petrovich Moussorgsky (1839–1881) and Nikolai Rimsky-Korsakov (1844–1908).

(Enoch) Arnold Bennett (1867–1931) is best known for his novels of the "5 Towns" – especially the *Clayhanger* trilogy. The 5 towns concerned were the members of the conurbation now known as Stoke: Burslem, Hanley, Longton, Stoke-on-Trent and Tunstall.

In Chinese art appear the "5 Blessings": easy death, longevity, serenity, virtue and wealth. The Blessings are represented visually by 5 bats.

One Greek school of thought had it that there were 5 Ages of Man, the 5th and current one being the Iron Age of sin and shame. (The others were, in order, the Golden Age of peace, the Silver Age during which Man discovered sin, the Bronze Age of war, and the Heroic Age during which all those demigods did their gallant derring-do.)

In their usual rather sour fashion, the Greeks conceived the Iron Age as enduring forevermore. Perhaps they were right.

Six

In 1932, the USSR ruled that in future there should be only 6 days in the week.

There have been 6 kings of Britain called George. Writing in 1855, after the reigns of 4 of them but before the accession to the throne of the 5th (1910), Walter Savage Landor came out with:

George the First was always reckoned
Vile, but viler George the Second;
And what mortal ever heard
Any good of George the Third?
When from Earth the Fourth descended,
God be praised, the Georges ended!

In *The Four Georges* (1855–6) Thackeray was rather kinder – in parts. He found George I flawed, but with redeeming qualities. Of George II he said: "Here was one who had neither dignity, learning, morals, nor wit – who tainted a great society by a bad example; who in youth, manhood, old age, was gross, low, and sensual . . ." He virtually eulogizes George III, though: "The heart of Britain still beats kindly for George III, – not because he was wise and just, but because he was pure in life, honest in intent, and because according to his lights he worshipped heaven." Edmund Clerihew Bentley was to disagree with this assessment:

George the Third
Ought never to have occurred.
One can only wonder
At so grotesque a blunder.

Thackeray saves his real spleen for George IV. One of his kinder remarks is: "*He* the first gentleman of Europe! There is no stronger satire on the proud English society of that day, than that they admired George." Charles Greville described George IV as "a despicable creature" who was "mean and selfish", among other things.

It all makes George V and George VI seem a little boring, doesn't it?

The element of atomic number 6 is carbon (C), the most important element of life as we know it: because of the way in which its atoms can serve as the backbones in long "chain" molecules or form "rings", it seems to be the unique element upon which our type of life can be based (but see *14). Leaving aside such discussions, which have filled not just books but libraries, carbon dioxide is a major component of the atmosphere (0.03%), carbon tetrachloride is important in dry-cleaning and in fire extinguishers (although the 1940s belief that it could make you pregnant is erroneous), many important minerals are carbonates (e.g., limestone, which is almost entirely calcium carbonate), carbon monoxide is a major waste product of the internal combustion engine . . . the list is endless. Carbon itself, as graphite, is the primary constituent of the "lead" in pencils; another of its 3 allotropes, diamond, is useful for drill bits and the like.

Although carbon makes up only a minute fraction of the Universe it is, as far as we're concerned, a very important fraction – and we know of more compounds which contain carbon than compounds which do not.

6 has attained certain numerological importance from at least the time of the Pythagoreans, since it is the smallest of the *26 known perfect numbers (its factors, 1, 2, 3, add up 1 + 2 + 3 = 6). Its qualities are balance and harmony. It has acquired additional numerological importance since God created Man (Adam) on the 6th day. So it's slightly surprising to find it mentioned only once in *Revelation* (except where, for example, the 6th of *7 trumpet-blasts is talked of); this is in *iv* 8, where we learn that each of the *4 animals around God's throne has 6 wings. One of the symbols of the Christian Church is a 6-winged dove.

The odds on dying in a game of Russian roulette are not 1 in 6, as you might think. Because of the weight of the bullet, the chances are slightly in favour, as the chamber is spun, of the bullet's ending up at the bottom. If you really want to kill yourself, the thing to do is to hold the revolver upside-down.

The 6th president of the United States was John Quincy Adams (1767–1848), son of the 2nd president, John Adams – a unique double-act. A Democratic-Republican, he served from 4th March, 1825, until 3rd March, 1829. An unpopular compromise candidate, most of his efforts were blocked by Congress. He became the only ex-president ever to sit in the House of Representatives.

Samuel Johnson, whose reputation far outstrips his wit, on Shakespeare: "Shakespeare never had six lines together without a fault. Perhaps you may find seven, but this does not refute my general assertion."

The original British florins, issued during the reign of Edward III, were worth 6 shillings. Not until 1849 did the florin become a 2-shilling piece.

The 6 wives of Henry VIII were: (1) Catherine of Aragon) married 1509; marriage annulled 1533); (2) Anne Boleyn (married 1533; beheaded 1536); (3) Jane Seymour (married 1536; died 1537 giving birth to Edward VI); (4) Anne of Cleves (married 1540; marriage annulled 1540); (5) Catherine Howard (married 1540; beheaded 1542); and (6) Catherine Parr (married 1543; died 1548). Catherine of Aragon gave him Mary Tudor and Anne Boleyn bore him the future Elizabeth I; but it seems that he was little interested in these 2 tough females, preferring instead the non-entity Edward VI.

Massachusetts became the 6th state of the Union, ratifying the US Constitution on 6th February, 1788.

In French musical history "The 6" (or "*Les Six*") was a group of composers who turned their backs on the lushness of the likes of Debussy and on the ponderous romanticism of the likes of Wagner. The 6 were: Georges Auric (1899–), Louis-Edmond Durey (1888–), Arthur Honegger (1892–1955), Darius Milhaud (1892–1974), Francis Poulenc (1899–1963) and Germaine Tailleferre (1892–).

Foreshadowing the advent of particle physics, Lewis Carroll's White Queen remarked in *Through the Looking-Glass* (1872): "Why, sometimes I've believed as many as six impossible things before breakfast."

Seven

A mediaeval superstition from Central Europe had it that a woman could "regain" her lost virginity by the bearing of 7 bastards.

7 is without a doubt the most popular number of all. Why? No one knows for certain, but we can make a few inspired guesses.

The most likely answer is that, to the ancients, there seemed to be rather a lot of sets of 7 around. Most important of these sets was the week of 7 days, especially once it began to be believed that the Lord had created the Universe in 7 days. The reason for the week being 7 days long is probably because it was deemed important to have a week-length which could be divided into the length of the lunar month, about 28 days. 7 was the obvious number of days to opt for, since the week then corresponded to one of the phases of the Moon: where we might say "I'll see you on Tuesday the 31st of June" our ancestors probably said something like "I'll see you 2 days after the next full Moon".

Other sets were: the 7 notes of the scale, the 7 vowels of the Greek alphabet, the 7 classical planets (Moon, Mercury, Venus, Sun, Mars, Jupiter, Saturn) and various others which we shall meet during the next few pages.

7 was thus a source of magical power – people who were 7th sons of 7th sons were especially gifted with magic and clairvoyance. Even today there seems to be some belief in this: the cinema has given us *Seven Brides for Seven Brothers*, *The Seven Samurai* (adapted as *The Magnificent Seven* and its sequels, and later as the sf movie *Battle Beyond the Planets*) and *The Seven Faces of Dr Lao*. Clearly, 7 sells.

The 7 Deadly Sins are avarice, envy, gluttony, lust, pride, rage and sloth. It is an interesting comment on humanity that there are, by contrast, only 4 Cardinal Virtues: fortitude, justice, prudence and temperance. Sometimes faith, hope and charity are added to redress the balance.

According to the Theosophical Society, mankind will have in its history a total of 7 "root races", of which we are the 5th – the 3rd root race was the Lemurians and the 4th lived on Atlantis. Each root race has produced/will produce in turn 7 subraces: so far our root race has had 5 subraces, although the 6th is at the moment making its appearance in California.

☆

The 7 Wonders of the Ancient World were Phidias' Statue of Zeus at Olympia, the Colossus of Rhodes, the Pharos of Alexandria (in some cases rejected in favour of the walls of Babylon), the Temple of Artemis at Ephesus, the Hanging Gardens of Babylon, the Mausoleum at Halicarnassus, and the sole survivor, the Pyramids of Egypt.

The 7 Wonders of the Mediaeval World were regarded as Stonehenge, the Great Wall of China, the Catacombs of Alexandria, the Coliseum of Rome, the Leaning Tower of Pisa, the Mosque of St Sophia at Constantinople, and the Porcelain Tower at Nanking.

☆

For some reason, 1-eyed people have often been considered sinister, and it is probably from this fallacy that the emotive expression "you dirty, no-good 7-sided sonuvabitch" was born, in the 19th century. The 7 sides of a 1-eyed person are: the frontside, the backside, the left-side, the right-side, the inside, the outside – oh, yes, and the blindside.

☆

The 7th day after the full Moon is believed to be the ideal time for a couple to meet and fall in love. This seems to be curiously linked with another time of inflamed passions: statistical research published in 1968 showed that the 7th day after the *new* Moon is the most popular day for arsonists (generally male, and generally teenagers) to strike. As the folksong has it:

It was the candle, not desire,
That set the bed on fire . . .

☆

The 7th state of the Union was Maryland, which ratified the US Constitution on 28th April, 1788.

The element of atomic number 7 is nitrogen (N), a colourless, odourless gas whose inert molecule N_2 makes up 78% of the atmosphere. Nitrogen is important to life in many ways: the amino acids are characterized by the presence of the NH_2 group, and without amino acids there would be no proteins, and without proteins . . .

Nitrates are important fertilizers – but the most interesting nitrate, nitroglycerin, is well known for other reasons. Aside from its use in blowing things up, it can be taken in pill form to relieve angina pectoris ("Do NOT Shake Bottle Before Use").

The alchemists identified 7 "bodies" (i.e., metals) with the 7 classical planets: gold corresponded to the Sun, silver to the Moon, quicksilver to Mercury (this metal is now generally called "mercury"), copper to Venus, iron to Mars (in the UK the symbol for both Mars and iron, ♂, can still sometimes be seen in ironmongers' windows), tin to Jupiter and lead to Saturn.

In his *The Famous Historie of the Seven Champions of Christendom* (*c*1597) Richard Johnson listed as the champions: (1) St Andrew of Scotland, who released from their bondage 6 women who had for 7 years lived in the shape of swans; (2) St Anthony of Italy; (3) St David of Wales, who slept for 7 years in an enchanted garden, then to be luckily awoken by St George (who features elsewhere in the tales of the champions); (4) St Denis of France, who for 7 years lived as a hart; (5) St George himself, the patron saint of England, who amongst his many exploits was gaoled by the King of Morocco for 7 years; (6) St James of Spain, who fell in love with a Jewess and was unable to speak for 7 years (I promise I'm not making this up); and (7) St Patrick of Ireland who, imprisoned, considerately dug his own grave using his fingernails.

The legend of the 7 Sleepers of Ephesus concerns 7 Christian Ephesians called Constantine, Dionysius, John, Malchus, Martinian, Maximian and Seraption. During the persecution of Decius (*c*250) these 7 hid in a cave – in which, by the order of Decius, they were then immured. They fell into a deep sleep, and didn't wake up until, 187 years later during the reign of Theodosius II, the obstructing stones were removed from the cave-mouth. Little realizing that they had slept through the alarm, they sent one of their number into Ephesus to buy food. In no time it was generally realized that a miracle had taken place, and the locals hurried to the cave to be blessed.

The 7 Sleepers of Ephesus than all dropped down dead.

☆

The 7 Sacraments are baptism, communion, confirmation, penance, ordination, marriage, and extreme unction.

☆

The phrase "in 7th heaven", signifying "ecstatically happy", comes from the geocentric idea that each of the 7 classical planets went around the Earth embedded in a separate sphere or "heaven". According to some elements of Judaism and to the Koran, the 7th and highest of these "heavens" was occupied by God and the angels.

☆

The Pleiades, or 7 Sisters, is a northern-hemisphere cluster of young, hot stars: 6 can be seen easily with the naked eye, and a 7th with rather more difficulty. Use of a telescope reveals hundreds more, as well as traces of the gaseous nebula from which the stars have (comparatively) recently condensed.

The bright stars are named for the 7 daughters of Atlas, of whom 6 (Alcyone, Celaeno, Electra, Maia, Sterope and Taygete) took gods for lovers; the 7th, Merope, instead married Sisyphus, and so is represented by a less bright star.

☆

The Endless Peace Treaty, signed in AD533 between Persia and the Holy Roman Empire, kept the peace for 7 years.

☆

The 7 Sorrows of the Virgin Mary were: (1) the prophecy of Simeon ("You see this child: he is destined for the fall and for the rising of many in Israel, destined to be a sign that is rejected – and a sword will pierce your own soul too – so that the secret thoughts of many will be laid bare" – *Luke ii* 34–5); (2) the Flight into Egypt; (3) Christ missed; (4) the betrayal of Christ by Judas; (5) the Crucifixion; (6) the removal of Christ's body from the cross; and (7) the Ascension.

Her 7 joys were: (1) the Annunciation; (2) the Visitation; (3) the Nativity; (4) the adoration of the Magi; (5) the presentation of Christ in the temple; (6) the discovery of Christ among the doctors; and (7) the Assumption (her transport to Heaven at the age of 75).

Findchu, a legendary Irish ascetic, believed so much in the power of 7 that he made 7 smiths construct 7 sickles with which he flogged himself for 7 years. In so doing, he won a new place in Heaven.

The 7th president of the United States was Andrew Jackson (1767–1845), a hero of the War of 1812 known as "Old Hickory". In the elections of 1824 Jackson received most electoral votes, but failed to get an overall majority; the House of Representatives chose instead of him the runner-up, John Quincy Adams, a decision which Jackson . . . resented. However, on 4th August, 1829, he became the country's 1st Democrat president; he served until 3rd March, 1837. In an attempt to root out bureaucratic corruption, he introduced the potentially even more corrupt "spoils system", whereby the winning political party after an election places its supporters in all the key administrative positions.

A US one-time Park Ranger called Roy Sullivan has been 7 times struck by lightning – in 1942, 1969, 1970, 1972, 1973, 1976 and 1977 – and still lives to tell the tale. He admits to no mortal sins, and cannot understand why he should be the target for so many thunderbolts.

Like *40 and *42, in mystic thinking there seems to be some sort of "aura of trial" about 7: the Ark of the Covenant was in the land of the Philistines for 7 months; some astrologers held that the soul descended to Earth *via* the 7 planetary spheres, in due course to return by the same route to reach the 8th Heaven (mentioned by Dante), the sphere of the fixed stars; Jacob worked for . . . but this grows complicated.

Jacob worked for Laban for 7 years in order to earn the hand of Rachel, but at the end of that time he was tricked by Laban into sleeping with Rachel's elder sister, the rather unmarriageable Leah. So he worked for Laban for a further 7 years in order to be allowed to marry Rachel for real; he then worked a *further* 7 years for Laban. Leah bore Jacob 7 children in all, the last a daughter. When Jacob fled with his by now 4 wives from Laban, the latter pursued him for 7 days. And so it goes on.

7's multiples have the same characteristic. For example, until very recently in the UK the "period of initiation into adulthood" was a multiple of 7 – 21 years.

The legend of the Flood, as described in *Genesis*, is packed with 7s. From *vii* 1–10: "Yahweh said to Noah, 'Go aboard the ark, you and all your household, for you alone among this generation do I see as a good man in my judgement. Of all the clean animals you must take seven of each kind, both male and female; of the unclean animals you must take two, a male and its female (and of the birds of heaven also, seven of each kind, both male and female), to propagate their kind over the whole earth. For in seven days' time I mean to make it rain on the earth for forty days and nights, and I will rid the earth of every living thing that I made.' . . . Seven days later the waters of the Flood appeared on the earth . . ."

A curious thing is that, in the same part of *Genesis*, we find that Noah took on board the Ark only 2 of each kind of creature, even the "clean" ones – although he did take 7 human beings with him (his wife, his 3 sons, their 3 wives).

More 7s appear in the Flood story. Noah's 3 releases of the dove occurred at 7-day intervals. The Flood started on the 17th day of a month and ended on the 27th day of a month. At the end of the Flood Noah's son Shem was aged 98, which is a multiple of 7 (an especially interesting one: it's 7 × 14). In short, reading *Genesis* with a calculator at your elbow is a sobering experience.

There are 7 holy angels: Abdiel, Gabriel, Michael, Raguel, Raphael, Simiel and Uriel.

The 7 Spirits of God are the spirits of counsel, divine awfulness, knowledge, power, righteousness, understanding and wisdom.

There are 7 canonical hours: matins, prime, tierce, sext, nones, vespers and compline.

The 7th or Sabbath day commemorates, of course, the final day of the week of Creation, on which God rested. On the 1st day, according to the more famous of *Genesis'* 2 accounts of those early times, God created the heavens and the Earth, light, and the succession of day and night; on the 2nd day He created the vault of Heaven to separate the waters of the skies from the waters of the Earth; on the 3rd day He drew the seas together so that dry land emerged from them, and he populated the land with seed-bearing plants and fruit-bearing trees; on the 4th day He created the Sun, Moon and stars; on the 5th day He created the creatures of the water and of the air; and on the 6th day He created the beasts of the land and, finally, in His own image, Man. (The word "day", in this context, means simply "period of time".)

☆

The demon Asmodeus understandably became known as the "Demon of Matrimonial Unhappiness" after he fell in love with Sarah, the daughter of Raguel, and caused the deaths of her first 7 husbands on their wedding nights. Tobias, son of Tobit, was her 8th husband, and was made of sterner stuff. On the advice of the angel Raphael he concocted a charm from the heart and liver of a fish, which he placed upon burning incense. The demon fled, choking and spitting, from the noxious stench ("noxious tench", I'm tempted to write), to be captured and enshackled by Raphael in Egypt. The lucky Tobias lived happily to the age of 117.

☆

The association of the number 7 with the image of the dove is a profound one in Christian symbolism. In particular, the dove may represent the Holy Ghost, which is why in Church art you often see a dove with 7 rays issuing from it (especially in stained-glass windows) or a flight of 7 doves. Here the 7 represents the 7 Gifts of the Holy Ghost: counsel, fear of the Lord, fortitude, knowledge, piety, understanding and wisdom. (See 7 Spirits of God on page 53.)

☆

The 7 Churches of Asia, founded by the apostles, were at Ephesus, Laodicea, Pergamum, Philadelphia (in Turkey!), Sardis, Smyrna, and Thyatira. It is to these 7 Churches that *The Book of Revelation* is addressed and it is tempting to think that the many recurrences of sets of 7 in *Revelation* are a result of the attempt to symbolize these churches. At a guess, such a supposition is oversimplistic. *Revelation* is a mystic work, and it is clear that its author(s) were steeped in numerological lore: they would have been fully aware of the significance of 7.

Here is a list of 7-ish things in *Revelation* (references are in the main to first appearances only):

The 7 Churches of Asia (*i* 4); the 7 spirits before God's throne (*i* 4); the 7 golden lampstands (*i* 12); the 7 stars (*i* 16); the 7 flaming lamps burning (*iv* 5); the scroll sealed with 7 seals (*v* 1); the lamb with 7 horns and 7 eyes (*v* 6); the 7 angels who stand in the presence of the Lord and the 7 trumpets they blow (*viii* 2 to *x* 19 *passim*); the 7 words like thunderclaps which the seer must not record (*x* 3–4); the 7 thousands who shall die by the wrath of God (*xi* 13); the 7-headed dragon (*xii* 3); the 7-headed Beast who appears in *xiii* (this is the Great Beast – see Appendix I); the 7 angels who bring the 7 last plagues (*xv* 1), who are given 7 bowls of God's wrath (*xv* 7) which they spill upon the Earth (*xvi*); yet another 7-headed beast (*xvii* 3ff).

Astride this last beast there rides a whore (the "Whore of Babylon"). An angel explains to the seer (*xvii* 9) that its 7 heads represent the 7 hills astride which sits a whore (clearly Rome); also that the 7 heads represent, in addition, 7 emperors. (See also *10.)

The 7 hills upon which the city of Rome was built were the Aventine, Caelian, Capitoline, Esquiline, Palatine, Quirinal and Viminal. It is not so well known that the city of Sheffield in South Yorkshire, UK, shares with Rome the distinction of having been built on 7 hills.

According to 14th- and 15th-century legend 7 bishops, driven with their followers by the Moors from 8th-century Spain, fled to an island in the Atlantic, where they founded 7 cities. This "Island of the 7 Cities" is *still* occasionally to be found on maps.

Another bishop story. In 1688 the "7 Bishops" – Sancroft, Archbishop of Canterbury, and bishops Ken (of Bath and Wells), Lake (of Chichester), Lloyd (of St Asaph's), Trelawny (of Bristol), Turner (of Ely) and White (of Peterborough) – signed a petition urging that the clergy should not be obliged to read out in church James II's Declaration of Indulgence, which sought to grant religious freedom to Dissenters and Catholics. The 7 Bishops were brought to trial on a charge of seditious libel, but were acquitted – "to the intense joy of the nation", notes one source. Not to the intense joy of Dissenters and Catholics, presumably.

We've seen that 7 features in the Christian Creation myth; it features, too, in an early Chinese one. Tao (God) created a hairy dwarf called P'an Ku; from his eyes shone light and from his mouth came forth the winds. P'an Ku created the Sun and planets by saying their names 7 times.

When P'an Ku died his feet formed the mountains of the west, his arms those of the north and south, and his head the mountains of the east. His coursing blood became the rivers, his hair the plants; and the insect pests on his skin evolved to become the animals, including Man.

In Korean mythology there is a figure called Kim Su Ro who was born out of a golden egg and reached adulthood in only 7 years. Today, some 6 million of South Korea's 33.5-million population bear the name Kim and claim direct descent from him.

According to Pythagoreans, 7 was the number of opportunity. This was apparently because 7 seemed to turn up so often in the process of individual human development: a boy-child could be born 7 months after conception, cut his teeth 7 months after birth, reach puberty $2 \times 7 = 14$ years after birth, grow a beard 7 years later, etc., etc., etc.

That the boy-child would probably take 9 months to be born, might already have some teeth by that time, could reach puberty at 12 and grow a beard at 16 – all this doesn't seem to have caused the Pythagoreans any doubts about the essential *rightness* of the system.

John Wesley (1703–1791) claimed that every 7 years he burnt all his old sermons – on the basis that "it is a shame if I cannot write better sermons now than I did seven years ago".

In Japanese mythology we find the 7 Gods of Luck; they feature in songs, stories, folk tales and the theatre. Often they are found sailing in a treasure ship and making use of magical objects, such as a purse that never becomes empty and a cap of invisibility. The group consists of 1 goddess – Benten – and 6 gods: Bishamon, Daikoku, Ebisu, Fukurokuju, Hotei and Jurojin.

The Greek legend of the 7 Against Thebes is rooted in the disputes between Oedipus' twin sons, Polyneices and Eteocles, whom he had cursed before his death. They were unable to agree as to which of them was to occupy the throne of Thebes following their father's death, and so decided that each would reign in alternate years. However, at the end of Eteocles' 1st year he refused to let his brother Polyneices take over. King Adrastus of Argos, Polyneices' brand-new father-in-law, took up arms against Eteocles, the 7 generals of his army being (according to Aeschylus' version) Amphiaraus, Capaneus, Eteoclus (confusing, isn't it?), Hippomedon, Parthenopaeus, Polyneices and Tydeus (another of Adrastus' sons-in-law). In the ensuing war, Polyneices and Eteocles killed each other – thereby fulfilling Oedipus' curse.

The Thebans won the war, though. A generation later Adrastus returned to the attack, aided by the sons of the great 7, the Epigoni. This time he was successful, but unfortunately died on his way back home to Argos.

The 7 Sages of Ancient Greece and Asia Minor were: (1) Thales of Miletus (early 6th century BC), Bias of Priene (6th century BC), Cleobulus of Lindus in Rhodes (6th century BC), Periander of Corinth (*c*625–*c*585BC), Solon of Athens (*c*639–559BC), Pittacus of Mitylene (*c*650–*c*570BC) and Chilon of Sparta (*fl*560BC).

The "7 Liberal Arts" was a system of education bequeathed by Ancient Greece to Rome and thence to mediaeval Europe. The 7 Liberal Arts were dialectic, grammar and rhetoric (together comprising the *trivium*), and the more advanced arts of arithmetic, astronomy, geometry and music (the *quadrivium*).

The 7 Years' War, known also as the 3rd Silesian War, was waged between 1756 and 1763. On one side was Frederick the Great,

assisted by England and Hanover; on the other, France, Austria, Russia, Saxony, Sweden and Spain.

In 1866 Austria and Prussia fought the 7 Weeks' War – Prussia won.

The 7 Seas (or, more accurately, the 7 Oceans) are traditionally given as the Antarctic, the Arctic, the Indian, the North Atlantic, the North Pacific, the South Atlantic and the South Pacific.

In the early 16th century there were reported from the southwest of North America 7 golden cities, the "7 Cities of Cibola", and the tales drew many fortune-seeking expeditions, among them that led in 1540 by Coronado, 1300 men strong. The "golden cities" were never found, and it seems likely that the reports were corrupted accounts of a group of pueblos.

The heptagon, or 7-sided polygon (plane geometrical figure), is the polygon with the least number of sides which cannot be constructed in the classical geometric fashion – that is, by the use of straight-edge and compasses alone.

According to Thomas Nash (1567–1601) there are 7 stages of drunkenness, each having a different bestial characteristic. The 7 were: ape-drunk, lion-drunk, swine-drunk, sheep-drunk, Martin-drunk, goat-drunk and fox-drunk. "Martin-drunk?" you cry.

Well, Nash violently opposed Puritanism, especially as enshrined in the satirical pamphlets written in 1588–89 by "Martin Marprelate". The 3 authors of these (the 3 original Martinists), Penry, Throckmorton and Udall (*not* the author of *Ralph Roister Doister* and headmaster of Eton) were brought to trial for dissent. Penry was executed, Udall died in prison, and Throckmorton perjured himself in order to obtain release.

Adolf Hitler was convinced that his lucky number was 7. His preference for ordering army assaults on the 7th day of months was a contributory factor to his downfall.

In the UK pubs are often called "The 7 Stars". Readers who have puzzled over this may be interested to find that the 7 stars in question are the 7 bright stars of the Plough (part of the constellation Ursa Major, the Great Bear), and *not* the Pleiades, as one might expect.

In popular superstition – and indeed in *Revelation* (see page 55) – this subconstellation is associated with the Virgin Mary. Like many other pub names, therefore, this one is of religious origin.

☆

At the special request of my 4-year-old daughter Jane I must include one of her favourite nursery rhymes, which is heavily 7-oriented (she wanted "Snow White and the 7 Dwarfs" to be put in, but even someone as indulgent as I baulked at that). The nursery rhyme in question is a riddle:

As I was going to St Ives
I met a man with 7 wives.
Each wife had 7 sacks,
Each sack had 7 cats,
Each cat had 7 kits.
Kits, cats, sacks and wives –
How many were going to St Ives?

The answer is, of course, I – see the last line of the riddle if large numbers are still swirling around in your brain. For interest, the total number in this curious party met by the narrator was $1 + 7 + 7^2 + 7^3 + 7^4 = 2801$ (including the sacks).

Eight

The world's 1st mail-order catalogue, produced in 1874 by Aaron Ward, was a mere 8 pages long.

☆

The 8th president of the United States was the Democrat Martin Van Buren (1782–1862), a politician with all the "political skill" of a Richard Nixon. He served from 4th March, 1837, until 3rd March, 1841, being defeated after only 1 term. In 1848 he ran for the presidency under the banner of the Free Soil Party, which was opposed to slavery.

Since 4 is a very material number, numerologically 8 is doubly so; however, 8 carries with it also the strong possibility of failure. Alternatively, 8 is a symbol of birth, or new birth, since children are born from the 8th orifice of woman, which is not possessed by man.

In the Great Fire of London in 1666, it is generally accepted that only 8 people lost their lives.

In palmistry there are 8 "mounts" or "mounds" (i.e., fleshy bits) on the hand: the Mount of Venus at the base of the thumb; the Mount of Mars Positive between the thumb and the 1st finger; the Mount of Jupiter at the base of the 1st finger; the Mount of Saturn at the base of the 2nd finger; the Mount of the Sun (or of Apollo) at the base of the 3rd finger; the Mount of Mercury at the base of the little finger; the Mount of Mars Negative, directly opposite that of Mars Positive; and the Mount of the Moon, the bulge near the wrist more-or-less opposite the Mount of Venus.

The 8th pope was probably called Telesphorus, holding office *c*125–*c*136. It seems probable that he was a martyr (unlike most of the other early popes, although they are venerated as such), put to death during the reign of Hadrian.

Before the rise of Christianity, there were 8 days in the Graeco-Roman week.

It has often been suggested that counting to the base 8 would be a marked improvement on our present system of counting to the base *10 – although still not as good as counting to the base *12, of course. 8 has the advantage of being 2^3. What we would recognize as the number 100 would be, if written to the base 8, 144.

The element of atomic number 8 is oxygen (O), which makes up about 21% of the atmosphere and about 50% by weight of the Earth's crust (but see *94). The oxygen we breath is in the form O_2; less common is ozone, O_3, which some people still think is what gives the seaside air its distinctive tang (in fact, it's rotting seaweed). To say that all living creatures depend in one way or another on oxygen would be not merely to state the obvious, it would also be untrue: some bacteria actually curl up and die if exposed to it.

Winston Churchill's mother Jeanette (*née* Jerome; 1854–1921) was one 8th Iroquois.

The group of US painters called "The 8" exhibited together only once; in so doing, though, they founded the "ashcan" school of art. The 8 artists originally involved were: Arthur Bowen Davies (1862–1928), William James Glackens (1870–1938), Robert Henri (1865–1929), Ernest Lawson (1873–1939), George Benjamin Luks (1867–1933), Maurice Brazil Prendergast (1861–1924), Everett Shinn (1876–1953) and John Sloan (1871–1951).

South Carolina became the 8th state of the Union by ratifying, on 23rd May, 1788, the US Constitution.

In Scandinavian mythology there were 8 "bests": (1) Yggdrasil, the best of trees; (2) Garm, the best of hounds; (3) Skidbladnir, the best of ships; (4) Habrok, the best of hawks; (5) Odin, the best of the *12 or so Aesir; (6) Bragi, the best of bards; (7) Sleipnir, the best of horses; (8) Bifrost, the best of bridges.

According to Indian mythology, the Earth is supported on the backs of 8 white elephants.

For symmetry fans, a little arithmetic. The number 8 has the interesting property that

$$
\begin{gathered}
1 \times 8 + 1 = 9 \\
12 \times 8 + 2 = 98 \\
123 \times 8 + 3 = 987 \\
1234 \times 8 + 4 = 9876 \\
12345 \times 8 + 5 = 98765
\end{gathered}
$$

and so on, right up to $123{,}456{,}789 \times 8 + 9 = 987{,}654{,}321$!

Nine

An old Turkish proverb seems to have been especially tailored to offend everybody: "Among any 10 men, 9 are women."

According to the false Dionysius the Areopagite (the real one was a disciple of Paul, the false one lived in the 5th century), there are 9 orders of angels arranged in 3 circles. The 1st circle contains cherubim, seraphim and thrones; the 2nd dominions, powers and virtues, and the 3rd angels, archangels and principalities.

The element of atomic number 9 is fluorine (F), a yellow gas between which and yourself it is wise to put a large distance as swiftly as possible. It reacts with virtually anything in sight to produce fluorides – often themselves extremely nasty chemicals; this is not to say that the very small quantities of fluorides put in drinking-water are dangerous – indeed, you can often find higher quantities of fluorides in well-water than in any artificially fluoridated water.

Its principal mineral, fluorite or fluorspar, comes in many colours. Some types are fluorescent – that is, they glow in visible colours when bathed in (invisible) ultraviolet light.

"Possession is 9 points of the law," they say. The 9 points of the law used to be listed as follows: (1) enough money; (2) enough patience; (3) a good cause; (4) at least as good a lawyer; (5) a good counsel; (6) good witnesses; (7) a sympathetic jury; (8) a good judge; and (9) good luck. So now you know.

The lamprey is known alternatively as the 9-eyed eel.

The 9th president of the United States was William Henry Harrison (1773–1841), a Whig who took office on 4th March, 1841, and, having delivered his inaugural address in the middle of a rainstorm, died exactly 1 month later of pneumonia. His is the shortest period of office of any US president.

And the shortest reign of any British monarch was the 9 days clocked up by Queen Jane, better known as Lady Jane Grey. She was proclaimed queen on 10th July, 1553, apparently reluctantly. On the 19th of the same month Mary Tudor was proclaimed queen in her place. With her usual feminine sweetness, Mary had Jane and her husband beheaded, for treason, the following year.

The 9 Muses were daughters of Mnemosyne and Zeus, and were born at the foot of Olympus; they became attendants on Apollo and, more importantly, goddesses of various branches of the arts and sciences. The 9 were Calliope (epic poetry and eloquence), Clio (history), Erato (love poetry), Euterpe (lyric poetry and flute-playing), Melpomene (tragedy), Polyhymnia (sacred song and the mime), Terpsichore (dancing), Thalia (pastoral poetry and comedy) and Urania (astronomy). There's an interesting imbalance between the arts and the sciences, there – but then the Greeks seem ever to have believed that science was too close to technology for respectability.

In Macaulay's *Lays of Ancient Rome* we find:

Lars Porsena of Clusium
By the nine gods he swore
That the great house of Tarquin
Should suffer wrong no more.

The 9 gods of the Sabines were Aeneas, Aesculapius, Bacchus, Fides, Fortuna, Hercules, Romulus, Santa and Vesta. The 9 gods of the Etruscans were Hercules, Juno, Mars, Minerva, Tinia, Saturn, Summanus, Vedius and Vulcan.

The number 9 has the interesting property that the sum of the digits of any of its multiples is always divisible by 9. For example, $9 \times 1{,}698{,}724 = 15{,}288{,}516$, and $1 + 5 + 2 + 8 + 8 + 5 + 1 + 6 = 36$, which is indeed divisible by 9.

To the numerologist 9 is an extremely important number for various reasons: the 9 months of pregnancy, 9's position as the last of the series before the transition to 10, 9's value of 3×3, etc.

Its properties therefore include both childish and maternal traits, completeness, initiation, and all the properties of 3, only more so.

The 9th state of the Union was New Hampshire, which ratified the US Constitution on 21st June, 1788.

Charlemagne had 9 wives – Hamiltrude, Desiderata, Hildegarde, Fastrade, Luitgarde, Maltegarde, Gersuinde, Regina and Adalinda.

According to the mediaevals, the "9 Worthies" were Alexander the Great, King Arthur, Charlemagne the Great, King David, Godfrey of Bouillon, Hector, Joshua, Judas Maccabaeus and Julius Caesar. Another group of "9 Worthies" was the privy council of William III: Caermarthen, Devonshire, Dorset, Lowther, Marlborough, Monmouth, Pembroke, Nottingham and Edward Russell.

The "9 Worthies" of London were: Sir John Bonham, Sir Hugh Caverley (best known for having rid Poland of a giant bear), Christopher Croker (sidekick of the Black Prince), Sir John Hawkwood (known in Italian history as Giovanni Acuti Cavaliero), Sir Henry Maleverer (or Henry of Cornhill), Sir Henry Pritchard, Sir William Sevenoke, Sir William Walworth (who stabbed Wat Tyler, thereby halting the progress of social justice for at least a few decades, and was rewarded with the lord mayorship of London), and Sir Thomas White.

In the Japanese language "9" sounds much like "suffering", and so many hotels and hospitals in Japan eschew a room or ward numbered 9 – much as we behave towards the number *13. Similarly, rooms or wards 4 are likewise in short supply, because the word for 4 sounds suspiciously like that for death.

Ten

There were only 10 subscribers to the first London telephone exchange, opened in 1878. The figure for subscribers in London for the Spring of 1982 is 3.4 million (the number of *telephones* is 5.9 million).

The 10 Commandments brought to the Israelites by Moses were, in brief:

(1) Thou shalt have none other gods but me.

(2) Thou shalt not make to thyself any graven image, nor the likeness of any thing that is in heaven above, or in the earth beneath, or in the water under the earth. Thou shalt not bow down to them, nor worship them . . .

(3) Thou shalt not take the name of the Lord thy God in vain.

(4) Remember that thou keep holy the Sabbath-day. Six days shalt thou labour . . . but the seventh day is the Sabbath of the Lord thy God.

(5) Honour thy father and thy mother . . .

(6) Thou shalt not kill.

(7) Thou shalt not commit adultery.

(8) Thou shalt not steal.

(9) Thou shalt not bear false witness against thy neighbour.

(10) Thou shalt not covet thy neighbour's wife, nor his servant, nor his maid, nor his ox, nor his ass, nor any thing that is his.

An interesting variant of the 7th Commandment was rendered in a 1632 edition of the Bible: "Thou shalt commit adultery." Not unnaturally, this edition became known as the "Wicked Bible".

The discoverers of iron were called, in Greek mythology, the Daktyls. Originally there were only 3 of them – the smelter, the hammer and the anvil – but their numbers increased over time until they were 10. They were then christened the Daktyls, or fingers.

The 10th president of the United States was John Tyler (1790–1862), who served briefly as Vice-President before Harrison's untimely death. He was the 1st vice-president to take over the presidency in this way; although the Constitution's ruling in such an event was unclear, he elected to sit out the remainder of the term. Quarrelling with his own party, the Whigs, over his repeated vetoing of its nationalistic moves, he was expelled from it and threatened with impeachment. His most important act was probably his backing of Morse's telegraphy system.

He served from 6th April, 1841, until 3rd March, 1845.

The element of atomic number 10 is neon (Ne), an inert gas which glows an orange-red colour when excited by an electric current. This property has given us the neon light, invented in 1910 by the French chemist Georges Claude.

It was not only the Pythagoreans who held 10 to be in some way a perfect, holy number (see page 10); the idea of 10's perfection and completeness occurs throughout religious thought. For example, the biblical statement that there are *9 orders of angels was, to the mediaevals, confirmed by the notions that, taken together with the godhead, the number 10 was generated; or alternatively that, originally, there were 10 orders of angels but that, when Lucifer and his cohorts fell, there remained only 9 so that God had to create Man in order to make the number back up to 10.

The latter theory was backed by reference to a passage in *Luke*: "Or again, what woman with ten drachmas would not, if she lost one, light a lamp and sweep out the house and search thoroughly till she found it? And then, when she had found it, call together her friends and neighbours? 'Rejoice with me,' she would say; 'I have found the drachma I lost.' In the same way, I tell you, there is rejoicing among the angels of God over one repentant sinner."

By analogy, then, Man is clearly the lost, 10th, drachma – and is due to be both found and saved.

In *The Book of Revelation* the number 10 turns up only occasionally, though. For example, the church in Smyrna is warned not to fear a 10-day ordeal (*ii* 10); this is generally taken merely to mean that it should not fear a minor, short-lived ordeal – the period of time for a full-scale ordeal being usually given as *42 months.

Of greater interest is that each of the *7-headed beasts bears 10 horns (*xii* 3, *xiii*, *xvii* 3, and elsewhere; the 2nd of these references relates to the Great Beast 666 – see Appendix 1). In the case of the

3rd beast, the whore astride which represents Rome, the horns are explained as each representing the king of a satellite nation.

Between 1310 and its fall in 1797, the Republic of Venice was ruled by the Council of 10, a body originally created to counter crimes against the state. Consisting of, all told, 17 members (the doge, 10 members elected by the grand council and 6 elected by the lesser council), it gained greater and greater powers, controlling a secret police and a team of inquisitors, and empowered to pass sentences against which there was no appeal. Despite its apparently despotic nature, the Council of 10 seems to have been a refreshingly incorrupt body – just brutal.

A group of painters who exhibited together for a couple of decades from 1898 onwards, and who exerted a fair influence on the development of US 20th-century art, were known as "The 10" or "The 10 American artists". Those involved were Frank Weston Benson (1862–1951), William Merritt Chase (1849–1916), Joseph 1938), Childe Hassam (1859–1935), Willard Leroy Metcalf (1853– because, on Twachtman's death, Chase was brought in to make 1925), Robert Reid (1862–1929), Edward E. Simmons (1852–1931), Edmund Charles Tarbell (1862–1938), John Henry Twachtman (1853–1902) and Julian Alden Weir (1852–1919). Attentive readers will notice that there are 11 painters named in this list: this is because on Twachtman's death, Chase was brought in to make up the number.

The 10th state of the Union was Virginia, which ratified the US Constitution on 25th June, 1788.

10 is of course the base of our everyday decimal system of counting, in use almost throughout the world. It seems certain that 10 was selected because it is the number of digits on a pair of hands. Other systems have been or are based on 5, the number of digits on a single hand; 20, where you take in the feet, too; and so on. (For further discussion of different bases for counting see *8, *12 and *60.)

The press baron Lord Northcliffe had notices put up in his office which said: "They are only 10." These were to remind him of his assessment of the public's mental age. More recently, *The Sun* in the UK has been demonstrating that Northcliffe was, at least in its view, vastly overestimating the wit of the population.

Eleven

The name "11" comes from the Anglo-Saxon *aendlefene*, Old English *endleofon*, meaning literally "one left over" – that is, after you've used all the 10 digits of both hands in the counting of a collection of objects, there's still one object left over.

☆

The quasireligious legend of Ursula and her 11 thousand virgins has it that the British Ursula, in order to avoid marriage to a pagan, fled from her royal father's court to Rome, taking with her 10,999 virginal chums. As this vast collection of unsullied femininity headed home again, they were intercepted by the Huns at Cologne, and slaughtered.

The origins of the legend are obscure – although certainly some young women did become religious martyrs at Cologne – but by the 9th century it was popularly accepted that 11 virgins, led by one of their number called either Pinnosa or Ursula, had been killed for their beliefs and their determined retention of their virtue. Our ancestors were never impressed by small numbers (the number of people recorded as having died in the Black Death actually exceeded the population of Europe), and so the figure of 11 virgins was promptly multiplied 1000-fold. In the 12th century an old cemetery at Cologne was unearthed, and its contents claimed as the remains of Ursula and her virgins.

In the 1982 (football) World Cup – a contest which brought into footballing reportage a new use of the word "cynicism", to mean fouling – there were 100 bookings exactly. Of these, the Italian team was responsible for the greatest number, 11. Curiously, the Italian team also won the contest. One wonders, cynically, if there might be any connection between these two facts.

A pickpocket named James Hardy Vaux was sentenced during

the reign of George III to 7 years' hard labour in exile in Australia. His crime had been the theft of a handkerchief, valued at 11 pence.

He was lucky: had the handkerchief been worth a shilling, just 1 penny more, he would have been sentenced to death.

The element of atomic number 11 is sodium (Na), a metal much loved by intelligent schoolchildren the world over because, if you drop a lump of it into a bowl of water, it bursts into flames with exciting ferocity. (Use of tweezers is advised when doing this, since the lump is likely to settle instead for the moisture on your fingers.) Many sodium compounds are embarrassingly familiar: sodium chloride is common salt, sodium bicarbonate is baking soda, sodium carbonate is washing soda, sodium hydroxide is caustic soda, sodium thiosulphate is the photographers' "hypo", and sodium pentothal is the famous "truth drug".

Confusingly, soda water has nothing to do with sodium at all. It's made, basically, by dissolving carbon dioxide in water.

Franklin D. Roosevelt was related, by blood or by marriage, to no less than 11 other US presidents: George Washington, John Adams, James Madison, John Quincy Adams, Martin Van Buren, William Harrison, Zachary Taylor, Ulysses Grant, Benjamin Harrison, Theodore Roosevelt and William Taft. Since Roosevelt was the *32nd president, this means that he was related to more than one 3rd of his predecessors.

☆

But he wasn't related to the 11th president, James Knox Polk (1795–1849), a Democrat who took office on 4th March, 1845, having been elected on a platform based on the notion of Manifest Destiny: although it was bad news for the Red Indians, God wanted the USA "to overspread the continent allotted by Providence for the free development of our multiplying millions". There was a chap in Germany in the 1930s who had the same sort of idea.

Owing to ill health, Polk retired on 3rd March, 1849, at the end of his 1st term of office. He died shortly afterwards.

On 26th July, 1788, the state of New York ratified the US Constitution, thereby becoming the 11th state of the Union.

11 devils were named by Dante in his *Divine Comedy*: Alichino, the allurer; Barbariccia, the malicious; Calcobrina, the scorner of grace; Caynazzo, the snarler; Ciriato Sannuto, the tusked boar; Dragnignazzo, the fell dragon; Farfarello, the scandalmonger; Grafficane, the dog-like; Libicocco, the ill-tempered; Rubicante, the rage-reddened; and Scarmiglione, the baneful.

In 1753 there was rioting in Britain when the Gregorian Calendar supplanted its Julian predecessor, the necessary adjustment being made by having September 14th following immediately after September 3rd. The riots came about because the people were clearly being robbed of 11 days of their lives . . .

A happy-go-lucky little creature is the marsupial known as the "big bang" mouse. The males of the species are born in September, and in the following August start their sex life. For 11 solid days they copulate for up to 12 hours per day – and then they promptly die, presumably of exhaustion.

Translated into human terms, this would imply a man living to the age of 68, copulating nonstop throughout his waking hours for a solid 2 years, and then dying at three score years and ten. Women, on the other hand, would live to be about 130. Well, women *do*, on average, live several years longer than men. It makes you think, doesn't it?

Twelve

In 1757 the then Prince of Condé (1717–1776), a French aristocrat and descendant of the "Great Condé" who had served with such distinction in the *30 Years' War, managed to make love 12 times in a single night with one Mme Deschamps. Brimming with understandable pride concerning his achievement, he became – and for the rest of his life remained – obsessed by the number 12: he had it marked on his clothes and stamped on his buttons, always had 12 courses at dinner, and never gave a tip other than

12 *louis d'or*. Mme Deschamps seems to have displayed no such obsession, which makes one wonder.

12 runs is the lowest score ever achieved in an innings in 1st-class cricket. The feat was performed in 1907 by Northamptonshire in a match against Gloucestershire. In fact, Northamptonshire, admitted to 1st-class cricket only in 1905, were to take the silver medal in quite a few matches over the next 4 decades: between 1930 and 1948 the side never appeared higher than 2nd bottom in the county championship, and during that period they once achieved a run of coming bottom 5 years in a row, between 1934 and 1938. Their fortunes have since improved somewhat.

The 12th president of the United States was Zachary Taylor (1784–1850), a Whig and military hero known to his soldiers as "Old Rough and Ready". He took office on 4th March, 1849, and at once took a bold stance against the expansion of the practice of slavery: he was courageous enough to accept civil war as the lesser of 2 evils. However, he died on 9th July, 1850, and so the argument was postponed for a decade or so.

There's a curious Italian legend concerning 12th Night. A fairy called Befana comes on that night to fill the stockings of the children with goodies. This is because, long ago, she was too busy to look after the 3 Magi as they went to view the newborn Christ; to make up for it, she promised that she'd give them hospitality on their return journey. But the 3 Magi, of course, returned to their country by a different way, and so she was unable to keep her promise. Ever since, every year on 12th Night, Befana looks out for them, ready to shower gifts upon them – but the kids get the gifts instead.

The name "Befana" comes from the same root as "epiphany", and is probably a comparatively recent corruption.

The 12 signs of the Zodiac, the band of the heavens through which the Sun appears to pass during the course of the year, are Aries, Taurus, Gemini, Cancer, Leo, Virgo, Libra, Scorpio, Sagittarius, Capricornus, Aquarius, Pisces. It's conventional to put Aries at the head of the list, because the Sun used to be in that constellation at the time of the Spring equinox; in fact, owing to precession (see *26), the so-called "1st Point of Aries" is currently in the constellation Pisces or even, by popular belief, Aquarius (since the constellation boundaries are not precisely marked out, the view is a reasonable one).

A recently published attempt to show that the ancients knew of a 13th zodiacal sign, Arachne, is reputed to be a hoax.

The original US Bill of Rights contained 12, not 10, amendments to the Constitution: the 2 that failed to be adopted concerned the salaries of senators and congressmen and the size of the House of Representatives.

The element of atomic number 12 is magnesium (Mg), an element of interest to metallurgists. Its discovery (i.e., isolation) *was* interesting, though, in that it formed part of a remarkable series of such feats by the man generally reckoned to have been the most handsome of all Great Scientists, Humphry Davy (1778–1829). Various naturally occurring substances – e.g., magnesia – were thought to be compounds of unknown metals, but no one could succeed in reducing them to those metals. Davy's approach was to build the strongest battery then known (it had over 250 metal plates) in order to pass electric currents through the materials. In 1807–8 he succeeded in isolating potassium, sodium, barium, strontium, boron, calcium and magnesium, all for the 1st time.

The 12 major deities of the Greek and Roman pantheons were known, to the Romans, as the *Dii Majores* (or *Consentes Dii*); of *Dii Minores* there were of course a vast number (30,000, according to Hesiod). The *Dii Majores* of the Greeks (*Romans*) were: (1) Hera (*Juno*), (2) Aphrodite (*Venus*), (3) Artemis (*Diana*), (4) Athena (*Minerva*), (5) Demeter (*Ceres*) and (6) Hestia (*Vesta*) – all goddesses – and (7) Zeus (*Jupiter*), (8) Apollon (*Apollo*), (9) Ares (*Mars*), (10) Hephaistos (*Vulcan*), (11) Hermes (*Mercury*) and (12) Poseidon (*Neptune*).

According to Greek mythology, near the dawn of time Gaea, the Earth Mother, and her son Uranus mated to produce the 12

Titans: (1) Mnemosyne, (2) Phoebe, (3) Rhea, (4) Theia, (5) Tethys and (6) Themis – all females – and (7) Coeus, (8) Crius, (9) Cronus, (10) Hyperion, (11) Iapetus and (12) Oceanus. Before Cronus rather brutally put a stop to further activities on the fathering front, the prolific Uranus and Gaea produced also the *3 Cyclopes and the 3 Hecatoncheires.

To the numerologist 12 ranks with *7 in importance: where the one is 3 × 4 the other is 3 + 4 (3 is a spiritual number, 4 a material number), and so it is only to be expected that they should be expressed in such similar ways in the workings of the Universe around us – the year of 12 months and the week of 7 days. That 12 is a number of completeness and perfection is reflected in the selection of 12 disciples by Christ (but see *14!), the 12 days of Christmas, the 12 labours of Hercules, the 12 tribes of Israel (see *13), the 12 gods of Olympus, the 12 Aesir of the Norse Asgard, and the 12 signs of the Zodiac. In addition, of course, there were the 12 hours of day and the 12 hours of night: while we think in terms of the standard hour, so that only at the equinoxes do both night and day have 12 hours, the Romans, for example, had the system of "temporary hours", the 12 daylight hours each being longer during the summer and shorter in the winter, with the 12 nocturnal hours varying conversely.

But before one gets carried away and starts attaching numerological importance to the fact that there used to be 12 pence to the shilling (in real money) and still are 12 inches to the foot, it's worth having a look at 12 itself. It is divisible by 2, 3, 4 and 6, which makes it an extremely useful number in mathematics and in such practical matters as measuring – a foot and a sixth is 14 inches, but a metre and a sixth is 1,166.666666666 . . . millimetres. True, a foot and a fifth is $14\frac{2}{5}$ inches, which isn't too convenient, but the point is that 12 can give whole-number results when divided by *more* numbers (4) than can 10 (2). In fact, 12 is so much better a base for our counting that it has often been said that, had we by chance had 6 rather than 5 digits on each hand, we would probably have been able to travel among the stars by now; and there are occasional calls from the dedicated for moves towards adopting 12 as the base for the future. The response has been, of course, to drop the 12d shilling in favour of the

100p pound and the 12″ foot in favour of the 1000mm metre. (See also *240 in this context.)

According to the Talmud, Adam lived in Eden for a mere 12 hours before his expulsion with Eve.

North Carolina became the 12th state of the Union by its ratification of the US Constitution on 21st November, 1789.

The 12 Tables, in Roman Law, were the 12 wooden tablets on which around 450BC (possibly quite a lot later), the legal code of Rome was painted or engraved for exhibition in the Forum for everyone to see (originally there were only 10 tablets, but a further 2 were added the following year).

This measure followed protests by the plebeians that they were vulnerable to discrimination against them by the judges, who were of course patricians, because the legal code was preserved only orally and only within a small, elite group. The modern equivalent of such secrecy is to allow public access to the laws of the land, but to have so many of them that, in practice, it is often hard to know whether your acts are illegal or not: if you guess wrongly, then "ignorance of the law is no defence".

According to *Genesis*, Joseph had, all told, 12 sons: by his 1st wife Leah he had 6 (Reuben, Simeon, Levi, Judah, Issachar and Zebulun); by his 2nd wife Rachel he had 2 (Joseph and Benjamin); by Leah's slave Zilpah he had 2 (Gad and Asher); and by Rachel's slave Bilhah he had 2 (Dan and Naphtali). All but Joseph would become a patriarch to one of the 12 tribes of Israel (see *13).

In *Revelation* 12 appears often, often overtly in recognition of the 12 tribes of Israel. 12,000 from each are saved on the Day of Apocalypse (*vii* 5–8); and the City of God has 12 gates, one for each tribe (*xxi* 12). The City's walls have 12 foundation stones, one for each of the 12 Apostles (*xxi* 14), and the City is 12,000 furlongs in length, breadth and height (*xxi* 16). (See also *144.) Other 12 references in the book are the 12 stars on the woman's head (*xii* 1), and the description of the trees of life, on either side of the River of Life, which bear 12 crops each year (*xxii* 2), one for each month.

Calamity Jane (Martha Jane Burke; *c*1852–1903), the noted adventuress, prostitute and transvestite of the Wild West, worked her way through no fewer than 12 husbands.

Thirteen

Before plunging into all the general gloom created by 13's unluckiness, let us pause to smile admiringly at the US rationalist association which stubbornly meets on fridays the 13th. It is called the National Society of 13 Against Superstition, Prejudice and Fear.

The Chaldean hero Amelon is reported to have ruled for a full 13 sares. Since a sare is a period of time equal to 3600 years, this means that he must have lived for over 46,800 years. By comparison Methuselah, who lasted a mere 969 years, died young.

There is a popular superstition that the 1st person to rise from a dinner table at which 13 people are seated will die before the year is out. This could obviously create a tricky situation for a hostess who suddenly realizes that she shouldn't have let someone bring along a friend, but there is in fact one traditionally "approved" solution to the dilemma. This is for all 13 diners to leap from their seats at exactly the same moment. It just takes a little practice and teamwork, that's all.

One rival tradition has it that 13 is, by contrast, an extremely lucky number. The supportive tale has it that Pope Gregory the Great (reigned 590–604; see *64) was in the habit of giving breakfast to 12 of Rome's poor each morning. One day Jesus appeared in the guise of a beggar, making the number at the breakfast table up to 13, and ever since then it has, of course, been positively *good* luck to have 13 people at your table.

Of course, it was only to be expected that the only Apollo mission to have to abort would be Apollo-13 (1970). However, before we get carried away we should realize that there was a tremendous amount of luck involved in the survival of the astronauts concerned. One of the 3, Jack Swigert (his colleagues were James Lovell and Fred Haise), had been substituted at a comparatively late stage as the pilot of the Lunar Module – and, by sheer chance, he had earlier made a specialized study of the possible use of the Lunar Module as a "lifeboat" in case of accident. The result was that, while we learnt little about the Moon from the Apollo-13 mission, we learnt a great deal about nuts-and-bolts spaceflight – the sort of thing that mankind might have had to learn the hard way, through the loss of lives.

The irrational fear of the number 13 is technically termed "triskaidekaphobia".

The composer Arnold Schönberg was a triskaidekaphobe of the first water – but in his case one wonders if there really *is* something in the superstition. Born on 13th September, 1874, he concluded that he would die in his 76th year (because 7 + 6 = 13). Not only did this prove to be true, but he died on Friday 13th July, 1951, at 13 minutes to midnight.

Of all dates on which ventures are doomed, Friday the 13th is paramount. This is an example of two "bad lucks" working together, for in many cultures Friday is regarded as an unlucky day. The Christian explanations, that this is a result of Christ's having been crucified on a friday (hence the Catholic idea of Friday as a fast-day), or even that it was on a friday that Adam and Eve ate from the Tree of the Knowledge of Good and Evil, are appealing, but give no reason for the day's reputation for unluckiness in other cultures (e.g., Buddhism). In Scotland, however, it is traditionally regarded, curiously enough, as a lucky day. Modern office-workers seem to agree, having christened the day "Poet's Day" (because you can "*p*ush *o*ff *e*arly, *t*omorrow's *S*aturday").

It is generally accepted that there are 13 witches in a coven; but in fact it seems likely that covens were nothing more than figments of the Inquisitors' imaginations: the unfortunate accused, of course, confessed to exactly what they were told to confess to, and so supported the story. It's rather disturbing to think that all those modern suburban witches, who cavort nakedly around campfires at bank holiday weekends, may well be continuing a tradition that never existed in the first place . . .

The reasons for 13's widely assumed unluckiness are much in doubt. One theory is that it was because Jesus and the 12 disciples together made a group of 13 people (a coven, Margaret Murray and others have suggested), the 13th of whom, Judas, was a traitor. Alternatively, but in the same vein, it might have been because there were 13 at the Last Supper.

Both of these explanations suffer one major drawback: the idea that 13 is unlucky dates from long before the time of Christ, and extends far beyond Christendom. One possible reason for the *importance* of 13, it has been suggested, is that there are 13 lunar months in the year; but in fact there are 13.37 to the year, not 13, and if anything the figure would have been slightly higher in ancient times. The best suggestion available – and it is not a particularly convincing one – is that 13 is both important and unlucky because it immediately follows *12. If 12 is a number of completeness and perfection, then 13 is the first step into the trans-12 region, while also symbolizing necessarily the sin of excess, of gluttony, of the greed that makes men tyrants. I'm not convinced.

The 13th of the 13 "original colonies" to ratify the US Constitution, on 29th May, 1790, and therefore by definition the 13th state of the Union, was Rhode Island.

The 13th president of the United States was Millard Fillmore (1800–1874), who took over on 10th July, 1850, on the death of the 12th president, Zachary Taylor (obviously the 13 curse was just a little off-target), and served out the rest of the term, until 3rd March, 1853. A moderate man opposed to slavery, Fillmore nevertheless supported the fence-sitting Compromise of 1850 (concerned with the extension or otherwise of slavery to new territories) in order temporarily to avert civil war.

He later became a member of the Know-Nothing Party, whose principles were the exclusion from politics of Catholics and naturalized citizens, and the restriction of immigration. The party split in 1856 over its attitude towards slavery, but not before Fillmore had had a chance to run as its presidential candidate – unsuccessfully.

The element of atomic number 13 is aluminium (Al), the commonest metal of the Earth's crust, comprising about 8% of it. Corundum, one of the forms of alumina (aluminium oxide), is the hardest naturally occurring substance after diamond, being used as the reference for the 9 on the Mohs scale.

13 is called the bakers' dozen because, in the days when bakers faced severe penalties if they supplied a short weight of bread, they gave a 13th loaf for the price of a dozen for fear of falling foul of the law. But 13 is known, too, as the Devil's dozen, as reflected in the Scots proverb: "Man's twal is nae sae guid as the De'il's dizzen." The meaning is clear: Man, unaided, has little chance against the Devil, who will always have an unfair advantage.

In Norse mythology Loki, the Principle of Evil, the "Wizard of Lies" (although originally conceived as a benign entity), was often considered to be a 13th member of the Aesir (the 12 gods of Asgard). His connection with the number 13 is underlined by the tale that, at the banquet in Valhalla where Balder was to be killed by Loki, there were 13 valkyries in attendance rather than the more conventional 12.

Between June 1962 and January 1964, Albert DeSalvo murdered 13 women in the Boston area, thereby earning for himself the nickname of the "Boston Strangler". Peter William Sutcliffe earned his nickname, the "Yorkshire Ripper", by killing 13 women in the north of England between October 1975 and November 1980.

The famous "12 Tribes of Israel" in fact numbered 13. 11 were the descendants of Jacob's sons Asher, Benjamin, Dan, Gad,

Issachar, Judah, Levi, Naphtali, Reuben, Simeon and Zebulun, while 2 were descendants of Joseph's sons Ephraim and Manasseh. The 13th, the odd tribe out, was that of Levi, who were not initially given a share in the parcelling out of the newly conquered Canaan, the Promised Land. However, the Levites pleaded for justice and were given various towns and pasturelands.

The 13 Years' War lasted from 1454 until 1466. It was fought between the Teutonic Knights, rulers of Prussia, on the one hand, and Poland, on behalf of the Prussian people, on the other. Poland won; the Prussian people didn't.

The 12th-century Jewish philosopher Moses Maimonides attempted to summarize the fundamental tenets of Judaism in clear and uncluttered form, in order to reduce the risk of the faithful sinning simply because they didn't understand what they were supposed to be doing or not doing. The resulting document is known as the 13 Principles or as the 13 Articles of Faith.

On 7th May, 1921, a football match at the Manchester United stadium between Stockport County and Leicester City had a total "gate" of 13 people. Ignoring matches at which, for reasons of earlier crowd hooliganism, teams have had to play in front of an empty stadium, this is believed to be a record low for the professional game. It is not recorded whether or not the crowd mobbed the pitch after the final whistle.

Fourteen

Eugène Ionesco is responsible for this, not me: "When I was born I was nearly 14. That's why I found it easier than most people to realize what life was all about." Understand it? No, nor I.

All told, there are 14 different species of albatross.

According to the Argentinian writer Jorge Luis Borges, there was an encyclopaedia in Ancient China which classified the animal kingdom according to the following 14 categories:

(1) those belonging to the Emperor;
(2) those embalmed;
(3) those which are tame or domesticated;
(4) suckling pigs;
(5) sirens;
(6) those which are mythological or fabulous;
(7) stray dogs;
(8) those which are included in this scheme of classification;
(9) frenzied creatures;
(10) uncountable ones;
(11) those drawn with a fine camel-hair brush;
(12) etc.;
(13) those which have just broken the water-pitcher; and
(14) those which, from a distance, look like flies.

There were 14 Apostles, according to the Bible, not 13 or 12 – the distinction being, of course, that there were only 12 *disciples*. The disciples were Andrew, Bartholomew (or Nathanael), James the Greater, James the Lesser, John, Judas, Jude, Matthew, Peter, Philip, Simon and Thomas. The 13th Apostle was Matthias, chosen by lot after the Ascension to take the place of Judas, and the 14th was of course Paul.

According to numerologists, 14 was the "fadic number" of the Bourbon kings of France – which is to say that it was involved in all the unlucky things that happened to them.

At first sight the evidence seems reasonably impressive: Louis XIV became king in 1643, nearly lost his life in 1652, took full control of France in 1661, was driven out of Italy and Holland in 1706, and died in 1715 at the age of 77 – the point being that

$$1 + 6 + 4 + 3 = 14,$$
$$1 + 6 + 5 + 2 = 14,$$
$$1 + 6 + 6 + 1 = 14,$$
$$1 + 7 + 0 + 6 = 14,$$
$$1 + 7 + 1 + 5 = 14,$$

and
$$7 + 7 = 14.$$

It would be a churl who pointed out that the two major international events in Louis's reign were the War of Devolution (1667–1668) and the War of the Spanish Succession (1701–1713), in both of which he gained little more than an economic crisis, and that

$$1 + 6 + 6 + 7 \neq 14,$$
$$1 + 6 + 6 + 8 \neq 14,$$
$$1 + 7 + 0 + 1 \neq 14,$$
and
$$1 + 7 + 1 + 3 \neq 14.$$

The numerologists' case for 14 being the fadic number of the Bourbons becomes a little desperate when we look at the case of Louis XVI. In 1788, 14 years after becoming King of France (in 1774), he issued the edict to convoke the States General, thereby precipitating the Revolution. The Bastille was stormed on 14th July, 1789, and the Constitution was accepted on 14th September, 1791. Louis was beheaded 28 (14 × 2) years after becoming Dauphin of France (1765), in 1793.

We're struggling. The Revolution actually began *15* years after Louis succeeded to the throne, and he was executed 19 years after becoming *King*. The trouble is that, by suitable selection of the events to be considered, and by varying the way in which one interprets the various dates and numbers, it is possible to "prove" that 14 – or any other reasonable number – is the fadic number of just about anyone.

Me? Well, I'm thoroughly convinced that my own fadic number is 1 . . .

☆

Quartodecimans – or "14-ers" – were so-called in the wake of a minor disagreement within the early Christian Church. The pope of the time, Anicetus, believed that Easter ought always to be held on a sunday, while some branches of the Church, notably in Asia Minor, had traditionally celebrated Easter on the 14th day of Nisan, whatever day of the week that might be, and saw no reason to change their ways. Refreshingly, in the light of the way in which this and similar trivialities would later disrupt the Church (can you see God gnashing His teeth in fury because His children are celebrating Easter on the *wrong day*?), the two sides in the debate simply agreed to differ.

At least, that was the case under Anicetus. But the argument reappeared during the reign of the 14th pope, Victor I, who held office from *c*189 until *c*199. Victor seems in many respects to have been a rather unpleasant character, and his solution to the quartodeciman problem was simply to excommunicate all quartodecimans. Fortunately St Irenaeus dissuaded him from such buffoonery.

☆

The element of atomic number 14 is silicon (Si), at 27.72% the 2nd most abundant element of the Earth's crust (after oxygen). Since silicon is capable of forming chain and ring molecules in much the same way as does carbon (see *6), an intriguing possibility is that somewhere there might be lifeforms based on silicon rather than on carbon chemistry, as we are. The odds are not good – for example, the analogue to carbon dioxide would be silicon dioxide, and exhaling quartz might be painful (quartz registers 7 on Mohs' scale) – but this view may be totally an Earth-chauvinist one.

☆

In January, 1918, President Woodrow Wilson outlined his proposals for a post World War I peace settlement; these proposals became known as the "14 Points". 9 of them concerned specific points, but 5 have a more general interest:

> (1) that covenants between nations should be open, and openly arrived at;
> (2) that all should have freedom of the seas, not only in peacetime but also during wartime;
> (3) that economic barriers between nations should be removed – insofar as is possible;
> (4) that countries' armaments should be reduced to the level where they can be used only for domestic purposes;
> (14) that there should be an "association of nations" with "specific covenants".

Point 14 was to give rise to the League of Nations (see *63), but most of the others were merely glossed over in the Treaty of Versailles. In particular, points 1 to 4, taken in conjunction with point 14, clearly comprised a sort of blueprint for the encouragement of future world peace, and so it is a very great pity that they were not given more serious attention.

In February, 1918, Wilson qualified his list by producing the "4 Principles"; in July, by the "4 Ends"; and in September by the "5 Particulars".

☆

The 14th president of the United States was Franklin Pierce (1804–1869), a relatively young and inexperienced compromise candidate of the Democratic Party who took office on 4th March, 1853. Elected on an expansionist platform, he signally failed in all such attempts owing to vacillation. He produced the Kansas–Nebraska Act (1854), which said that territories subsequently added to the Union could decide for themselves whether or not they wanted to permit slavery: this led to a mini civil war in Kansas. Pierce left office on 3rd March, 1857, to live out his remaining years in virtual obscurity.

In the USA, new guns are sold at an average rate rather greater than 1 every 14 seconds.

Fifteen

The element of atomic number 15 is phosphorus (P), a highly reactive nonmetal of extreme importance to life: the nucleic acids are phosphates. Phosphorus has 3 allotropes, one of which is well known to schoolchildren: a yellowish, waxy substance, if left exposed to the air it smoulders for a while and then bursts into flames – what fun!

Purists may wish to know that the fertilizer Superphosphate should correctly be called "calcium dihydrogenphosphate". Try that one at your garden centre.

There are fifteen books in the Book of Mormon, although 1 of these, *The Words of Mormon*, should, strictly speaking, be regarded less as a book and more as an explanation of preceding books and a prefatory introduction to succeeding ones.

The Book, engraved in an unknown language on golden plates which have not been released to the public view, was revealed by Mormon's resurrected son Moroni in 1827 to one Joseph Smith, who had earlier had the occasional brush with the law as, essentially, a con-man; still, God may have seen virtues invisible to others. Smith translated the plates with Moroni's help, and the Book was published in 1830.

At the very least, the Book is a remarkable pastiche of the King James Bible to be produced by a little educated man aged 23. Members of the Church of Jesus Christ of Latter-Day Saints hold it, of course, to be written by God – their 8th Article of Faith reads: "We believe the Bible to be the word of God as far as it is translated correctly; we also believe the Book of Mormon to be the word of God."

☆

The 15th president of the United States was James Buchanan (1791–1868), a Democrat who presided over the disintegration of the Union in the years immediately prior to the Civil War; he served from 4th March, 1857, until 3rd March, 1861. Although loudly claiming to be personally opposed to slavery, he felt that the individual states had under the Constitution the right to decide for themselves on the issue – a pretty damned odd moral stance.

☆

Sir Edward Creasy (1812–1878) is known, if at all, for his book *The 15 Decisive Battles of the World* (1851). His choice of battles was: (1) Marathon (490BC); (2) Syracuse (413BC); (3) Gaugemala (Arbela; 331BC); (4) the Battle of the Metaurus River 207BC); (5) the Battle of the Teutoburg Forest (AD9); (6) the Battle of the Catalaunian Plains (451); (7) Tours (732); (8) Hastings (1066); (9) Orléans (1429); (10) the defeat of the Spanish Armada (1588); (11) Blenheim (1704); (12) Poltava (1709); (13) Saratoga (1777); (14) Valmy (1792); and (15) Waterloo (1815).

☆

Most readers will have good reason to curse the fact that the vast majority of modern nonfiction books are either poorly indexed or not indexed at all: perusal of the Journal of the (UK) Society of Indexers, *The Indexer*, will reveal an often hilarious, often depressing, section of review-quotes concerning lousy indexes.

The phenomenon is not new, although every reasonable human being will warm to the hyperthoroughness of the indexer of *The Origin of Human Reason* (1889) by St George Jackson Mivart (1827–1900). This indexer, according to *Curious Facts* (1981), by John May *et al.*, listed an improbable tale about a cockatoo under no less than 15 headings. Here are some of them:

> "absurd tale about a cockatoo",
> "anecdote, absurd one, about a cockatoo",
> "cockatoo, absurd tale concerning one",
> "incredibly absurd tale of a cockatoo",

"invalid cockatoo, absurd tale about",
"preposterous tale about a cockatoo",
"very absurd tale about a cockatoo" and
"wonderfully foolish tale about a cockatoo".

Sixteen

A highwayman called John Rann, executed in 1774, was a famous dandy. Especially noted were the 8 ties on each leg of his breeches, which earnt him the popular nickname of "16–string Jack". It is to this character that Johnson referred when asked if Gray's poetry did not "tower above the common mark". "Yes, Sir, but we must attend to the difference between what men in general cannot do if they would, and what every man may do if he would. Sixteen-string Jack towered above the common mark."

The 16th president of the United States was Abraham Lincoln (1809–1865), a compromise Republican candidate. It is hard to assess the strength of his feelings against slavery. Although he spoke frequently and vehemently against the extension of slavery into newly acquired territories, he was never an abolitionist as such; and, while his 1863 Emancipation Proclamation, made during the Civil War, abolished slavery in the rebel states, he had earlier, in 1860, the year of his election, pledged without apparent qualms that he would not interfere with the practice of slavery in those states. It is likely that he undertook the Civil War in order to preserve the Union, with the issue of slavery as a secondary matter or as a convenient unifying cause.

He took office on 4th March, 1861, by which time 7 of the southern states had already seceded from the Union to form the Confederate States. On 12th April, 1861, Confederate guns opened fire on Fort Sumter, in South Carolina, thereby launching the Civil War. Lincoln's forces initially suffered considerable reverses against the Confederate States, now numbering 13; however, brilliant officers such as Grant and Sherman changed the picture.

Lincoln was reelected in 1864 with the war looking as good as won: on 9th April, a few weeks after he had taken office for this 2nd term, the war ended with Lee's surrender at the Appomattox Court House in Virginia.

He did not long enjoy his victory. On the night of 14 April, while at the theatre, he was shot by John Wilkes Booth, dying the following morning.

In *Revelation xiv* 19–20 we learn of the fate of the faithless of the Earth. They are harvested by angels bearing sickles and placed in the huge winepress of God's wrath. From this so much "wine" flows that it comes clear up to the horses' bridles as they work a full 16 hundred furlongs (200 miles) away.

The element whose atomic number is 16 is sulphur (S), known in the USA as "sulfur". Its presence is noted in the names of the sulphonamides, or sulpha drugs, which inhibit the reproduction of invading bacteria and are generally used in conjunction with antibiotics. The initial discoveries which led to the development of the sulphonamides were made by a German pharmacologist called Gerhard Domagk, who was consequently awarded the 1939 Nobel Prize for Physiology or Medicine. However, Hitler was in a fit of pique with the Nobel committee at the time, and so Domagk was unable to collect his medal until 1947 – by which time the cash prize had automatically reverted to Nobel Foundation funds.

In global terms, sulphur dioxide is probably the most important of sulphur's compounds, unfortunately. This particularly nasty pollutant – it reacts with water to give sulphurous acid which, while not as bad as sulphur*ic* acid, is still pretty unpleasant – is pumped into the atmosphere in large quantities all the year round because it makes "good economic sense" to continue doing so.

The 16th pope was called Callistus or Calixtus, and reigned from 217 until 222. While archdeacon to his predecessor, Zephyrinus, he established the cemetery on the Appian Way in which were to be buried all the 3rd-century popes except – ironically – himself.

He seems to have been a fairly forceful liberal, allowing absolution to penitent adulterers, fornicators, murderers and apostates. This "moral laxity" and his leanings towards the monarchian heresy caused St Hippolytus to set himself up as antipope (the only antipope ever to be accorded sainthood).

☆

According to an 1857 report in the medical journal *The Lancet*, out of every 16 female Londoners of the time, whatever their age or their marital status, 1 was engaged in prostitution.

Seventeen

"Sybil Dorsett", born in 1923, whose biography was written by Flora Rheta Schreiber (*Sybil*, 1973), possessed, over the years, a total of no less than 16 different personalities. Finally, over a decade after starting psychotherapy with Dr Cornelia Wilbur, her 16 personalities were fused into a 17th, the real Sybil.

The element of atomic number 17 is chlorine (Cl), a toxic and corrosive gas which has been used in warfare – as has its compound phosgene (carbonyl chloride). For long enough chlorine was thought to be merely a compound of oxygen: so said the notable 18th-century Swedish chemist Karl Scheele, and everyone believed his prestigious words until, in the early 19th century, Davy showed that Scheele had been talking nonsense.

The 1st chain reaction discovered was not a nuclear one, as you might have expected, but that of a mixture of chlorine with hydrogen, which goes off with a satisfying bang on being exposed to light. In 1918 Hermann Nernst showed that what happens is this: the light breaks the chlorine (Cl_2) molecule down into its 2 atoms; each of these combines with a hydrogen (H_2) molecule to produce 1 molecule of hydrogen chloride (HCl) and a free atom of hydrogen; the atom of hydrogen combines with a chlorine molecule to give a molecule of hydrogen chloride plus a free atom of chlorine . . . and so it goes on. Thus a single flash of light can cause quite a pleasing explosion.

One of the most incomprehensible of mass murderers was a certain Richard Rosse, the cook of the Bishop of Rochester. In 1531, for reasons which have never emerged, he killed 17 people at one of his master's dinners, using poison. For this crime the miserable unfortunate was boiled to death – a punishment thought fitting for a murderous cook. He may have been innocent.

The planet Saturn is now known to have at least 17 moons, whereas less than a handful of years before the time of writing it was believed to have only 10. The additional knowledge has of course come to us thanks to the Voyager probes, which have also revealed details of Saturn's ring structure sufficiently surprising to demand the reexamination of some of our basic laws of physics.

The 17th president of the United States was Andrew Johnson (1808–1875), a Democrat elected as Lincoln's vice-president on a "National Union" ticket only to find himself, 6 weeks later, on 15th April, 1865, taking over as president.

He immediately faced the problems of Reconstruction in the wake of the Civil War, and handled matters badly. Rather than force the southern states to accept the abolition of slavery – which, under the circumstances, would not have been difficult – he compromised, against the wishes of Congress, by merely insisting on an "oath of loyalty", and by condoning the notorious "black codes", laws drawn up by the southern states to ensure that the freed slaves enjoyed few of the benefits of their freedom.

Johnson was impeached in March, 1868, by a now thoroughly hostile Congress, but, by a single vote, unfortunately escaped conviction. However, he failed to secure the Democratic nomination for the 1868 election; his term of office ended on 3rd March, 1869.

To date there have been 17 poets laureate, the 1st being John Dryden, appointed in 1668 by Charles II (although in 1616 Ben Jonson had been appointed laureate in all but name by James VI & I), and the 17th being Sir John Betjeman (1906–   ).

It is pleasing to discover that the integers in 17^3 – that is, 4913 – add up to 17. Put another way, this means that $(4 + 9 + 1 + 3)^3 =$ 4913!

Eighteen

The 18th president of the United States was the Republican Ulysses Simpson Grant (1822–1885), the most notable Unionist hero of the Civil War. Although he had an impressive record as a soldier he proved an ineffectual president – despite his personal integrity, his administration was riddled with corruption, and this hardly helped him. He attempted to annex Santo Domingo, but failed; and he introduced Force Acts to ensure the rights of blacks under the 14th and 15th Amendments, but these failed because of southern obduracy and northern apathy.

He served 2 terms, from 4th March, 1869, until 3rd March, 1877, then went off to tour the world – only to be swindled out of all his capital. His Civil War memoirs, written when he was nearly penniless and suffering from throat cancer, fortunately ensured the economic security of his family.

The night before he went into his final coma, Dylan Thomas ignored the protests of his friends and went out on the town, staggering home a while later to tell them proudly that he had just drunk 18 straight whiskies.

In fact, this was almost certainly a lie: his health was by this stage so poor that he would have dropped dead long before reaching the 18th.

In the early days of golf, the number of holes in a round depended entirely on the size and topography of the course. It is only comparatively recently that the standard round has been fixed at 18 holes, and this was the result of an accident. The old course at St Andrews used to consist of 11 holes, so that by playing each hole on the way out and on the way home players could complete a round of 22 holes. In 1764 the Royal and Ancient Golf Club of St Andrews elected to convert the 1st 4 holes of the course to 2, so that golfers now played only 9 holes each way. The Royal and Ancient went on to achieve supremacy in matters golfing, and so 18 was fixed as the number of holes in a full round.

The element whose atomic number is 18 is argon (Ar), an inert gas which is relatively common in our atmosphere (0.934%).

The tale of its discovery is of interest in that it shows the value of examining discrepancies between theory and practice. During the 1880s Baron Rayleigh did some very important work on the exact atomic weight of the elements, concentrating particularly on oxygen. He noticed that the oxygen he used always had the same atomic weight, wherever he had got it from (e.g., from the air, from compounds), but that the nitrogen he got from the air seemed to have a slightly higher atomic weight than that obtained from other sources.

Enter William Ramsay, the Scots chemist. He recalled an experiment performed in 1785 by Henry Cavendish which had seemed to show that air did indeed contain small quantities of some inert gas; at the time, because the experimental results didn't seem to fit in with the theory, they were quietly forgotten about. Ramsay performed a variant of Cavendish's experiment, and turned the spectroscope onto the bubble of this strange gas. Sure enough, it proved to be a hitherto unknown element, argon.

Ramsay wasn't content with this, and went on to discover all but one of the other inert gases. Helium had been detected in the spectrum of the Sun, but in 1895 he isolated it on Earth; and in 1898 he and an assistant discovered neon, krypton and xenon. The final inert gas, radon, was not to be discovered until 1900, with advances in studies of radioactivity, by Friedrich Dorn. Ramsay salved his hurt by being the first to determine its atomic weight.

Nineteen

Joan of Arc, arguably the most famous martyr of all time, was only 19 when she was condemned and burnt at the stake. King Charles VII of France, whom she had put on the throne, made no move to save her from her fate.

The element of atomic number 19 is potassium (K), a metal rather like sodium but bursting into flames even more enthusiastically when dropped into a bowl of water. It's important to both plant and animal life, and its radioactive isotope K^{40}, which decays into Ar^{40} (argon-40) with a halflife of 1.28 billion years, is important in the dating of rocks.

It was the rejection by Charles I of the "19 Propositions" put to him in 1642 by Parliament, calling upon him to renounce the doctrine of the Divine Right of Kings and make way for the parliamentary rule of the country, which set the stage for the start of the Civil War.

☆

The 19th president of the United States was the Republican Rutherford Birchard Hayes (1822–1893), who came to office after one of the most dubious elections in presidential history. Although the Democrat Samuel Tilden won a popular majority, there were disputed results in 4 of the states. A special electoral commission, the majority of whose members were Republicans, decided that all the disputed states should be awarded to Hayes, who thereby won the election by one electoral vote.

He took office on 5th March, 1877, and, perhaps because of the irregular nature of his election, proved to be one of the better presidents the country has had. His integrity can be assessed by considering his reversal of the previous practice of appointing all one's political cronies to the plum civil-service posts on attaining presidential office, insisting that recruitment should instead be by competitive examination. For similar reasons of integrity, he refused to stand for a 2nd term, retiring on 3rd March, 1881, having done much to reunite his country.

Twenty

The word "canard" means, of course, a hoax or a fraudulence. The original canard (French *canard* = "duck") was, according to Littré's great French dictionary (published 1863–72), bruited about by Cornelissen, who claimed to have had 20 ducks. These, he said, he had killed off one by one, in each case feeding the carcase to the survivors. The marvel was that, by the time he had only 1 duck left, that doughty bird had eaten all of the other 19 – and yet still remained normal duck-size! How could this have come about?

In Lincolnshire, UK, can be found the place called Twenty.

The Society of the 20, or *Les Vingt*, was a group of Symbolist artists who exhibited together between 1891 and 1893 in Belgium. Later they were to effect the transition from Symbolism to Art Nouveau.

The 20th pope was Fabian, who reigned from 236 until 250. There is a persistent tradition that he was a layman who just happened to be there during the elections for a successor to poor Antherus. In flew a white dove to settle on his head – a sure sign that there was one more voter than everybody had thought. Under the persecution of Decius, Fabian was tortured and eventually beheaded for refusing to make a sacrifice to Decius' "genius".

The element whose atomic number is 20 is calcium (Ca), a metal, the 5th most abundant element of the Earth's crust. Many of the invertebrate animals have shells made of calcium carbonate, and some limestones are made almost entirely of the ground and compressed remains of these shells.

The mineral gypsum is the hydrated sulphate of calcium, which sounds pretty complicated until you look at the chemical formula: $CaSO_4.2H_2O$. When you heat gypsum to 128°C it loses most of the water, leaving a powder called plaster of paris. Adding water to this reforms the gypsum as a hard plaster – the ideal medium for drunken signatures.

Britain's worst mass murderess was probably Mary Ann Robson (1832–1873); her surname was successively Mowbray, Ward, Robinson and Cotton. She had probably 20 victims to her credit – the lack of precision in this figure is due to the fact that some of her "victims" may have died of natural causes, especially the younger ones. Her accredited victims, all of whom died by arsenical poisoning, are:

> (1–9) William Mowbray, her 1st husband, and her 8 children by him;
> (10) George Ward, her 2nd husband;
> (11–13) John Robinson, the son of her 3rd husband, and 2 others of his children;
> (14) her mother;
> (15–19) Frederick Cotton, her 4th (bigamous) husband; Margaret Cotton, his sister; her child by Cotton; Cotton's 2 sons by an earlier marriage; and
> (20) Joseph Nattrass, her lover.

It is a sign of those times that she was able to continue her career for so long before people started asking questions. It is also a sign of those times that this obviously desperately sick woman was hanged.

The 20th president of the United States was James Abram Garfield (1831–1881), selected as a compromise candidate by the Republicans after Hayes had refused to stand for reelection. He continued Hayes' reforms of the civil service, and extended these to the postal services. However, on 2nd July, 1881, a French-Canadian called Charles Jules Guiteau shot him twice in a railway station in Washington for reasons which are still obscure (suffice it to say that "divine inspiration" played its part) and, although Garfield clung to life for a few weeks, he died on 19th September, 1881.

It is a sad reflection on human nature that, thanks to his assassination, the introduction of the reforms he had been trying to bring about was considerably advanced.

The Maya and the ancient Gauls used a counting system which worked to the base 20 – as opposed to our familiar system of counting to the base *10. Clearly these people used as their base the number of digits on a full set of 2 hands and 2 feet, whereas our system was born from the use of the number of digits on a pair of hands. For higher numbers, the Maya switched to the base *60 – but then they were not the only ones.

Twenty-One

At the time of writing, 21 of Elvis Presley's albums have sold more than 1 million copies each.

The 21st president of the United States was Chester Alan Arthur (1830–1886), who, as vice-president, took up the reins after Garfield's death. Arthur's history was a patchy one: as an attorney he had won some important civil-rights cases, but as an administrator he had been removed from his position as head of customs collection in the port of New York after a corruption investigation prompted by Hayes. The former instance seems to give a more accurate picture of the man: he proposed the heretical notion that the welfare of the country ought to come before narrow party interests, and so did not gain the Republican nomination for the election of 1884. He left office on 3rd March, 1885.

In the old days, when money was money, there were 21 shillings to the guinea (= £1.05). It was a guinea which put paid to the life of the poet Thomas Otway (1652–1685). Penniless and starving, he accepted the philanthropic gift of a (20-shilling) guinea, bought himself a loaf of bread with a small part of it, and choked to death on the first mouthful.

The popular card-game pontoon is known also, variously, as *vingt-et-un*, blackjack, and 21.

The element of atomic number 21 is scandium (Sc), a metal which is one of the "rare-earth elements", grouped together because all have much the same properties.

When the great Russian chemist Mendeléev first drew up his Periodic Table of the Elements (1st version published 1869) he realized that the patterns of the properties of the elements involved varied in such a way that he could predict the existence of further elements which had yet to be discovered. 3 he described in some detail (in 1871), one of them being "eka-boron". In 1879 Lars Nilson discovered a new element which he christened scandium (he was Swedish), and in the same year Per Cleve showed that this element was in fact Mendeléev's "eka-boron".

Mendeléev's other 2 predictions were "eka-aluminium", which proved to be gallium, discovered in 1875, and "eka-silicon", now known as germanium, discovered in 1886. All 3 of his predicted elements were thus given nationalistic names.

The great French astronomer Charles Messier (1730–1817), best known for his catalogue of *103 nebulous objects, was primarily an enthusiastic comet-hunter. He discovered no less than 21 "new" ones – a figure not far short of a record.

Twenty-Two

In *No Orchids for Miss Blandish* (1939) by James Hadley Chase, arguably the 1st of the modern school of "realistic" thrillers in which violence is so much the main object that it is often used as a direct substitute for sex, 22 of the characters, all male, are "rubbed out": 15 are shot (6 with a machine-gun, to make it especially titillating), 3 stabbed to death, 2 beaten to death with a blackjack, 1 kicked to death, and 1 forced to commit suicide.

The element of atomic number 22 is titanium (Ti), a metal much used in metallurgy for the creation of corrosion- and temperature-resistant, strong, light alloys popular in the aerospace industry. Titanium dioxide is a white pigment used in paints, plastics and the like.

The 22nd pope was Lucius I, whose pontificate lasted less than a year, between 253 and 254. Banished under the persecution of the Emperor Gallus, he seems to have been positively annoyed that he was shortly afterwards allowed to return to Rome without having been martyred.

The Order of the Knights of St Patrick was founded in 1783 by George III. It is restricted to the monarch, a grand master (the lord lieutenant of the day), the princes of the blood royal, and 22 knights. Its motto is *Quis separabit?*

The 22nd president of the United States was Stephen Grover Cleveland (1837–1908), a Democrat of legendary honesty and integrity; he was nominated and elected despite the opposition of some of the less ethical elements of his own party, taking office on 4th March, 1885. It is probably because of this honesty of his – which naturally earnt him many enemies – and his determination to expose graft and corruption that he lost the election of 1888 to Harrison. However, Cleveland was to return as *24th president, in due course.

There are 22 major trumps in a pack of Tarot cards, normally given as follows: (0) the Fool, (1) the Juggler, (2) the Female Pope, (3) the Empress, (4) the Emperor, (5) the Pope, (6) the Lovers, (7) the Chariot, (8) Justice, (9) the Hermit, (10) the Wheel of Fortune, (11) Strength, (12) the Hanged Man, (13) Death, (14) Temperance, (15) the Devil, (16) the Falling Tower, (17) the Star, (18) the Moon, (19) the Sun, (20) the Day of Judgement and (21) the World. The meanings ascribed to the various trumps – as to the rest of the cards in the Tarot pack – depend upon whether the cards appear the right way up or upside-down. In not all cases does the upside-down appearance of a trump imply a simple reversal of meaning: the Hanged Man, the right way up, has meanings such as suffering, sacrifice and early death, while its meaning when "reversed" include pain and punishment.

Twenty-Three

If you have 23 people at your party, there is a 50:50 chance that 2 of them will share the same birthday.

☆

The unorthodox psychologist Wilhelm Fliess (see *284) believed that virtually everything to do with Man and his little Universe could be explained or expressed in terms of the important numbers 23 and 28. He based this belief on his theory that the normal male has a sexual cycle of 23 days and the normal female one of 28 days (this is *not*, however, the menstrual cycle, which for some reason is *quite different*). Eager mathematicians will note that their own and their spouses' cycles should therefore be "in step" only once every 644 days – a depressing thought.

Numerologically speaking, Fliess was delighted to find that so many "important numbers" could be expressed in the form $23a + 28b$, where a and b are whole numbers. He seems not to have realized that in fact *any* whole number can be expressed in this way – by adjusting the values of a and b. In order to test this, choose at random any whole number and set to work. For my part I picked mystic 7, and within a few moments found that the equation worked if I substituted the values $a = -7$ and $b = 6$.

This is not a special property of 23 and 28. Again choosing 7, but this time selecting at random the coefficients 15 and 17, I swiftly found that $15a + 17b = 7$ when $a = 5$ and $b = -4$.

Freud believed in Fliess's ideas – or at least had a considerable amount of time for them – for a number of years, and was quite surprised when he did not drop down dead at the age of 23 + 28 = 51 years.

Although the most recent pope called John was Pope John XXIII, there have in fact been only 22 popes called John; the 23rd reckoned in the counting was one of the 3 antipopes of that name, "John XVI", who "reigned" from 997–998 before being deposed, imprisoned and blinded by the Holy Roman Emperor Otto III.

The element of atomic number 23 is vanadium (V), a metal which has the distinction of having been discovered twice. The first time was by the Spanish–Mexican mineralogist Andrès Del Rio, who found this new metal in 1801 and called it "erythronium". Unfortunately, everybody else said it was just chromium, which had already been discovered. Not unnaturally, Del Rio stamped his foot, went off in a huff, and stopped discovering elements. It wasn't until 1831 that the Swedish chemist Nils Sefström discovered vanadium all over again.

Christine Sizemore is probably the most famous multiple personality of all times, the subject of Corbett Thigpen's bestselling book, *The Three Faces of Eve,* which was subsequently made into a successful movie. Later Sizemore admitted that far more than the 4 personalities described in the book had inhabited her body: in all, there had been 22 which, in 1975, fused together to form a stable 23rd.

The 23rd president of the United States was the Republican Benjamin Harrison (1833–1901), the grandson of William Harrison, the 9th president. A hero from the Civil War, he was nevertheless either an incompetent or an unlucky president, depending upon how charitable you feel. The single noteworthy achievement of his administration on the domestic front was the Sherman Antitrust Act, which sought to curb the powers of the great monopolies: the act didn't work very well, but it was a start.

When the Democrats captured Congress in 1890 it spelt the end of Harrison's credibility as President, although the Republicans nominated him for reelection. Even the death of his wife a couple of weeks before polling day failed to pull in enough votes for his reelection. He had served from 4th March, 1889, until 3rd March, 1893.

The official figure for the number of deaths during the 1976 US swine 'flu epidemic is given as 23. The tragedy is that these people lost their lives not as a direct result of the disease – the epidemic never really got off the ground – but as a result of symptoms caused by the vaccine.

The national vaccination programme had been championed by President Gerald Ford, and budgeted to cost $135 million.

Twenty-Four

Initially it may seem surprising that 24 does not have at least some of the numerological importance of 7, the number of days in a week, and 365, the number of days in a year. This is probably because, to the ancients, the notion that there were 24 hours to the day was far less important than the practice of having 12 hours of daytime and 12 of night, the lengths of the hours being adjusted to fit in with this scheme (see *12). 24 does gain a certain measure of importance from the fact that it is highly divisible – it gives whole-number results when divided by 2, 3, 4, 6, 8 and 12, and so acquires some of the properties of each of these numbers.

The 24th president of the United States was once again Grover Cleveland, who had earlier served as 22nd president; he is the only president ever to have "returned from the dead".

His resurrection was not a success. The USA was facing economic depression and Cleveland's efforts to help the situation had little or no effect. Moreover, he lost popular support by his hamfisted attempts to deal with labour troubles. At the end of his term he failed to secure the Democratic nomination, and so left office on 3rd March, 1897.

The Democratic candidate in that election, William Jennings Bryan (1860–1925), is of more than passing interest. Although he supported women's suffrage, he opposed the theory of evolution on fundamentalist grounds, and acted as the (successful) prosecuting attorney at the infamous Scopes Trial of 1925, in which a biology teacher was brought to court for having broken the Tennessee law against discussing the theory in class. (The verdict was later overturned.) Bryan ran for the presidency in 1896, 1900 and 1908 – never with success.

In *The Book of Revelation*, from chapter *iv* onwards, a recurring role is played by the 24 elders, initially encountered seated on 24 thrones in the presence of the Lord (*iv* 4).

The element whose atomic number is 24 is chromium (Cr), an important metal used in the making of hard and stainless steels.

Chromium was discovered in 1797 by the French chemist Louis Vauquelin, and a few months later by the German chemist Martin Klaproth, who had been working quite independently. Don't waste too much sympathy on Klaproth, though, for having missed out on fame and recognition this time: he discovered so many other elements, including uranium (see *92), that the odd one here and there can't have mattered much to him!

The purity of gold is expressed in terms of carats, a single carat representing one 24th part. Thus 24-carat gold is pure gold, 12-carat gold only 50% gold and 50% base metal, and so on. These carats mustn't be confused with the carats used in the weighing of precious stones – those are quite different. For gems, the generally accepted standard is the metric carat, which equals 0.2 grams.

In the USA the distinction is often made between karats (gold) and carats (gems).

Twenty-Five

When he was aged only 2, W. S. Gilbert (1836–1911) was kidnapped and held to ransom in Naples. Luckily his parents were able to find the cash to pay for his return. Even allowing for inflation, the sum demanded seems unusually modest: £25.

The element of atomic number 25 is manganese (Mn), a useful metal employed in making alloys. But there is a problem: manganese ore deposits on the land are not especially common. This problem will to a large extent be solved should Man continue to explore and exploit the deep ocean floors, for lumps of manganese are lying around there for the taking. These manganese nodules form by the straightforward accretion of the metal onto an initial "seed", in much the same way that pearls are formed.

The 25th president of the United States was the Republican William McKinley (1843–1901); his election occurred largely as a result of the efforts of Marcus Alonzo Hanna, an industrialist who successfully eased McKinley into various political offices, culminating in the presidency (Hanna raised $3.5 million to effect this last little feat).

In 1900 McKinley was elected for a 2nd term, but on 14th September, 1901, in Buffalo, NY, he was assassinated by an anarchist called Leon Czolgosz. Later that year Czolgosz was put to death for the crime.

25 scholars were involved in the production of the Revised Version of the Bible, begun in 1870; of these, 10 died before the work was completed in 1885. It is interesting to note that the New Testament, finished before the Old, in 1881, was not favourably received by the critics because of recurring stylistic flaws; such flaws were largely avoided when the Old Testament appeared. This response to adverse criticism poses all sorts of questions about how literally we should interpret any version of the Bible available to us.

The 25th pope was Dionysius, elected a full 11 months after the death of his predecessor, Sixtus II; the reason for the delay was the persecution of Christians under the Emperor Valerian. Dionysius was elected in 259 and died at the end of 268. Interestingly enough, he is the 1st pope whom tradition accepts as not having suffered martyrdom.

Twenty-Six

There are only 26 known perfect numbers. A perfect number is one whose factors, including 1, when added up equal the number itself. The smallest and best known example of a perfect number is 6 (1 + 2 + 3 = 6); then come *28, *496 and 8128 (1 + 2 + 4 + 8 + 16 + 32 + 64 + 127 + 254 + 508 + 1016 + 2032 + 4064 = 8128).

After that, things become a little more mathematical. All perfect numbers have the general form $2^{n-1}(2^n - 1)$, where n is a prime number (i.e., a number like 29 which has no factors); in the case of 6, n has the value 2. The 26th perfect number, discovered only in 1979, is $2^{44,496}(2^{44,497} - 1)$. This number is of the order of $3.2 \times 10^{26,788}$ and would fill about 12 pages of this book if written out in full.

In the state of Kentucky can be found the settlement called Twenty-Six.

There is a dice game called 26 in which the player selects a number between 1 and 6 and then throws a set of 10 dice 13 times (i.e., 130 die-throws all told) in the attempt to "show" his selected number at least 26 times. Clearly he has a 130/156 = 5/6 = 0.83333 . . . chance of succeeding in this venture.

The element of atomic number 26 is iron (Fe), a metal of such economic importance that the subject is barely worth going into – after all, a whole age of our cultural development is named after it. Much more interesting are its magnetic properties and, in particular, its high abundance in the Earth's core: taken together, these give our planet a magnetic field.

Studies of iron-bearing rocks allow us to determine the position of the magnetic poles of the Earth in ages past – and examining rocks from different continents has given a dramatic proof of the theory of continental drift (on the basis that, had the continents all stayed in the places they occupy today, then the magnetic poles throughout history would have had to be in several places at once). Moreover, examination of the rocks around midocean ridges, where material is welling up molten from the mantle below and solidifying, has shown that the direction of the Earth's magnetic field periodically reverses – so that the "north" pole of your compass would, after a reversal, point south. We're "due" for a reversal about now.

By playing with a top or a gyroscope, one can easily witness the phenomenon known as precession: while the top or gyroscope is spinning rapidly, its "pole" more slowly traces out a circle. The Earth, the great gyroscope upon which we all live, acts in a similar way: its north pole (and its south pole, of course) traces out a circle every 26 thousand years or so. In astrology, this has given rise to the notion of the "Platonic Year", which runs from the start of one "Age of Aquarius" (say) to the start of the next (see *12); the Platonic Year is, of course, equal to 26 thousand conventional ones. (A possibly more accurate figure for all this is 25,776 years, but there are so many imponderables involved that such accuracy is spurious and so 26 thousand years is generally accepted.)

Some thinkers have recently combined the reversals of the Earth's magnetic field and the phenomenon of precession to produce a new version of the "poleshift" theory – the notion that, from time to time, the Earth flips over to operate "upside down". When the Earth flips over, its magnetic field stays in the same place, they explain, which is why we see apparent reversals in the field recorded in the rocks.

Normal precession is not much use in turning the Earth swiftly upside-down – and the flip obviously has to be a swift one if you're to have a really good cataclysm. The poleshifters therefore invoke "fast precession" which can most easily be seen by playing with a toy called a tippe-top. This looks rather like an idealized apple with a thick stalk; when spun, the tippe-top very quickly turns over to stand spinning on its stalk. The interesting things are that (a) unlike a gyroscope, which will strongly resist being turned upside-down, the tippe-top is only too eager to do so; and (b) the direction of the tippe-top's spin, as viewed from the outside, is unchanged by the inversion, which means that, for the mites standing on the tippe-top, the direction of the spin has apparently reversed. Some old catastrophe accounts tell of the Sun rising in the west and so, say the poleshifters, clearly the Earth has suffered tippe-top, or "fast-precession", inversions in the past.

The trouble is that the tippe-top does its stuff when spun on a surface such as the top of a table. The Earth is not sitting on a table, however . . .

☆

The 26th president of the United States was the Republican Theodore "Teddy" Roosevelt (1858–1919), the youngest president and probably the most remarkable. He took office on 14th

September, 1901, following McKinley's assassination, and served until 3rd March, 1909.

A prodigious traveller, explorer and writer, he became a national hero in the Spanish–American War (1898); with Leonard Wood he led the famous "Rough Riders" or 1st Regiment of US Cavalry Volunteers, a unit made up of cowboys and ranchers. It's therefore not surprising that McKinley had selected him as running-mate in 1900.

His foreign policy was aggressive – in 1903 gunboat diplomacy won the USA the Panama Canal Zone – although he himself was proudest of his conservation efforts: 250 million acres were added to the national forests. He received the 1906 Nobel Prize for Peace for his mediatory role in the Russo-Japanese War.

He chose not to stand for a further term in 1908, making way for Taft; but in 1912 he ran for the presidency once more, this time as a candidate of the Progressive Party (the Bull Moose Party, a short-lived dissenting offshoot of the Republicans); he was unsuccessful. Deciding, therefore, to give up politics, he instead mounted an expedition to South America.

The honour of achieving the lowest innings total ever in Test cricket goes to the New Zealand side which faced England in March 1955. No less than 5 of their batsmen each contributed 0 to the total of 26 runs, while the top scorer, Sutcliffe, managed 11.

Twenty-Seven

For some considerable while the ampersand, &, was often considered to be the 27th letter of the English alphabet.

The 27th president of the United States was William Howard Taft (1857–1930), a Republican who served from 4th March, 1909, until 3rd March, 1913. An extremely inept politician, he had the presidency thrust upon him by Roosevelt, his predecessor, in comparison with whom he suffered yet further. His ineptitude wrecked his popularity, and a dissident wing of the Republicans broke away to form the short-lived Progressive Party, whose candidate against him was none other than . . . Roosevelt. The result of the dissent was Wilson's landslide victory.

In 1921 Taft was appointed Chief Justice of the Supreme Court; no one else has ever held both this and the presidential office.

27 seems to be a murderers' number! Both Petiot and Mudgett were executed for 27 murders, although both certainly committed far more than that (see *63 and *200). Another such killer was discovered in 1973 when a youth called Wayne Henley confessed to Pasadena police that he had shot dead a friend of his – Dean Corll, aged 33, locally regarded as a "real good guy" – in order to stop Corll murdering more young boys. At the rate of $200 per head, Henley had been bringing boys to Corll's house; there, with or without Henley's help, they were filled with drink and/or drugs, tied down to a wooden board, sexually assaulted, tortured and murdered. In the wake of Henley's confession the police found the remains of 27 corpses, although it seems certain that Corll must have killed over 30 boys in these repellent circumstances.

One is tempted to take 27's macabre qualities to ridiculous extremes. The birthdates of 3 of the best known (and perhaps greatest living) horror-movie stars of our time are: Vincent Price, 27th May, 1911; Peter Cushing, 27th May, 1913; and Christopher Lee, 27th May, 1922.

The element of atomic number 27 is cobalt (Co), the first metal to be discovered – in about 1730, by George Brandt – which had been unknown to the ancient world. Its compounds are used as blue pigments, and the metal itself is used in alloys – one such is Alnico, made of cobalt, aluminium, nickel and iron, which is used to make magnets.

In medicine, so-called "cobalt bombs" are used as sources of gamma rays in the treatment of cancer. The military, excited by the emotive term "cobalt bomb", are keen to develop a nuclear weapon using the same radioisotope (cobalt-60); the isotope's advantage is that it has a longish halflife, so that the bomb's fallout would remain deadly for years. What a nice bunch of people.

As an experiment, in 1977 a US writer retyped Jerzy Kosinski's prize-winning novel *Steps*, published in 1969, and began submitting it to publishers and literary agents as just another unsolicited manuscript by an unknown. At the time of reporting (in *The Book of Lists 2*) this manuscript had been rejected 27 times.

Twenty-Eight

In June, 1950, at the Desert Inn Casino in Las Vegas, a punter made 28 consecutive passes at the craps table – a 1 in 268.44 million chance. Had he let his winnings carry over from roll to roll, he would have walked away from the table over $500 million the richer for his initial $2 bet. Sadly, he bet only $2 per throw and so came away with only $756.

The element of atomic number 28 is nickel (Ni), a metal whose alloys are important. Best known is cupronickel, the alloy of copper and nickel used in most countries of the world to make "silver" coins – such as the US 5-cent piece known as the nickel.

Churchill's "antidisestablishmentarianism" is a word much beloved of schoolchildren, because it is "of course", with 28 letters, the longest word in the English language. Unfortunately, this is not true; readers are advised to see *29, just for starters.

The *88 constellations are used by astronomers as a convenient way of labelling the stars we see in the sky – ∝ Centauri, for example, is the brightest star in the constellation Centaurus. In oriental astronomy there grew up a system which served a similar function, that of the 28 "lunar mansions" – *nakshatra* to the Indians and *hsiu* to the Chinese. As you might guess, the Moon entered a new lunar mansion each day; after a complete circuit of 28 days, the Moon began the cycle once again in the first. The system in its complete form was certainly in use by 800BC, and had been in existence for perhaps 1000 years before that.

These very early dates erode the definitive statements of those archaeologists who consider it "impossible" that ancient peoples in Europe could have built megaliths such as Stonehenge for purposes related to astronomical observation.

Because of the link between the menstrual cycle and the lunar cycle, both being of 28 days, some odd theories have cropped up in numerological and other fields. (For Fliess's theory, see *23.) My favourite is the theory of a certain Professor A. Gerson, writing in 1920. Apparently, primitive males hunted for their women only on nights when the Moon was bright. The women fled from the eager men, but nevertheless became sexually excited at the thought of what might happen if they were caught. This rush of blood to the uterus became, over the aeons, exaggerated until it became a monthly bloodletting.

The theory could only have come from a man – and from a man whose ideas of women were fixed firmly in the Victorian mould. But what alarms me is this: why didn't the same thing happen to the male of the species?

☆

28 is the 2nd smallest of the *26 known perfect numbers (1 + 2 + 4 + 7 + 14 = 28).

☆

The 28th president of the United States was Woodrow Wilson (1856–1924), a Democrat who served from 4th March, 1913, until 3rd March 1921. He made countless worthwhile reforms, the least successful of which was Prohibition (introduced in 1919 by the 18th Amendment; it was scrapped as unworkable in 1933, by the 21st Amendment).

Wilson brought the USA into World War I in 1917 with considerable reluctance; in the war's aftermath he played a dominant role in setting up the League of Nations (see *14 and *63). For this he received the 1920 Nobel Prize for Peace. However, in his own country a Republican-dominated Senate refused, for questionable reasons, to ratify the League – thereby, eventually, dooming it. Wilson set out on a countrywide tour to drum up popular support for the League, but collapsed with a stroke under the strain. During the last 18 months or so of his presidency the government was run by his cabinet, aided by his wife.

☆

In 1973 Pat Coombs managed effectively to scupper the launch of a new breakfast cereal after 28 unsuccessful "takes" of a planned television commercial. Unfortunately, in each case, when it came to the moment she was unable to remember the cereal's name. At that point the crew gave up, and the ad was never completed.

Twenty-Nine

On 19th March, 1955, in Texas, Carolyn Wharton was kidnapped. At the time Carolyn was only 29 minutes old.

Although the specific criticism is untrue, in his "Soliloquy of the Spanish Cloister" Browning certainly caught something of the tenor of St Paul's message for us all:

There's a great text in Galatians,
Once you trip on it, entails
Twenty-nine distinct damnations,
One sure, if another fails.

February initially had 29 days, but in 8BC Augustus Caesar took the month called "*Sextilis*" and renamed it "August" in honour of himself. However, he was concerned that, if he did no more than this, the month named for him would have 1 day less than July, the month named for Julius Caesar, and so he added an extra day to its existing 30, taking that day from February.

This in no way explains a rather curious English proverb which runs, roughly: "Reckon right, and February has one and thirty days." This sounds suitably incomprehensible to have been uttered by one of Stella Gibbons' Starkadders, but is in fact traditional. It's unlikely that it refers to a lost dating system; the best explanation seems to be that, by the power of intellect or will, the least may be made as great as the greatest.

The element of atomic number 29 is copper (Cu), a metal as beautiful as gold, almost as useful in electrical work, and more useful in most other applications (it is, for example, harder than gold). However, it is considerably cheaper than gold – simply because it is commoner and tarnishes more easily. That rarity rather than usefulness or beauty should determine the value of a natural resource is a curious comment on the nature of the human animal.

Copper is a vital trace element in our diets since without it our bodies couldn't manufacture haemoglobin.

The human skull consists of 29 bones, 8 of them being fused together to form the cranium, the dome which protects the brain. Sir Richard Owen, the famous but startlingly unsuccessful 19th-century biologist and palaeontologist, had a theory that the skull is in fact just an extension of the backbone – i.e., that it is a vertebra with specialized modifications.

The 29th pope, Marcellinus, was elected in 296. Emperor Diocletian started his vicious persecution of the Christians in 303, and it is believed that in about 304 Pope Marcellinus publicly renounced his faith in order to save his own skin – and who could blame him? He is said later to have repented his apostasy and actually gone so far as to *martyr himself* – a rather extreme way of ensuring future honour as a saint.

The historical reliability of this tale is hard to assess.

The longest word in *The Shorter Oxford English Dictionary* (1965 edition) has a mere 29 letters: "Floccinaucinihilipilification. *joc.* 1741. (f. L. *flocci, nauci, nihili, pili* words signifying 'at little' or 'at nothing' (see Eton Latin Grammar) + -FICATION.) The action or habit of estimating as worthless."

Even by adding a rather desperate "istic" we still have only a 34-letter word, and we can do better than that (see *34).

The 29th president of the United States was Warren Gamaliel Harding (1865–1923), a Republican who served from 4th March, 1921, until his death on 2nd August, 1923, during a nationwide tour trying to drum up support for the League of Nations. After his death details emerged of the corruption of some of the highest officers of his administration (he had made the silly mistake of appointing political cronies to many important positions) as well as of a series of sexual affairs he had been embroiled in as an escape from the misery of his marriage. Such scandals have disguised the fact that he was a basically good man – if a poor president.

Lorenzo Castelli was knocked over and killed by a train in 1977, and you might have thought that then his troubles would have been over. But no! Because his actions had resulted in 3 trains being subjected to delays – the most serious of them being a full 29 minutes – his dead body was sued by the Italian railways.

When Albert Fish, the notorious cannibalistic sex murderer, was arrested in New York in 1934 it proved that he had 29 needles completely embedded in his body – most of them in the genital region. This seemingly gentle old boy produced confessions of a life so hideously bizarre that even the prosecution was unwilling for such matters to be introduced in court. Found guilty, Fish was electrocuted at the 2nd attempt: the failure of the 1st charge was probably because of a short-circuit among all the metal embedded in his body.

Thirty

The origins of the word "honeymoon" are not entirely clear, but it is generally accepted that the word records an old German custom of drinking hydromel (a type of mead, or honey-wine) more-or-less non-stop for 30 days after the wedding. Attila the Hun practised this custom so enthusiastically after his own wedding that he died before the 30 days were up.

30 is sometimes regarded as an unlucky number because of the account in Matthew's gospel of Christ's betrayal by Judas for the fee of 30 pieces of silver. Judas, of course, hearing that Christ had been condemned to death, took the silver and threw it at the feet of the priests before going away to hang himself. The priests recognized that what they had was blood-money, which could not really be added to holy funds, and so they bought with it the field of a potter to be used as a graveyard for foreigners.

Matthew claims that all of this was predicted in *Jeremiah*. Such is not in fact the case. The best I can find is that Jeremiah did buy a *field*, from his cousin Hanamel of Anathoth, for 17 *silver* shekels, and had the deeds placed in an earthenware *pot* for safekeeping (*Jeremiah xxxii*). Elsewhere the prophet is instructed by Yahweh to visit a potter (*xviii*) in order to buy a jug which he must smash in the place called Topheth which, it is predicted, will become a burial ground (*xix*). Equating Topheth with the potter's field seems to be stretching matters a little.

The 30th president of the United States was John Calvin Coolidge (1872–1933), a Republican who served from Harding's death on 3rd August, 1923, until 3rd March, 1929. He continued much as Harding would have done, although he replaced corrupt governmental officials by honest ones, rigorously pursuing administrational integrity.

The oligarchy which, under Spartan influence, ruled Athens briefly between 404 and 403BC, in the wake of the Peloponnesian War, was known to its detractors as the "Rule of the 30 Tyrants".

The element whose atomic number is 30 is zinc (Zn), a blue-white metal much used in alloys: brass is an alloy of copper and zinc. The metal is used also in batteries, in galvanizing, in dentistry, in fungicides, and so on. It is a vital trace element in our diets, being found in red blood cells and in insulin.

The Augeian stables, which housed 3000 oxen, had not been cleaned for 30 years when the strong-stomached Hercules was called upon to perform the task within 1 day; this he agreed to do on condition that he was given one 10th of the oxen. In fact, Hercules was able to avoid a singularly unpleasant task by diverting the courses of the rivers Alpheus and Peneius so that they ran through the stables. King Augeias promptly refused to give Hercules his 10% – an act of meanness which he was in later years to rue.

The 30 Years' War was in fact a series of wars, involving most of the countries of northern Europe. The wars started when the Protestants of Bohemia revolted against Catholic rule: they were rather swiftly put down. However, Denmark, fearing the might of the Hapsburg Empire, decided to invade northern Germany – only to be defeated in 1629, when the Holy Roman Emperor Ferdinand II (reigned 1619–37) issued the Edict of Restitution, which gave lands back to the Catholic Church. In 1630 Gustavus Adolphus, the Swedish king, led the Protestant German princes against the Holy Roman Emperor, only to be killed in 1632. The German states were ready to make peace, but then France decided to chance its hand . . . and so more and more

human beings were killed until eventually the Peace of Westphalia (1648) put an end to the whole nonsense.

Thirty-One

There are 31 letters in the Cyrillic alphabet.

The 31st president of the United States was the Republican Herbert Clark Hoover (1874–1964), one of the most inept men ever to have held the office; he served from 4th March, 1929, until 3rd March, 1933. He had been in office only a few months when the Wall Street Crash heralded the Depression, and it was at once obvious that he was totally incapable of handling the crisis. His most stupid move occurred in 1932 when the "Bonus Army", consisting of some 15,000 jobless war veterans, converged on Washington demanding that they should be allowed to cash bonus certificates issued to them in 1924 as a token of recognition of their war service. Hoover's response was to call in the military to drive the Bonus Army from the city – a clear breach of the pragmatic rule that "the government may welch, but it must not be seen to welch".

Largely as a result of this and of Hoover's general lackwittedness in the handling of economic affairs, Franklin Roosevelt had a landslide victory in the elections of 1932.

The outcome of the famous case of the Salem "witches" was that, in 1692, 31 of them were sentenced to death. 2 died before the sentence could be carried out, 19 were hanged, and 1 was pressed to death. In the spring of the following year it was realized that the entire case was a farce, and so the remaining 9 prisoners under sentence of death were simply released.

It seems likely that the "witches" were merely victims of mass hysteria. Today they could be rather simply cured – but then the 17th century was an ignorant one. We can say this from the smug vantage-point of the 20th century: what will the people of the 23rd century think of us?

The element whose atomic number is 31 is gallium (Ga), one of the 3 elements predicted by Mendeléev (see *21). It is a metal of few commercial uses, although it's of importance in the making of transistors and semiconductors, and it had a brief period of glory when calculators used illuminated displays: alloyed with arsenic and phosphorus, it was – and is – used in the manufacture of light-emitting diodes.

But gallium's special interest is that, with a melting-point of 29.78°C (85.6°F – it melts in your hand *and* in your mouth) and a boiling-point of 2403°C (4357°F), it is a liquid over a greater temperature range than is any other element.

Oddly enough, although it has somehow failed to achieve popular recognition, gallium is about as common as lead.

Thirty-Two

Philip III of Spain (1578–1621) probably set a royal record by fathering no fewer than 32 documented bastards.

☆

The 32nd pope was Miltiades, known also as Melchiades. He was elected in 311, some time after the death of his predecessor, Eusebius; his election immediately followed the issue of a decree of toleration of Christianity by the Emperor Galerius – who, ironically, had been primarily responsible for persuading Diocletian to start his hideous persecution of the Christians a little more than a decade before.

Galerius died in 310 and his antiChristian co-emperor, Maxentius, was killed in conflict against Constantine, who succeeded as Emperor. Of course, Constantine is a great hero of the Church, despite the fact that in many ways he was a rather unpleasant despot: first he declared that Christianity and other religions were lawful, and then he became a Christian himself. Moreover, he gave to Miltiades the Lateran Palace, the papal residence until 1309.

Miltiades died in January, 314. It was believed that he would have lived longer had it not been for the suffering to which he had been subjected before the start of his pontificate, and so he is accepted as a martyr. This is presumably because it became fashionable for early popes to be honoured as martyrs, and it was actually quite *difficult* to suffer martyrdom under Constantine.

☆

In the days of Edward II there was an Irish volumetric measure called the crannock, which equalled 32 gallons; sometimes, however, it equalled only 16 gallons – a situation which must have been confusing for all.

There are 32 letters in the Coptic alphabet, and 32 points to the compass.

The 32nd president of the United States was Franklin Delano Roosevelt (1882–1945), a Democrat, who served from 4th March, 1933, until 12th April, 1945 – the longest period ever served by a US president (he was the 1st and so far only president to serve a 3rd term).

The element of atomic number 32 is germanium (Ge), one of the 3 elements predicted by Mendeléev (see *21). A semiconductor, it was of some importance in the days before the silicon chip, being used in the manufacture of transistors.

In comparison with the oft-quoted mosquito (see *47), modern Man is comparatively underequipped with teeth. A full adult set has only 32: 8 incisors, 4 canines, 8 premolars and 12 molars (of which 4 are the wisdom teeth).

According to a recent survey, "Main Street" is only the 32nd most frequently used street-name in the USA.

The leading flat-Earther Wilbur Glenn Voliva (1870–1942) maintained that the Sun is only 32 miles in diameter and only about 3000 miles away. He proved this using the impeccable logic of the theory of Divine Design: since the sole purpose of the Sun must be to serve Man as a source of illumination, it would be ridiculous if it were any further away. After all, quipped Voliva, if you wanted a bedside light you wouldn't set up a searchlight in the next city. Yes but . . .

Thirty-Three

The 33rd pope was Sylvester or Silvester I, elected at the end of January 314 (he was to reign until 335). One legend about him has it that he cured the then still pagan Constantine of leprosy; Constantine was naturally an instant convert to Christianity. Other legends about Sylvester abound, but little is known for certain. The "Donation of Constantine", a document which purports to grant the papacy, in the shape of Sylvester, extensive temporal power in Italy and the West, is in fact a forgery dating from about the 8th century.

In Uruguay there is a place called Treinta y Tres. Keen Spanish scholars will instantly realize that this means that the place's name is, in English, 33.

The 33rd president of the United States was the Democrat Harry S Truman (1884–1972), who took over on the death of Roosevelt on 12th April, 1945, and served until 19th January, 1953.

Ironically, for the man who had guts enough to order the dropping of the atom bomb on Hiroshima and Nagasaki (a filthy, despicable decision perhaps, but a gutsy one nevertheless), he had throughout his presidency considerable difficulty in getting his measures through Congress. This was a particular pity in the case of his Fair Deal programme, which contained reforms in the fields of, for example, civil rights, education and the health service.

Although apparently vastly unpopular, he shocked all the pundits by successfully running for reelection in 1948; he then fell face-first into all the same old difficulties. His simplistic attitude towards Communism, which he regarded in any guise as the arch-enemy of Absolutely Everything, embroiled him in the McCarthyite witch-hunts of the early 1950s, and all their attendant evils (minor evils, perhaps, in comparison with what Stalin was up to, but evils nonetheless).

The "S" in the middle of his name is generally printed without a full point in that it did not stand for anything. It was inserted for purely cosmetic reasons, it being felt that Americans were more likely to vote for a man with a middle initial than for one without. It really makes you wonder . . .

The human backbone is made up of 33 vertebrae, the lower 9 of which are fused together while the upper 24 are joined with ligaments. As well as providing essential support to an upright creature such as ourselves, the hollow vertebrae protect the spinal cord, an important element of the central nervous system.

The element of atomic number 33 is the metalloid arsenic (As), known and loved by detective-story fans the world over. Everything to do with arsenic is poisonous: all its compounds are toxic.

It is, however, of some considerable medical note. In the early years of this century the German bacteriologist Paul Ehrlich and his team tested nearly 1000 arsenic compounds, looking for one which would kill the trypanosomes (bacteria) responsible for such diseases as sleeping sickness. In 1907 they investigated compound No. 606, dihydroxydiamino-arsenobenzene hydrochloride, and found it was useless for their purposes; but in 1909 one of his assistants discovered accidentally that compound 606 is extremely effective in killing spirochetes, the germs which cause syphilis – at the time a disease as dread as is cancer today.

Ehrlich devoted the remainder of his life to promoting the use of "salvarsan" (properly "arsphenamine"), despite loud criticism of him when idiot doctors "experimented with the doses". Nowadays penicillin is preferred.

Thirty-Four

When he was released in 1959, Stephen Dennison had spent 34 years in prison for having stolen $5 dollars' worth of confectionery – in 1925, when he had been only 16. His original sentence had been periodically extended owing to his having broken various minor regulations while inside.

The 34th president of the United States was the Republican Dwight David Eisenhower (1890–1969), one-time Supreme Commander of the Allied troops in Europe during World War II. He served from 20th January, 1953, until 19th January, 1961; on his retirement at the age of 70 he became the oldest president to complete his term of office (a record which Ronald Reagan may break).

One of his first actions was to achieve a truce in the Korean War (although a formal peace treaty has yet to be signed); by contrast, during his presidency "defence" spending rose to phenomenal levels. At home, his most important achievement was the passage of civil-rights legislation – although "Ike" himself seems privately to have been dubious about the enforceability of such legislation.

The element of atomic number 34 is selenium (Se), a metalloid discovered in 1818 by the Swedish chemist Jöns Berzelius – the man who introduced to the world the system of chemical symbols familiar to every schoolchild. A semiconductor, selenium has recently enjoyed something of a popularity boom since it is used in photoelectric cells, rectifiers, solar cells and in xerography and the vulcanization of rubber.

"Supercalifragilisticespialidocious" is, at 34 letters, certainly longer than the generally accepted longest word in the English language, "antidisestablishmentarianism" (see *28, but also *29). But then "supercalifragilisticexpialidocious" is a made-up word.

An iota higher up the acceptability scale is the name of a device reported by Martin Gardner in *Fads and Fallacies* (1957) as being in use by chiropractors: this object is called the "electroencephaloneuromentimpograph".

If you are unhappy with both of these, there is a perfectly reasonable word which is *45 letters long.

Thirty-Five

The elements which have the most known isotopes are xenon and caesium, each of which has 35.

The element of atomic number 35 is bromine (Br), a fuming red liquid which stinks and is well worth avoiding. While various bromides have such uses as in photography, as fumigants and as sedatives, their most popular reputed use is as anti-aphrodisiac additives to the tea served to British soldiers and schoolboys. There seems to be little truth underlying this belief – and anyway tea itself is a mild anti-aphrodisiac.

The 35th president of the United States was John Fitzgerald Kennedy (1916–1963), a charismatic Democrat who held office from 20th January, 1961, until his assassination in Dallas on 22nd November, 1963 (the same day on which Aldous Huxley less publicly died). The continuing controversy over his death (there was this conspiracy, you see) has tended to obscure the fact that he was an extremely interesting man: he won the Pulitzer Prize for Biography in 1957 for his *Profiles in Courage*; and during World War II he displayed heroism at sea.

As a president he displayed less wisdom than "instant history" has made out. One draws a veil over the Bay of Pigs fiasco of 1961 but can hardly do so in the case of the Cuban Missile Crisis of 1962, when Kennedy risked nuclear holocaust in a fit of *macho* posturing, generally described as a "diplomatic victory". In the field of civil rights and, on the international stage, in foreign aid and human rights issues, he was far more effective. Persistent rumour has it that he was grossly oversexed; in the gutter press this is regarded as an important issue.

Thirty-Six

There are 36 chapters in *The Book of Numbers* – the one in the Old Testament, that is.

The element of atomic number 36 is krypton (Kr), an inert gas used in arc lamps and the like. It is extremely unreactive: its only certainly known compound is krypton fluoride, which has properties interesting to chemists but distinctly less flamboyant than those associated with the "kryptonite" of the comics.

The largest winning margin in the history of 1st-class soccer was recorded during a match in September, 1885, in the Scottish Cup: Arbroath beat Bon Accord 36–0.

The 36th president of the United States was the Democrat Lyndon Baines Johnson (1908–1973), who served from Kennedy's death on 22nd November, 1963, until 20th January, 1969. Remarkably unpopular during his 2nd term of office, and despite his espousal of the extension of the futile Vietnam War, Johnson must nevertheless be regarded as one of the most competent and reforming presidents of recent decades.

Years before, he had secured Senate condemnation of McCarthy's anticommunist witch-hunts and effected the passage of important legislation on civil rights; as vice-president, although hardly in the media foreground, he made important political contributions to the space programme and to further civil-rights measures.

As president, he salvaged Kennedy's faltering programmes in fields such as civil rights (again) and tax reform; he pushed through, too, the Medicare Program, which gave free medical attention to people over 65 – a pale replica of other countries' national health systems, perhaps, but a major social advance in the USA.

He was a bit of an oddball so far as his initials, LBJ, were concerned: his wife became universally known as "Lady Bird", and his daughters were christened Lucy Baines Johnson and Linda Bird Johnson.

The 36th pope, Liberius, enjoys the (perhaps) dubious distinction of being the 1st not to be regarded as a saint. Consecrated in May, 352, he was soon involved in attempts to stop the Emperor Constantius (a son of Constantine) imposing the heresy of arianism – the idea that God had created Christ – on the Church and from hounding the rabidly anti-arian St Athanasius. The dispute led to Liberius being exiled in 355, to be replaced by the arian antipope Felix. In 358 Constantius allowed him to return as "joint pope" with Felix; shortly thereafter, Felix resigned.

At the top of Germany's highest mountain, Zugspitze, stands a 36m concrete tower whose purpose is not immediately apparent. But it is not merely a folly – honest! It was erected by a climber called Wolfgang Gorter, who was offended by the fact that the mountain was, untidily, only 2964m high – so had this tower built to make the figure up to a neat 3000m.

Thirty-Seven

The 37th president of the United States was the notorious Republican Richard Milhous Nixon (1913–), the best portrayal of whom is to be found in Philip Roth's "novel", *Our Gang* (1971).

Nixon played an important part in the Un-American Activities Committee, an earlier version of McCarthy's witch-hunts. His most celebrated achievement in this role was the conviction of the public official Alger Hiss on charges of being a communist and of perjury, charges which, although Hiss served 4 years in prison, may well have been concocted (there is a persistent rumour that Nixon knew they were indeed concocted, but it may be a mistake to give this too much credence).

He served as vice-president under Eisenhower, but then suffered various political setbacks, including being defeated by Kennedy in 1960; but in 1968, with Spiro Agnew (later to resign his vice-presidency over tax-evasion charges) as running-mate, he secured the presidency.

It would be folly to criticize Nixon's foreign policy – his achievements in relations with the USSR and especially Red China were momentous (although there is a perhaps dubious eye-witness account of an incident in which Henry Kissinger only just managed to persuade a drunken Nixon not to nuke North Vietnam). In this area he was a great president – but unfortunately he was irrevocably corrupt. In 1972, 5 men were discovered carrying electronic bugging equipment into the Watergate, the Democrats' Washington headquarters. Further investigation revealed that Nixon had had cognizance of various devious plots to secure his reelection which involved unusual interpretation of the duties of, e.g., the FBI, CIA and IRS (Internal Revenue Service). In July, 1974, the House of Representatives voted to impeach Nixon; in August of that year he resigned (just in time); and in September his successor, Gerald Ford (for whom, thanks to Agnew's earlier removal from the scene, no one had had the chance to vote), granted Nixon a full pardon. Nearly 30 of Nixon's co-conspirators went to gaol.

The transcripts of the tapes Nixon had paranoidly collected of his various discussions were published, bringing into the language the expression "expletive deleted".

One of the greatest comet-hunters of all time was the French astronomer Jean Louis Pons (1761–1831), who discovered no less than 37. The most important comet which he discovered – important because it has the shortest known orbital period (1206 days) – is unfortunately named after somebody else. Unfair! The object is known as Encke's Comet because in 1819, a year after Pons' discovery, Johann Encke (1791–1865) calculated its orbit.

The element of atomic number 37 is rubidium (Rb), a silvery white metal with properties not unlike those of sodium and potassium, only more so: it makes really quite a big bang when you drop a bit of it into a bowl of water.

The 37th pope was Damasus I, elected in 366. After his consecration rioting broke out over the arian question (arianism was the heresy that God had created Christ, who was therefore not coequal and coeternal with the Father) and the rights of the recently elected antipope, Ursinus. About 150 died, and Damasus was twice tried for his part in the rioting.

☆

37 has a pleasing property.

$3 \times 37 = 111$
$6 \times 37 = 222$
$9 \times 37 = 333$
and so on until
$27 \times 37 = 999$.

After that, one has to be satisfied with such less exciting products as $30 \times 37 = 1110$ and $33 \times 37 = 1221$ until reaching $3003 \times 37 = 111,111$, etc., and then $3003003 \times 37 = 111,111,111$ and *its* successors, and then . . .

Thirty-Eight

Although the Massacre of Glencoe (1692) is a notorious event in British history, one should retain a sense of proportion about these things: in fact, only 38 of the MacDonalds were killed – although right treacherously so. The reason for the notoriety of the crime is probably the taboo against murdering, or even harming, one's host – and the soldiers did indeed use every artifice of cowardice in their crime, killing not only the Chief and 33 of his men but also 2 women and 2 children.

There is still, today, a certain tension between Campbells and MacDonalds, but this is probably the result of historical distortion: although John Campbell, the Earl of Breadalbane, is generally cast as the villain of the piece, the leader of the murderous troops, it seems virtually certain that *at the very most* he had a supportive role in the affair.

The element of atomic number 38 is strontium (Sr), a silvery white metal whose maroon-burning compounds are much used in fireworks, tracer ammunition, etc. It was discovered in 1808 by the ubiquitous Humphry Davy.

The isotope strontium-90 is radioactive and has achieved a fame all of its own. It is the most notable of the long-lived radioisotopes produced in a nuclear explosion. By way of the stratosphere, the strontium-90 is deposited all over the world in the period following the explosion.

The 38th pope was Siricius, Bishop of Rome from 384 until 399. Unlike most of his predecessors, he was not admitted into the calendar of saints until as late as the 18th century. He is noted for his vigorous support of clerical celibacy – a matter which had not been of particular importance before.

The 38th president of the United States was the Republican Gerald Rudolph Ford (1913–   ), who served from Nixon's resignation on 9th August, 1974, until 20th January, 1977. Although the circumstances of his coming to office might have gathered for him a certain degree of popularity, he lost much of it by pardoning his predecessor in the office. He lost a good deal more of it through his talent for unexpectedly falling over, leading to the charge that he was intellectually incapable of walking and chewing gum at the same time.

In March, 1982, 38 people lost their jobs as a result of an illicit passion between a scoutmaster and a cub leader. The 22nd Oxford Sea Scouts had employed the 38 on a programme of public works on behalf of the Manpower Services Commission. Unfortunately, the scout leader then fell in love with the cub leader, and so the two of them were stripped of their warrants by the Scout Association. The group as a whole joined a rival organization, but continued to administer the scheme of public works.

The Scout Association retaliated by telling the MSC that the newly constituted group had no legal status, and the MSC responded by withdrawing the scheme's grant for the forthcoming year.

Ah, back on the dole go 38 at a time of recession, and all for the sake of love.

Thirty-Nine

On her 39th attempt to pass the UK driving test, Mrs Miriam Hargrave, of Yorkshire, drove straight through a set of red lights. Further glories seemed to be assured for her but, later in that same year, 1970, she accidentally passed the test – on her 40th attempt.

In the Mediterranean there is a little island called Trentanove. Translated, this means "39"!

To date there have been 39 antipopes (assuming you count Dioscuros as one of them – see *55). The practice of antipapacy seems to have dropped out of fashion in recent centuries, though: the last antipope was Felix V (Amadeus VIII of Savoy), whose antipontificate ran from 1440 to 1449.

The writer John Buchan (1875–1940), 1st Baron Tweedsmuir, was the author of a number of adventure novels popular to this day. Aside from *Prester John* (1910), his best known tales are those involving Richard Hannay, the 1st of which was *The 39 Steps* (1915). This tale has been filmed more than once.

The 39th president of the United States was James Earl Carter (1924–   ), a Democrat who served from 20th January, 1977, until 19th January, 1981. He instituted some important reforms, such as the linking of international arms sales to human-rights issues – a policy to be reversed by his successor. His finest achievement was probably the signing of the SALT (Strategic Arms Limitations Talks) II Agreement, which then failed to be ratified by Congress, for reasons which do not make sense.

Carter's reelection was scuppered by the issue of the US hostages in Iran. After a doomed attempt at using a military raid to bring the captured occupants of the US Embassy in Tehran home, Carter succeeded in securing their release *via* diplomatic means – not an easy task, since the Iranian administration's hold on sanity was weak. Unfortunately, the released captives were not actually back on US soil by election time, and this probably cost Carter his 2nd term.

This was a very great pity. Generally portrayed as a weak and vacillating president, Carter was in fact a man of considerable sense and sensibility who, in the main, coped with extremely tricky circumstances satisfactorily.

In *La Génération de l'Homme* (1690), Nicolas Venette cites the case of the "celebrated Tiraqueau", who by abstention from alcohol – he was a Muslim – and prolific use of a certain aphrodisiac was able to father no fewer than 39 legitimate children. The potent aphrodisiac in question was water.

The element of atomic number 39 is yttrium (Y), a silvery white metal whose best known use is in the phosphors of colour television screens (the yttrium phosphor gives the red).

According to Mosaic law it was forbidden for the unfortunate recipient of a flogging to receive more than 40 stripes, and so it became the custom to sentence offenders to 39 ("40 stripes save 1"), in order to safeguard the floggers against breaking the law by accident through having lost count.

The name "40 stripes save 1" is sometimes applied also to the 39 Articles of the Anglican Church, whose history is a tortured one.

With the divorce of England, under Henry VIII, from the Catholic Church in 1533–34, it was clearly necessary to draw up a list of articles of faith for the spanking new Church of England. The 1st attempt at this was produced in 1536 by a committee headed by Henry himself and Thomas Cromwell, Earl of Essex: the result was known as the "Bishops' Book" or, more correctly, the "10 Articles". In 1538, after disputes between Cromwell and Cranmer, these were replaced by the "13 Articles"; but in 1539 Parliament, at the suggestion of the Duke of Norfolk, complicated the whole issue by approving the so-called "6 Articles".

In 1552–53, some good while after Henry had had Cromwell executed on trumped-up charges, the "42 Articles" were produced under the guidance of Cranmer and Bishop Nicholas Ridley – only to be abolished in 1553 on the accession to the throne of the Catholic Mary Tudor: Cranmer and Ridley were among the countless burnt at the stake during the reign of "Bloody Mary". With Mary dead and gone, to general relief, the Convocation of Canterbury in 1562 rehashed the "42 Articles", and the results were passed through the Commons in 1566 – only to be dropped, on the orders of Queen Elizabeth, by the Lords. in 1571 the Convocation set to work to produce something more to Elizabeth's liking, and came up with the "39 Articles". In the same year, these were passed through Parliament.

Forty

In *A Midsummer Night's Dream* Puck says:

> *I'll put a girdle round the earth*
> *In forty minutes.*

In order to achieve this feat of circumnavigation, Puck would have to average about 37,500 mph. Since the Earth's escape velocity is only about 25,000 mph, Puck would run the serious risk of "boldly going where no elemental has gone before".

There are various theories to account for the numerological importance of 40, none of them completely satisfying.

The popular theory is that it is because of 40's frequent appearances in the Bible: Moses spent 40 days and 40 nights on Mount Sinai speaking with God; the Deluge lasted for 40 days and 40 nights; Jesus was tempted in the wilderness by Satan for 40 days and 40 nights; Elijah was fed for 40 days and 40 nights by ravens; the Jews wandered in the desert for 40 years; a mother is unclean, according to *Leviticus*, for 40 days after the birth of a boy and for $2 \times 40 = 80$ days after the birth of a girl; and so on, and on, and on. And, of course, there are 40 days in Lent.

Because of these, it came to be believed that the duration of a human pregnancy should be 40 times mystic 7 days – i.e., 280 days. From here and elsewhere developed the popular theory that 40 was a number in some way associated with health.

This numerological history is not particularly satisfying – and seems anyway to be built upon a misunderstanding. One of the early meanings of the word "forty" was simply "quite a lot" – a more sophisticated version of the primitive counting systems which run "1, 2, 3, lots" (see page 4n.) – and it is probably in this sense that the word is used in the Bible. Almost certainly, too, it would have been in this sense that the word was understood in the few centuries following Christ, and so to say that 40's reputation for healthiness, based on the Bible, gave rise to the Roman practice of quarantine – an enforced 40 days' isolation at ports – seems illogical. (This sense of the word gives rise, by the way, to phrases like our "40 winks".)

A far better theory involves tracing 40 back to the Babylonians. Each year the Pleiades (or *7 Sisters) were gone from the skies for 40 nights, and this absence coincided with the rainy period. On their return, the rainy season was pronounced officially over, and the New Year celebrated.

In the UK there is a persistent superstition that the weather on the feast-day of St Swithin determines what the weather will be like on the succeeding 40 days. The tradition has been shown hilariously erroneous a number of times, but still lingers on.

There is no trace of the theory's origins. Little more is known of St Swithin (or Swithun) than that he was the Bishop of Winchester, an adviser to kings Egbert and Ethelwulf, and died in 862; the basis of his claim to sainthood is unknown, and there is no obvious reason for his feast-day to be honoured in this way by the elements.

The 40th president of the United States is Ronald Wilson Reagan (1911–   ), an ex-B-movie actor who took office on 20th January, 1981, having defeated James Carter in a Bible-thumping militaristic campaign. Reagan has shown his own brand of Christianity by reducing welfare payments to the poor in line with income-tax reductions for the rich; and he has vastly increased US spending on "defence" while apparently countenancing the possibility of a "limited" nuclear war in Europe which would kill only a few tens or hundreds of millions – and hardly any of them Americans. No wonder they call him "Raygun".

☆

In May, 1982, a 27-year-old Georgia man, John Lacey, received 2nd- and 3rd-degree burns over 95% of his body in a domestic accident, and was rushed to one of the hospitals in his hometown, Savannah. The doctors there decided that he required specialist treatment which they could not provide, and began to contact burn-treatment centres.

Unfortunately, Lacey had no medical insurance. The doctors contacted 40 specialist hospitals, of which two-thirds said that they would accept no one who had no insurance, while the other third claimed to be full. Finally they found a place for Lacey in Baltimore City Hospital, but by then it was too late: he died of his injuries.

Roll over, Hippocrates.

☆

There are 40 letters in the Slavonic alphabet.

☆

The element of atomic number 40 is zirconium (Zr), a metal discovered in 1789 by the great German physical chemist Martin Klaproth. Its main minerals are zircon, a gem mineral, and baddelyite. It is used in flashbulbs and in the cladding of uranium fuel elements in nuclear reactors.

☆

The Académie Française, officially recognized in 1635, is France's premier literary and linguistic society and is responsible for producing *Le Dictionnaire*, generally regarded as the "Bible" of the French language. The society is limited to 40 members, the "Immortals".

Similarly, the number of Academicians of the Royal Academy of Arts – RAs – founded in 1768 by George III, is restricted to 40, plus the President.

☆

In old English law, the period of sanctuary was limited to 40 days. MPs were protected from arrest for 40 days after Parliament was dissolved and for 40 days before it was reconvened. A widow had the right to remain in her husband's house for 40 days after his death.

The 40th pope was Innocent I, who reigned from 401 to 417; his pontificate saw the sacking of Rome by the Visigoths, in 410. He is noted for having considerably reinforced the idea of papal supremacy throughout the entire Church.

Also, he condemned the ideas of the British monk Pelagius (*c*355–*c*425) as heresies, and excommunicated Pelagius and other pelagian leaders. To modern eyes, this seems like a very great pity, for pelagianism, with its rationalistic approach to religion and its search to reduce rather than increase the number of "mysteries" – e.g., discarding the notion of original sin – if adopted, even if only as a debating point, into the main body of Churchian lore might, in the centuries to come, have saved humanity from some of the hideous consequences of blind dogmatism.

The well known rhyme

Lizzie Borden took an axe
And gave her mother 40 whacks;
When she saw what she had done
She gave her father 41

refers to the case in 1892 in which Lizzie Andrew Borden (1860–1927) was believed to have murdered her father and stepmother. Public opinion had decided before the trial that she was guilty, and so there was a considerable public outcry when she was acquitted: hangings are fun, after all. Nobody was ever convicted of the killings, and Lizzie herself lived on to the ripe old age of 67, still protesting her innocence but still generally believed to be a murderer. Various case studies have been made which tend to support her claim.

Forty-One

The oldest goldfish known to the editors of the *Guinness Book of Records* (1982 edn.) was one called Fred, which died in 1980 at the age of 41.

The element of atomic number 41 is niobium (Nb), sometimes called columbium. It was first discovered in 1801 by the English chemist Charles Hatchett, who called it columbium because the sample he had been working on came from the fledgling United States, or Columbia. Another English chemist, William Wollaston, in 1809 declared that columbium was the same stuff as tantalum, discovered in 1802 by Anders Ekeberg. Since Wollaston was famous and Hatchett wasn't, Wollaston's verdict was accepted; in high dudgeon Hatchett retired from research.

In 1846 it was shown that Hatchett had been quite right: the two elements were different. In what can most charitably be viewed as an astonishingly brutal act of tactlessness towards a by now 80-year-old man, Hatchett's suddenly acceptable element was rechristened niobium. It is only in comparatively recent times that US scientists have accepted this name in place of columbium.

☆

Because of the Earth's motion through space, light from the stars is affected by the phenomenon known as aberration, so that the stars appear to be in a slightly different position in the skies from their real one: the net effect is that a star lying on the ecliptic (the plane of the Earth's orbit around the Sun) appears to move backwards and forwards through an angle of 41 seconds of arc during the course of the years.

Forty-Two

On Goldsmith complaining that James Beattie (1735–1803) was being lionized as a result of the publication of his *Essays on Truth* – "Here's such a stir about a fellow that has written one book, and I have written many" – his companion, Dr Johnson, is said to have waspishly replied: "Ah, Doctor, there go two-and-forty sixpences, you know, to one guinea."

According to the Ancient Egyptians, there were 42 demons present at the "last judgement" of each human being.

The element of atomic number 42 is molybdenum (Mo), an important catalyst in the process of the fixation of nitrogen by soil bacteria and an essential trace element in the diets of plants. Some paint manufacturers are beginning – tardily – to turn to nontoxic molybdenum compounds for use as pigments in place of the toxic chromium and lead ones.

The famous Gutenberg or Mazarin Bible, the 1st complete printed book extant from Western culture, printed around 1455 on the presses of Johann Gutenberg (*c*1397–1468), is often known as the "42-line Bible" because it has 42 lines to the column.

In *Revelation* the period of 42 months occurs several times (sometimes in the form 1260 days). Notably, it is the period for which the pagans shall trample on the Holy City (*xi* 3), and that for which the Great Beast (see Appendix I) shall enjoy its unhindered rule. Before leaping to numerological conclusions (42 can be represented as 1 × 2 × 3 × 7 – 4 important mystical numbers), we should note that 42 months is 3½ years, or half a "week of years", and appears elsewhere often to indicate the length of a "longish" persecution.

A survey made in 1967 measured the amount of stress involved in various important changes in the subjects' lives. Altogether 43 categories emerged, from death of one's spouse through being being fired to leaving school. Surprisingly, Christmas appeared as only the 42nd most stressful experience.

Forty-Three

The element of atomic number 43 is technetium (Tc), the lightest element to have isotopes all of which are radioactive, and the 1st element ever to be created artificially. The discovery of technetium was made in 1937 by Emilio Segrè, who found it in a lump of molybdenum which he had had bombarded with deuterons (proton-neutron pairs).

The 43rd pope was Celestine I, who reigned from 422 to 432. He is chiefly remembered for his firm stance against the heresy of nestorianism. Nestorius, the Patriarch of Constantinople, held that Christ had been 2 people, although inseparably involved together in the single body; and objected to the description of Mary as the "Mother of God" on the grounds that, when she bore Christ, she bore him as a human baby. Nestorius was excommunicated by Celestine, and his teachings damned.

Forty-Four

The most popular trees in the Bible are the cedar and the fig, both of which are mentioned 44 times. Next comes the olive, with a mere 37 appearances. Curiously, despite this popularity, not a single biblical quotation concerning either cedar or fig (or even olive) appears in *The Oxford Dictionary of Quotations* (1970 edn.).

The element of atomic number 44 is ruthenium (Ru), a hard metal used in metallurgy and as a catalyst in organic chemistry.

It was a sad day when the religious reformer John Wycliffe was burnt at the stake in 1428, following his condemnation as a heretic in 1415. Unfortunately, Wycliffe himself was unable to be present, having died 44 years earlier, in 1348, and so the executioners had to make do with his bones.

Forty-Five

"45" became a potent political slogan in 1763 when John Wilkes published, in issue 45 of *The North Briton*, a vitriolic attack on the government and on the poorly negotiated Peace of Paris (of which he remarked that, like the peace of God, it "passeth all understanding"). Wilkes was promptly tossed into the Tower of London, at which the London mob went wild, destroying large amounts of property, waging war against the forces of law and order, and daubing or scratching "45" on every available flat surface.

The 45th pope was St Leo I, who reigned from 440 until 461. He is one of only 3 popes to have earnt the sobriquet "the Great".

In 452 Attila the Hun invaded Italy only to be met by Leo, with whom he made his peace before withdrawing his forces back across the Danube: considerable bloodshed and human misery were thus saved by Leo's act of courage. He tried the same trick in 455 with the Vandal Gaiseric, but was less successful: although there was little bloodshed or destruction of Church property, Rome was looted by the Vandals and many prisoners taken.

There is in the US a card game of fluctuating popularity called 45, a variant of the Irish game Spoil 5. Both are primitive forms of bridge.

If you've decided that "electroencephaloneuromentimpograph" is, at *34 letters, the longest word in the English language, then it's surely about time you turned your attention to the 45-letter "pneumonoultramicroscopicsilicovolcanoconiosis", which first appeared in *Bedside Manna* (1936) by Frank Scully, and refers to a lung disease caused by ultramicroscopic particles of sandy volcanic dust. If this word *still* isn't long enough for you, see *83.

The element of atomic number 45 is rhodium (Rh), a metal discovered in 1804 by the English chemist William Wollaston. He called his discovery rhodium because some of its compounds are rose-coloured.

Forty-Six

The Order of the Bath was founded in 1399 by Henry IV, who created 46 Knights of the Bath at his coronation; it was revived in 1725 by George I, and today the number of knights is at the discretion of the monarch. Contrary to one popular misconception, the name of the Order has nothing to do with attendance on the monarch as he or she bathes: it refers to the ritual ablution, symbolizing purification, of knights immediately prior to their installation in the Order.

The crushing defeat at Cardiff of the Welsh by the Scottish at Rugby Union on 20th March, 1982 (Scotland 34, Wales 18) – a victory achieved in the teeth of all the betting – was of especial interest to the veteran Scottish back Jim Renwick. He had appeared no less than 46 times before for his country, and this was the 1st time they had won a match away from home.

The element of atomic number 46 is palladium (Pd), discovered by Wollaston at the same time as rhodium (see *45); he named it for Pallas, the asteroid, which had been discovered only a couple of years earlier by Heinrich Olbers. Theatres such as the London Palladium owe their names not to the element but to the image of the goddess Pallas upon which the safety of Troy was supposed to depend.

Palladium has the interesting property of being able to absorb some 900 times its own volume of hydrogen, and so is used in hydrogen purifiers.

In 1912 it took the Democratic Party 46 ballots to settle on a candidate for the forthcoming presidential election. Finally they picked on a compromise candidate, Woodrow Wilson, who swept to power and became one of the country's best and most visionary presidents (see *28).

Forty-Seven

Mosquitoes have 47 teeth.

The element of atomic number 47 is silver (Ag), a precious metal much used for ornament, in coinage, etc. Because it is the best heat and electricity conductor of all, it is much used for electrical contacts and in printed circuits. Silver nitrate is a noted wart-remover.

Were it not for predators such as mankind, the mating of a single pair of houseflies, and then the mating of their offspring, etc., etc., would within a year result in the Earth being entirely covered in a 47-foot layer of houseflies. The fact that this doesn't occur is a measure of the low life-expectancy of the average housefly.

In 1961 Henri Matisse's painting *Le Bateau* was put on exhibition in New York's Museum of Modern Art. 47 days later somebody noticed that it had been hung upside down.

Forty-Eight

When Copernicus' astronomical system, in which the Sun rather than the Earth was the centre of the Universe, was first introduced, it required the use of 48 epicycles (minor circles) to explain the observed motions of the planets. The system replaced the more cumbersome Ptolemaic one, which was based on the idea that the planets, including the Sun, went around the Earth. But the most sophisticated versions of the Ptolemaic system at the time of Copernicus' writing (1543) required the use of only 40 epicycles, and produced much more accurate tables of planetary positions – essentially because Copernicus believed that the orbits of the planets must be of a basically circular nature. In this light, it is surprising that the theory ever established itself.

The element of atomic number 48 is cadmium (Cd), whose only significant mineral is greenockite. The metal was first discovered almost by accident by the German mineralogist Friedrich Strohmeyer in 1817 as a result of coming across a mislabelled jar in an apothecary's shop.

Although the genuine meaning of a "hairsbreadth" clearly varies from head to head, the defined unit of measurement is such that there are 48 hairsbreadths to the inch. In botany, the unit has been used to mean one 12th of a fibre.

The legend of Sawney Bean or Beane is poorly substantiated but seems to have some basis in fact. Bean and his common-law wife set up home in Galloway, on the west coast of Scotland, in the early 15th century (so the story goes). Finding the bleak countryside there short of food, they hit on the notion of attacking passing strangers and eating them.

James IV himself brought the clan to justice in 1435: by this time there were 48 of them – 8 sons, 6 daughters, 18 grandsons and 14 grand-daughters. They were tried at Leith. The men and boys were mutilated and left to bleed to death, while the women and girls were burnt alive. Of course, this was pathetically unjust to the children and grandchildren, who must have thought that eating people was the normal way of subsisting, but then 15th-century justice was not known for its clemency.

In lottery superstition, the number 48 stands for death.

The 48th pope was Felix III and held office from 483 to 492; actually he was only the 2nd pope to be named Felix – the cause of the confusion is the antipontificate of Felix between 355 and 365.

There are 48 extant copies of the Gutenberg *42-line Bible out of an initial print run of 300 – that is, assuming that the 2 that were in Nazi Germany survived World War II and are now living somewhere in South America. The most ever paid for a copy was (in 1970) $2.5 million.

Enthusiasts for the number 48 are advised to spend their next vacation in the region of Eight-and-Forty, Yorkshire.

It is not uncommon for there to be a delay of a few hours between the births of twins, but Dougie and Debbie Schee probably clocked up a record in 1955 in Delaware, Ohio: they were born 48 *days* apart.

Forty-Nine

The infant prodigy Marjorie Fleming (1803–1811), who died at such a tragically early age, left behind her some poems, letters and a journal. In the journal we find a comment that seems hardly fair to the innocent 49 (or the equally innocent 64, for that matter): "The most devilish thing is 8 times 8 and 7 times 7 it is what nature itselfe cant endure."

Alaska was the 49th state of the Union, achieving its statehood on

3rd January, 1959. It had been bought by the USA from Russia in 1867 for $7.2 million – or roughly 2 cents an acre.

The element of atomic number 49 is indium (In), a very soft rare metal with properties not unlike those of aluminium.

Its discovery in 1863 was marred by controversy. The German mineralogist Ferdinand Reich was keen to discover a new element, and thought that he'd probably done so when he examined a precipitate he'd obtained from a zinc ore. The thing to do was to check it by spectroscope, but Reich suffered from an unfortunate disadvantage – he was colourblind! His assistant, Hieronymus Richter, looked through the spectroscope for him and spotted an indigo line which betrayed the presence of the hitherto unknown metal – hence its name. Afterwards Richter claimed that he, not Reich, was the true discoverer of the element.

49 is an especially sacred number in that it is the product of sacred 7 times sacred 7. According to Jewish tradition, every 50th year is a jubilee year since it marks the end of a preceding age of $7 \times 7 = 49$ years. In exactly similar fashion, since the sacredness of 7 meant that critical periods in life occurred every 7 years, the 49th year of life was regarded as one of the 2 minor "climacterics", the other being *81 (9^2). Neither of these, of course, compared with the Grand Cimacteric of *63.

The 49th pope was Gelasius I, who reigned from 492 until 496 and is best known for not having written the so-called "Gelasian Sacramentary".

In a cavern, in a canyon,
Excavating for a mine,
Dwelt a miner, forty-niner,
And his daughter – Clementine

wrote Percy Montrose in one of the most popular songs of all time – and I'm sure all of us can remember as children puzzling away over what on Earth a "49-er" might be. In California, on 24th January, 1848, gold was struck, and from all over the world people converged on the region, hoping to make a quick fortune.

The bulk of them arrived during the year 1849, and so the participants in this gold rush became known as Forty-niners. Incidentally, between 1848 and 1849 the population of California roughly quintupled, from about 20,000 to over 100,000.

Fifty

According to the *Majorca Daily Bulletin* in Spring 1982: "The storm was one of the worst spring onslaughts in memory to plague Massachusetts, triggering traffic accidents that included a 50-cat [sic] pile-up south of Boston."

On 21st August, 1959, Hawaii rather belatedly became the 50th, and to date last, state of the Union. Progress towards statehood was delayed by US involvement in World War II – ironically initiated by the Japanese attack on the US base at the Hawaiian port of Pearl Harbor.

There are 50 acknowledged authors in the Bible. In fact, of course, since many of the books are clearly by more than one hand, and since many of them have been subjected to later revisions and covert interpolations, there must have been many more than this.

When tossing a coin, your chance of throwing a tail is of course 50% (ignoring for a moment the fairly slender chance of the coin landing on its edge). Since these odds aren't too bad, it might seem that throwing tails 50 times in a row might be reasonably feasible. If you tossed a coin every 5 seconds during the course of a 35-hour working week, you could expect to throw 50 tails in a row once in every 860 million years or so. The world's very first multicellular organism, if it had started flipping its coin not long after its birth, would have roughly a 70% chance of having performed the feat by now.

The element of atomic number 50 is tin (Sn), normally thought of as being a white metal although, below 13.2°C, it can change to a powdery metalloid. Its main use is in the form of tinplate, especially for cans, although nowadays these are increasingly being made of aluminium instead.

The 50 daughters of Danaos, King of Argos, married the 50 sons of his brother Aegyptos; but Danaos, who nurtured a deep hatred for his brother, armed each of his daughters with a knife. On their joint wedding-night, 49 of the Danaids despatched their husbands, only Hypermnestra sparing her husband Lynceus and fleeing with him.

The 50th pope was Anastasius II, who reigned from 496 until 498; he was a peace-maker who, because he took into communion the near-heretic Photinus, was himself widely regarded as a heretic until the Middle Ages (for example, Dante tells of his tomb aflame in Hell). For this reason Anastasius, unlike most of the early popes, has not been admitted to the Roman Martyrology – that is, is not recognized as a saint.

In the book of *Esther* we find the tale of how the Jewish Queen Esther, wife of King Ahasuerus (probably Xerxes I, King of Persia 486–465BC), saved the Jewish people of Persia from a plan by the king's favourite, Haman, to slaughter them. Haman begged Esther to spare his life; but the king, entering suddenly to find him kneeling before Esther in supplication, conceived that Haman was in fact trying to rape her – and that sealed Haman's fate.

By happy coincidence, Haman had not long ago built a 50-cubit-high gallows-tree upon which to hang the old Jew (now saved) who had brought news of the plot to Esther. With a pleased eye on economy, the king's adherents now used it to hang its creator.

Why bother recounting this story? Well, there's one odd element to it. A cubit is a measure derived from the length of the forearm, and lies in the range 18–22 inches. This means that the gallows-tree was at least 75 and possibly 91⅔ feet high – an ostentation which seems barely credible.

In 1813 the *Morning Post* described the then Regent, later King George IV, as an "Adonis of Loveliness". This was too much for most people, including the editors of *The Examiner*, the novelist Leigh Hunt and his brother John. They printed the remark that "this Adonis of Loveliness was *a corpulent gentleman* of 50!". For this great sin, the two were fined £500 each and sentenced to 2 years' imprisonment. But the nickname "Adonis of 50" was to stick . . .

Fifty-One

The 51st pope was Symmachus, who reigned from 498 to 514. The election during his reign of the antipope Lawrence seems to have been utterly justified: while all accounts from a date as early as this must be considered questionable, it seems certain that Symmachus' behaviour was likewise: he was a fornicator, and a promiscuous one to boot (although his regular lover was a woman called Conditaria, if you really want the *News of the World* details), as well as a man to whose eager fingers rather a lot of Church money stuck. Incredibly, 15th-century enthusiasts decided to recognize him as a saint.

The element of atomic number 51 is antimony (Sb), a silvery white metal with a surprising number of uses: for example, it is a legal requirement for automobile upholstery in the USA to be fireproofed using antimony oxide. Its compounds turn up in paints, medicines, explosives, etc., and it is alloyed in Babbitt metal, pewter and type-metal. It is used also in lead-storage batteries and in semiconductors.

Joseph Bramah's famous lock, patented in 1784, is on record as having taken, during trials, an experienced locksmith 51 hours to pick.

Fifty-Two

When an unemployed Philadelphia heating engineer called Clarence Darrow first submitted the boardgame he had invented to Parker Brothers, Inc., it was rejected on the basis that it had "52 fundamental playing errors". Later the company relented and bought the rights in the game, Monopoly, from him. It proved so popular that it made him a millionaire.

Perhaps more strikingly, the face value of the Monopoly money printed each year by Parker Brothers is about twice as great as that of the real money printed by the US mint.

The element of atomic number 52 is tellurium (Te), discovered in 1782 by an Austrian mineralogist called Franz Müller. Initially Müller sent this new substance he'd found – which he was certain was a new element – to Torbern Bergman, a rather boring mineralogist who died before he could finish analyzing the substance. It was left to the great Martin Klaproth to validate Müller's discovery.

The bodies of women, because of their high proportion of fatty tissues, may contain as little as 52% water (by weight). By comparison, a thin man's body may be as much as 70% water.

In 1874, after a full 52 ballots, the jury was still unable to reach a decision about the innocence or guilt of Henry Ward Beecher (brother of Harriet Beecher Stowe, author of *Uncle Tom's Cabin*), the congregationalist leader, on charges of adultery. Beecher was therefore acquitted, and he went back to preaching.

It seems virtually certain that he *did* have an affair with Mrs Elizabeth Tilton, the wife of one of his flock. Apparently, he used the well tried seducers' technique of claiming that God had willed them to have sex.

Fifty-Three

The UK currently (1982) has 53 Roman Catholic bishops.

The element of atomic number 53 is iodine, whose symbol is I throughout most of the world but J, for *Jod*, in Germany. It is a vital trace element in the human diet, deficiency leading to goiter (swelling of the thyroid gland); it is found in most plants and especially seaweeds – a good reason for eating seaweed.

The element was discovered in 1811 by one of the most modest scientists of all time, Bernard Courtois; although he'd discovered the stuff, he decided that he wasn't a good enough chemist to analyze it and so passed his samples along to prominent scientists such as Davy and Gay-Lussac.

Iodine was until 1896 thought not to occur in animal tissues; then Eugen Baumann discovered that the thyroid gland is rich in it. Most adults will recall its use as an antiseptic – dabbed on to a wound it hurts like hell.

According to Tennyson's poem *The Revenge*, Sir Thomas Grenville, in his ship of that name, in 1591 fought off 53 Spanish vessels all night long before finally being mortally wounded, his ship lost. In fact, a more realistic figure – although it detracts not one whit from Grenville's heroism – is that *The Revenge* held out against 15 Spanish ships, for 15 hours. The incident occurred when *The Revenge* became isolated during a British attempt to intercept the Spaniards off the Azores.

Fifty-Four

There are approximately 54,000,000,000,000,000,000,000,000,000 possible bridge hands.

The element of atomic number 54 is xenon (Xe), the heaviest stable member of the family of inert gases (the others are helium, neon, argon, krypton and the radioactive radon). Xenon is the least inert of the family. Although Linus Pauling had suggested that there could exist compounds of the inert gases, it was not until 1962 that anyone actually succeeded in preparing one – xenon platinofluoride ($XePtF_6$, should you be even remotely interested). Other compounds of xenon and of some of the rest of the family of inert gases are now known.

Only 54 lines remain of a poem composed in a dream by Coleridge: that poem is, of course, "Kubla Khan", probably written in 1798. In the poet's own words: ". . . On awaking he appeared to himself to have a distinct recollection of the whole, and taking his pen, ink and paper, instantly and eagerly wrote down the lines that are here preserved. At this moment he was unfortunately called out by a person on business from Porlock, and detained by him above an hour, and on his return to his room, found, to his no small surprise and mortification, that though he still retained some vague and dim recollection of the general purport of the vision, yet, with the exception of some eight or ten scattered lines or images, all the rest had passed away . . . Yet from the still surviving recollections in his mind, the author has frequently purposed to finish for himself what had been originally, as it were, given to him."

It's customary to lambast the philistine "person on business from Porlock" and to rate "Kubla Khan" as one of the great fragments of English literature. But the whole story, on closer examination, begins to look fishy. The house where Coleridge was staying is some distance from Porlock, and it seems unlikely that someone would travel this distance on the offchance of catching Coleridge there. The poet claims that the incident took place in 1797, yet he did not visit the farmhouse in that year. Moreover, if one looks at the poem as an account of a lost dream, rather than as a straightforward account of the contents of the dream itself, it suddenly takes on the aspect of a complete, finished work of art – not a fragment at all!

One wonders, though, how many words – including those above – have been devoted to those 54 lines . . .

☆

During the Siege of Paris (1871), the beleaguered naturally found it difficult to correspond with allies, relatives and friends. The solution was the "balloon post". In all, there were 54 flights, and it is reckoned that they carried between them some 2½ million letters.

Fifty-Five

The 55th pope was Boniface II; he held office from 530 until 532, having been selected by his predecessor, Felix IV. In fact, most of the Roman clergy (60 out of 67) refused to recognize him, and so in September, 530, they elected a rival, Dioscuros, as antipope . . . or should one say pope? Clearly there are valid arguments in favour of both descriptions, and historians are still uncertain on the issue. 23 days later Dioscuros died, thus ending the brief schism: clearly God had Spoken in no uncertain terms.

Tactlessly, Boniface publicly mocked the pro-Dioscuros set,

and in turn designated his own successor, the extremely unpleasant Vigilius (see *59). This was so vehemently and generally opposed that Boniface had to back down.

55 delegates representing the 13 original states of the Union signed the US Constitution in the summer of 1787; but it was not until the summer of 1788 that the necessary 9 states had ratified it, and not until the spring of 1789 that it came into effect. In 1791 the Bill of Rights, consisting of 10 amendments (originally there were 12) advocated by James Madison, was added. Since 1791 there have been only 16 further amendments.

The element of atomic number 55 is caesium (Cs); we shall pretend not to know that in some parts of the world it is called "cesium". Like various other elements, it excitingly bursts into flames when dropped into a bowl of water: in fact it's so eager to do so that the chances are there'll be enough moisture in the air near your bowl for your lump of caesium to ignite before it ever gets to the water.

Fifty-Six

Henri IV of France (1553–1610) had a total of 56 recorded mistresses, not to mention 2 wives and countless one-night stands. He died the way he lived: when he was assassinated he was sitting in his coach with a mistress on each side.

In Stone County, Arizona, you can find Fifty-Six.

The element of atomic number 56 is barium (Ba). Its compound barium sulphate is highly insoluble and has the advantage of being opaque to X-rays: this is the stuff you eat on a "barium diet" so that your intestines can be examined from without. (Yes, here is the safe alternative for Japanese depressives who want to look at their guts but baulk at the idea of suicide.)

The discovery of radioactive barium could have changed the course of history, but fortunately didn't. The German physical chemist Otto Hahn noticed in 1938–9 that uranium bombarded by neutrons seemed to be decaying into radioactive barium; that is, that the uranium nucleus was splitting in two. Hahn was too shy to suggest that this could actually be what was going on, although his brilliant associate Lise Meitner, exiled from Germany by the Nazis, did. Very luckily, the Nazis seem not to have had the wit to realize that in the process of nuclear fission lay a way of killing large numbers of people: it was left to the Allies to do that.

Fifty-Seven

57 workers died during the construction of the Forth railway bridge, in Scotland (completed 1890).

The slogan "57 Varieties" came to H. J. Heinz in 1892 when he was travelling on an elevated train in New York. He was boredly looking at the ads in the train when he saw one that advertised "21 styles" of shoes, and immediately the phrase "57 Varieties" popped into his head. He mounted an advertising campaign on the strength of it – despite the fact that Heinz by this time were manufacturing over 60 varieties. As we know, the campaign was immensely successful. In 1902 the name of the Heinz house journal was altered from *Pickles* to *The 57 News*, and the company built for promotional purposes the Heinz Ocean Pier – "The Sea Shore Home of the 57 Varieties" – in Atlantic City.

In *The Good Provider* (1973) Robert C. Alberts tells of a telegram received by the company at the height of the initial campaign when it was (falsely) rumoured that Heinz had leased the side of Lookout Mountain, Chattanooga, for the erection of an enormous "57 Varieties" billboard: "IF YOU DARE TOUCH THAT SACRED SPOT WE WILL PICKLE YOU IN 57 WAYS."

The element of atomic number 57 is lanthanum (La), the 1st in the so-called "lanthanum series" of elements (running to lutetium, atomic number *71). Lanthanum itself, a metal, was discovered in 1839 by the Swedish chemist Carl Mosander, who named it from a Greek word, *lanthanein*, meaning "to lie hid", because he'd had considerable difficulty locating it amongst the mineral assemblage he'd been examining.

Fifty-Eight

The element of atomic number 58 is cerium (Ce), a metal discovered independently and almost simultaneously in 1803 by Jöns Berzelius, with the help of Wilhelm Hisinger, and by Martin Klaproth. It gained its name from the 1801 discovery by Giuseppe Piazzi of the 1st of the asteroids, Ceres.

Cardinal Mezzofanti (1774–1849) could speak 58 different languages, and so was dubbed the "Briaraeus of languages". More recently (1979), Isaac Asimov reports that Georges Schmidt, of the UN translation service, can translate from 66 languages, 30 of which he can speak fluently.

Fifty-Nine

The British writer Enid Blyton (1898–1968), the creator of Noddy, the Famous Five, etc., wrote more than 600 books for children – although one must remember that some of them were extremely short. Nonetheless, her bumper year of 1955 must have been quite an experience, with 59 books being published. Now imagine if the various publishers had thrown a launch-party for each of them . . .

The 59th pope was Vigilius, the type of pope you don't want to meet up a dark alley. His persistent strivings for the papal office, which had gone on for many years, were at last satisfied in 537; he was to die in 555. It is pleasing to find that he didn't have an easy time of it. Emperor Justinian decided to play at Church politics, and enlisted Vigilius' assistance in enforcing his wishes in the matter of condemning what he, Justinian, considered to be heresies. Every time Vigilius publicly obeyed orders the Church erupted; every time he tried to placate the faithful, Justinian came down on him like a ton of bricks – eventually even arranging for his excommunication, in 553.

Vigilius managed to claw his way back into imperial favour by the simple expedient of retracting everything he had said which had offended Justinian and saying that what had happened was that he had been misled by the Devil – an excuse I've used myself when late home from the pub. The humiliation broke Vigilius, and he was a pale remnant of his former self for the remaining 2 years of his life.

The element of atomic number 59 is praseodymium (Pr). In the 1840s the Swedish chemist Carl Mosander discovered the elements erbium, terbium and an apparent element called didymium (from a Greek word meaning "twin", because didymium was virtually a twin of lanthanum). It was not until 1885 that the Austrian chemist Karl Auer was able to prove that the twin was indeed twins, being a mixture of 2 hitherto unknown elements, praseodymium (which has a prominent green line in its spectrum) and neodymium (the "new" twin).

Sixty

Francesco Caraccioli (1752–1799) summed up the eating habits of one nation and the religious bigotry of another with acuity when he remarked: *"Il y a en Angleterre soixante sectes religieuses différentes, et une seule sauce."* ("In England there are 60 different religious sects, but only a single sauce.")

The "Diamond Wedding" is the 60th wedding anniversary.

Although it is rare, a few peoples through history have counted to the base 60, although generally only as an extension of a counting system using a more conventional base. There is good evidence that the Maya used the base 60, although their very complicated counting system was essentially to the base 20. In the writing of Mayan numbers one must pretend that one is building a wall: the bottom row of bricks represents the number of units; the next row represents the number of 20s; the next the number of 360s; and the next the number of 7200s. The number 9002 would therefore look like this:

·	(1 × 7200)
————	(5 × 360; "————" is 5)
O	(0 × 20)
· ·	(2 × 1)

This was fine for calculation, but clearly rather cumbersome in everday use, and so 60 seems to have been hit upon as a useful base to use for "largish" numbers – particularly those just less than a multiple of 360! 719, for example, would be

•	(1 × 360)
• • ——— ——— ———	(17 × 20)
• • • • ——— ——— ———	(19 × 1)

I leave it to the reader to work out how to write 14,399 (= (2 × 7200) – 1) in Mayan!

Sixty-One

61 workmen died when, during construction, the German battle-cruiser *Scharnhorst* rolled over on her side, and from this point onward she seems to have been jinxed. At her launching, watched by Hitler and other Nazi notables, the cables broke and she ploughed her way through several other ships to the sea; 20–25 of her crew died during her assault on Danzig, some from suffocation after being trapped in an unventilated gun turret, others when a gun blew up; later, after having suffered severe damage off Oslo, she accidentally sank the *SS Bremen*, then one of the world's largest passenger vessels; when she entered her final engagement she had a complement of nearly 2000, of whom only 36 survived; when these 36 reached shore and tried to light their emergency heater it exploded, reducing their number to 34 . . .

It's no wonder the *Scharnhorst* features so frequently in the Fortean literature on jinxes and curses!

Sixty-Two

The element of atomic number 62 is samarium (Sm), discovered in 1879 by the French chemist Paul Émile Lecoq de Boisbaudran, who discovered also the elements gallium (1874) and dyprosium (1886).

The greatest number of Knights of the Order of the Garter created in a single day is 62, by King James VI & I at his coronation as king of England and Scotland on 25th July, 1603.

Sixty-Three

The age of 63 is traditionally known as the "Grand Climacteric" of life, it being believed that hardly anyone who reached this age would struggle on until the age of 64. This belief was much more reasonable in times past, when Man's brutishness and medical ignorance conspired to maintain life expectancy at a low level. (This is not to say, of course, that modern medicine has extended the human lifespan: it's just that more people are living a full lifespan.)

The Grand Climacteric derives its name from the belief that critical periods in life occur every 7 and every 9 years – these critical periods are called climacterics. Clearly, then, the ages of *49 (7^2) and *81 (9^2), the minor climacterics, would be pretty important – although the latter is even today no more than academic for most of us. But the greatest of all would be the critical period at the age when the 2 "cycles" acted together for the first time since birth – and this was of course at the age of $7 \times 9 = 63$.

The year AD6300 has long been regarded as a plausible date for the end of the world for this reason, with centuries taking the place of years. Even more plausible in the Judaeo-Christian culture is the year AD2296, on the basis that the world was created in 4004BC and would last for only 6300 years. The fundamentalist magazine *The Plain Truth* has pointed out that, even if the scientists are right and the world was created a few years earlier than 4004BC, then all this does is advance the date of the Apocalypse. No comfort there.

On his arrest Dr Marcel Petiot confessed to 63 murders, although in the end he was charged with and convicted of only *27 of them. During World War II he made substantial sums of money out of his sadistically murderous career: he would offer rich Jews an escape-route from Nazi-occupied France, take their money (ostensibly to grease a few palms), kill them unpleasantly, and burn their bodies in his basement furnace. At his trial he claimed that all his victims had been members of the Gestapo – and, indeed, he did fight for a while in the Resistance – but his claim was given the lie by the vast quantities of personal clothing found carefully stored in his house. He was sent to the guillotine on 26th May, 1946.

It's ironic that some far worse and more sadistic murderers, whose careers were contemporary with Petiot's, are today respected elder citizens in countries such as Argentina.

Approximately 63 thousand trees are cut down to make the paper on which to print each Sunday's edition of the *New York Times*. Since the population of the USA is of the order of 204,770,000, this means that, every 62.5 years or so, the paper would cost 1 tree for each man, woman and child in the country (the equivalent figure for the population of New York State is about 5 years 7 months).

All told, 63 governments were members of the ill-fated League of Nations, which functioned from its foundation on 10th January, 1920, until its collapse by April, 1946; its highest membership at any one time, however, was 58 countries, in 1934. The notable exception from the membership list was the USA, whose Senate did a SALT II on poor Woodrow Wilson (see *28). This, the USSR's expulsion in 1939, and the withdrawal at various stages of 17 other states (including, notably, Germany, Japan and Italy) spelt doom for the League. It was to be replaced by the marginally more effective United Nations.

The 63rd pope was Pelagius II, who reigned from 579 until 590. He was largely responsible for ending the Lombard siege of Rome and for the general pacification of the region. Although his emissary in Constantinople, Gregory (later to be Pelagius' successor), was unable to persuade the Byzantine Emperor Tiberius to send help in the Lombard affair, Pelagius got round this difficulty adroitly. He persuaded the Catholic Franks to come instead of the imperial forces, and managed to get Tiberius to subsidise the venture. This friendly relationship with the Franks was to prove of immense importance in the centuries to come.

Pelagius died a victim of an epidemic of bubonic plague which swept Rome.

According to a calculation carried out by Aristotle, there are, all told, 10^{63} grains of sand in the Universe. This estimate is probably rather conservative.

Sixty-Four

The 64th pope was Gregory I, the Great (Gregorius I Maximus), who reigned from 590 until 604. Born a patrician, he became by age 30 a prefect of Rome; but he heard the call, converted several of his houses into convents and monasteries, and retired to one of the latter. After a few years of monasticism he was asked to serve his Church, acting as papal emissary to Constantinople under his predecessor, Pelagius. Later he set out on a missionary trip to Britain, but was called back to be pope; his task in Britain was to be carried out instead, at his behest, by St Augustine of Canterbury from 596 (from 601 Augustine was 1st Archbishop of Canterbury).

Gregory accepted the papacy with reluctance, but then threw himself into his task with vigour. As a landlord (the Church was the most powerful landlord in Italy) he ensured fair treatment for the peasants, efficient use of resources, and equitable distribution of food to the poor. As a Church leader, he enforced the supremacy of the papacy and stressed the necessity for clerical celibacy. As a statesman he dealt firmly with imperial meddling, and acted to save Rome from the marauding Lombards: not only did he pay for Rome's defences, he negotiated peace with the pagans. Emperor Mauritius was not amused by this demonstration of papal independence in temporal matters, although his successor, the usurper Phocas (reigned 602–10), was considerably more sympathetic.

Gregory carried out substantial liturgical reforms and left behind him an abundance of writings – certainly far more than any pope before him – which were immensely popular in his time and are often still of importance today.

The element whose atomic number is 64 is gadolinium (Gd), named in 1886 by Lecoq de Boisbaudran for a Finnish chemist called Johan Gadolin who had been the 1st to realize that there were "rare earths".

Naturally occurring oxides which were resistant to heat and insoluble in water were known as "earths". The common ones, such as silica, were well known, but in 1794 Gadolin identified a much more uncommon one. The group of elements involved in the rare earths are scandium, yttrium, lanthanum, cerium, praseodymium, neodymium, promethium, samarium, europium, gadolinium, terbium, dysprosium, holmium, erbium, thulium, ytterbium and lutetium.

☆

The *I Ching* is based upon the interpretation of 64 hexagrams of 6 lines each; the lines may be broken (*yin*) or unbroken (*yang*). Originally, the hexagrams were devised by repeatedly dividing a fistful of 49 yarrow stalks, but today it is more customary to toss coins. Take 3 coins and toss them: if the majority are tails, this represents a *yin* line; if heads, a *yang* line. One does this 6 times, drawing the appropriate lines, to build the hexagram from the bottom upwards.

Armed with the hexagram, you then have to consult an "index" to its meaning – these are readily available in bookshops. Unfortunately, to occidental rationalism, the given meanings are maddeningly vague – which is to say that they have to be interpreted with thought for the particular situation by the consulter of the oracle. I have just consulted the *I Ching* with the question "Will *A Book of Numbers* be phenomenally successful?" and have been told not to envy a jagged mountain peak jutting against the sky. Gulp.

Sixty-Five

The Lord's Prayer contains 65 words (according to the Authorized Version). This did not stop a certain Frank Watts of Felmingham demonstrating in 1968 that, without the use of magnifying glass, he could write it out in full no less than 34 times on the back of a standard-sized postage stamp. The amount of prose involved is equivalent to about 6 pages of this book.

☆

In July 1982 a Spanish naturist, Tomas Cameselle, was fined £65 in Pontevedra. His fine was broken down as follows: £60 for appearing nude on a public beach; £5 for failing to carry his identity papers.

Sixty-Six

The Protestant version of the Bible has 66 books, 39 in the Old Testament and 27 in the New.

Polymer 66 was 1st produced in 1931 by the US chemist Wallace Hume Carothers: he found that he had invented an artificial fibre which was stronger than silk. Sadly, Carothers committed suicide in 1937; not until 1938 did the Du Pont company put Polymer 66 into production. They called it "nylon".

Sixty-Seven

According to Brewer a German eccentric called Lieuben bet that he could turn up the cards of a standard pack in a particular order. Unsuccessful in his early attempts, he persisted doggedly, finally winning his bet 20 years later, having put in a steady 10-hour day, 7 days a week, shuffling the pack and turning it up – a total of 4,246,028 times, according to his records.

I have my doubts about Lieuben's honesty. The odds are about 8×10^{67} against him being able to turn up the cards of the pack in any prearranged order; at the rate Lieuben was going the task should have taken him, with even luck, about 200 million million million million million million million million million million years!

It seems that if you want your son to become a saint, one of the best things you can do is to christen him Felix. There are no fewer than 67 saints called Felix in the Roman Martyrology.

By way of comparison, there are only 64 Johns.

In 1969 Adriana Martines and Octavio Guillen wed, thus putting to an end an engagement which had lasted for 67 years.

Sixty-Eight

The element of atomic number 68 is erbium (Er), one of the rare earth elements discovered by Carl Mosander (see *59) in the 1840s. Both it and terbium were named by him for the quarry of Ytterby, where the relevant minerals were found. This quarry gave its name also to yttrium and ytterbium, and so is the most commemorated name in the Periodic Table of the elements.

Sixty-Nine

Of the famous Penny Black, the 1st postage stamp to be issued (with the Twopenny Blue), on 1st May, 1840, 69 million were printed.

In "In the Neolithic Age" Rudyard Kipling put forward the interesting hypothesis

> *There are nine-and-sixty ways of constructing tribal lays,*
> *And – every – single – one – of – them – is – right!*

As anyone who has ever had any contact with magic will confirm, Kipling's observation was rather more accurate than perhaps he thought. If people *believe* in a ritual then, whatever the ritual might be, it *is* right – and in certain cases it will work.

In *Judges ix* we learn of the great tyrant Abimelech, who managed to murder 69 of his 70 brothers, the sons of Jerubbaal, in order to ascend the throne of Israel. The survivor was his youngest brother, Jotham, who had wisely gone into hiding. Abimelech died the death of a true male chauvinist superhero. While he was attacking a fortified tower in Thebez, a woman dropped a stone on his head, fatally wounding him. As he lay there in his mortal agony, he had the presence of mind to call for his armour-bearer and ask to be run through with a sword, so that no one could ever say that he had been killed by a woman.

Seventy

The element of atomic number 70 is ytterbium (Yb), one of the rare earth elements. Its main occurrence is in the mineral gadolinite, sometimes called ytterbite for the Ytterby quarry in Sweden, after which the element is itself named.

☆

Traditionally 70 – threescore years and ten – is regarded as the natural span of the human life. Psalm 90 is typical: "The days of our age are threescore years and ten; and though men be so strong that they come to fourscore years: yet is their strength then but labour and sorrow; so soon passeth it away, and we are gone."

It is a common fallacy that, owing to the advance of medical science, this natural lifespan is increasing (see *63).

☆

The 70th pope was Honorius I, who reigned from 625 until 638. He is best known for his apparent support of the heresy of monotheletism – the notion that, while Christ had 2 natures, he had but a single will (orthodoxy maintained that he had 2 wills); this heresy has been well-nigh imposed upon the Church by the Emperor Heraclius I. For some decades, until 668, successive popes were to be in conflict with successive emperors over this seemingly trivial issue.

Posthumously, in 681, Honorius was declared a heretic. Notorious Honorius.

Seventy-One

The element of atomic number 71 is lutetium (Lu), the heaviest of the rare earth elements, discovered in 1907 by the French chemist Georges Urbain and named by him in honour of the village which, in Roman times, stood on the site now occupied by Paris.

In 1911 Urbain thought he'd discovered another element, which he called celtium and believed fitted the position in the Periodic Table of element 72 (hafnium had not yet been discovered). The brilliant British physicist Henry Moseley, who was soon to have his life thrown away at Gallipoli, by use of sophisticated X-ray techniques of analysis was soon able to show that celtium was merely a mixture of other rare earth elements.

Seventy-Two

Aside from its more commonplace meanings – as in paper-sizes – the word "folio" denotes a unit used in the reckoning of the length of a document. In conveyancing it is 72 words (but see also *90), which means that this page is approximately 4 folios in length.

72 people, mostly children, died at a Christmas party in Calumet, Michigan, in 1913 when a wag shouted: "Fire!" There was no fire, of course, but there was a panic . : .

The element of atomic number 72 is hafnium (Hf), a metal with properties much like those of zirconium (atomic number *40), with which, in nature, it is often found in close association. It was discovered in 1923 by Georg von Hevesy, who had set out specifically to try to find the element to occupy the vacant 72 slot in the Periodic Table. Niels Bohr had suggested to him that this "new" element might have properties like those of zirconium, which lies directly above it on the Periodic Table, and it was in following up this idea that Hevesy made his discovery.

The Cambodian alphabet, with 72 letters, is the longest in the world. Just before you stutter "B-b-but what about Chinese?" remind yourself that pictographic languages don't *have* alphabets, as such.

While Queen Victoria of Britain is popularly regarded as the longest-reigning monarch of all time (64 years – 1837–1901), the real record (in recorded history) is held by the Sun King, Louis XIV of France. He reigned for a full 72 years, from 1643 until 1715.

The Pharaoh Pepi II possibly outdid Louis, supposedly reigning from *c*2566BC until *c*2476BC – a grand total of 90 years. King Sobhuza II of Swaziland reigned for 61 years (1921–82).

The 72nd pope was John IV, who reigned from 640 until 642 under rapidly succeeding Byzantine Emperors: Heraclius I died in February, 641, to be succeeded by Constantine III, who died in May, 641, to be succeeded by Haracleonas, who abdicated in September, 641, to be succeeded by Constans II Pogonatus, who broke the pattern by remaining on the throne for the next 28 years.

With the benefit of hindsight we can see that, from the Church's point of view, this was a very great mistake on the part of the Almighty.

In *Luke x* it is recorded that, as Christ was making his final pilgrimage to Jerusalem, he appointed 72 messengers in addition to his 12 principal Apostles to go ahead of him to spread the word of his coming. Without shoes or money, they were to accept charity and to speak and act for Christ, curing the sick in his name. On their return, the 72 expressed a rather touching astonishment: even the devils submitted when Christ's name was used. It seems likely that much of the "curing of the sick" consisted of what we would now call "faith-healing" or "placebo medicine", but which is more correctly termed, in light of the cultural circumstances, "exorcism".

Seventy-Three

In 1940 Trotsky was killed by a sole assassin wielding an icepick (the murderer was probably Jacques Mornard, *alias* Raymond Mercader). This was the 2nd murder attempt on Trotsky that year: earlier his bedroom in Mexico City had been sprayed with no less than 73 bullets, and he escaped without a scratch.

The modern Roman Catholic version of the Bible has 73 books, 46 in the Old Testament and 27 in the New.

In the presidential election of 1800, at a time when the electors each voted for 2 candidates, so that the one with the most votes became president, the runner up vice-president, Thomas Jefferson and Aaron Burr each received 73 votes. The matter was put to Congress and, largely thanks to Alexander Hamilton's staunch opposition to Burr, Congress selected Jefferson to be president. Burr was so furious with Hamilton (and you can hardly blame him, can you?) that, some years later, in 1804, in which year he believed that Hamilton had also blocked his election to the governorship of New York, he challenged Hamilton to a contrived duel and killed him.

Brander's Swamp Deer is only 1 of many animal and plant species threatened with extinction as a result not only of inclement natural circumstances but also mankind's greed. In 1975 it was reported that the world population of Brander's Swamp Deer was 73.

The element of atomic number 73 is tantalum (Ta), a metal whose properties are very similar to those of niobium – a similarity which gave rise to a nasty squabble over the matter of niobium's very existence (see *41). Tantalum was discovered in 1802 by the Swedish chemist Anders Ekeberg.

There were 73 signatories to a letter published in *The Guardian* for 27th March, 1982, protesting about staff conditions in a major bookshop. The 73 represent the cream of modern British letters with an admixture of names from the stage and academia. Here is a personal selection: John Arden, Dame Peggy Ashcroft, Professor Sir A. J. Ayer, Beryl Bainbridge, John Berger, Edward Bond, Melvyn Bragg, Raymond Briggs, Brigid Brophy, Angus Calder, Angela Carter, Bernard Crick, Margaret Drabble, Michael Foot, John Fowles, Susan George, Michael Hamburger, Professor Eric Hobsbawm, Michael Horowitz, Lord Hugh Jenkins, Mervyn Jones, Paddy Kitchen, Lady Jennie Lee, Peter Levi, Edward Lucie-Smith, Ian McEwan, James MacGibbon, John McGrath, Sheila MacLeod, Lord Melchett, Jonathan Miller, Adrian Mitchell, Michael Moorcock, Angela Neustatter, Tom Pickard, Christopher Price, J. B. Priestley, Frederick Rafael, Vanessa Redgrave, Salman Rushdie, Sir Roy Shaw, Clancy Sigal, Dale Spender, Julian Symons, Emma Tennant, Paul Theroux, Ted Walker and Charlotte Wolff.

For authors to protest about a major bookshop is, of course, unusually courageous, since they are risking their livelihoods. The bookshop was Foyle's.

Seventy-Four

The element of atomic number 74 is tungsten, whose symbol is unexpectedly W: the element was initially called "wolfram" after the mineral wolframite, from which it was 1st isolated in 1783 by the Spanish mineralogist Don Fausto d'Elhuyar. Tungsten is very hard, and so is its compound tungsten carbide, used in cutting-tools. The compound is of even greater interest to schoolchildren – of all ages – because its chemical formula is WC. Snigger.

Seventy-Five

In 1976, 75 prisoners failed in their attempt to escape from Saltillo Prison in Mexico. The tunnel which they had been busily digging for several months unfortunately emerged in a nearby courtroom.

The element of atomic number 75 is rhenium (Re), a very rare and very hard silvery white metal with applications similar to those of platinum. Rhenium was the last of the nonradioactive elements to be discovered, in 1925 by Walter Noddack and Ida Tacke (later Ida Noddack). The Noddacks thought that they'd discovered also element *43, calling it masurium. They were wrong.

The 75th pope was Eugenius or Eugene I. He was elected in 654, actually before the death of his predecessor, Martin I, who nevertheless acknowledged him as a *bona fide* pope. After attempting to compromise with the Emperor Constans over the matter of the monothelete heresy (the idea that Christ had 2 natures but only 1 will), he faced a clerical rebellion in Rome and so promptly determined to stand firm against the continuing attempts of Constans to impose the heresy on the Church. He died in 657, just before Constans had had a real chance to retaliate.

Seventy-Six

There is in Kentucky a township with the unusual name of 76, christened thus in order to commemorate the Declaration of

Independence in 1776. Elsewhere – for example in Kansas and Missouri – people opted for the more conventional name of Independence.

The element of atomic number 76 is osmium (Os), a rare metal discovered in 1803 by the British chemist Smithson Tennant, who named it after the Greek word for "smell" because one of its compounds did. Osmium was the 1st metal to be used for an electric lightbulb filament, by Karl Auer in 1898, in preference to the carbonized thread of Edison; since osmium is alarmingly rare, its place in this application was soon taken by tungsten.

Osmium is the densest of all elements, weighing in at a healthy 22.48 grams or so per cubic centimetre.

The period (i.e., the time between successive passages close to the Sun) of the most famous comet of them all, Halley's, is approximately 76 years. Halley's name is associated with the comet because in 1705 he not only realized that at least some comets might be in orbit around the Sun, rather than simply appearing as if from nowhere and then vanishing back there again, but also noticed that the comet of 1682, which he had himself observed, was probably the same as those of 1456, 1531 and 1607. He predicted that it would reappear in 1758 or thereabouts – although he was not too definite about the precise year because he recognized that the gravitational attractions of the planets would affect his calculations. In fact, the comet reappeared in 1759 – by which time Halley had been dead for 17 years.

Mark Twain, born in 1835 – the next "year of the comet" – predicted frequently that, having come with the comet, he would go with it – which he duly did. The comet next appeared in 1910, the year of Twain's death.

The worst terrorist massacre in recent history has been the explosion in the central station of Bologna in August, 1980, reportedly the work of right-wingers. 76 people lost their lives.

Seventy-Seven

The highest recorded TV audience in Holland was in 1972, when 77% of the public was watching. The broadcast concerned? No, not the Apollo-16 or -17 landings on the Moon: it was a quiz show.

The element of atomic number 77 is iridium (Ir), a hard white metal of interest in that it is the element most resistant to corrosion at room temperature. It was discovered in 1803 by the British chemist Smithson Tennant, who gave it its name because its compounds seemed to display a whole spectrum of colours.

The worst recorded accident in the history of motor-racing occurred in 1955 at Le Mans, when the Mercedes of Pierre Levegh went out of control, hit a wall and exploded, killing 77 people (including Levegh himself). Unimpressed by all this carnage, the racing authorities insisted that the race continue.

Seventy-Eight

Although there may seem to be much more, because of UK television repeats *ad nauseam*, only 78 episodes of *Star Trek* were made (1966–68).

78 popes have been canonized, the most recent being Pius X, who reigned from 1903 until 1914. It should be recognized, however, that the vast majority of these papal saints were canonized virtually by accident or through custom, either in the early days of the Church or in later centuries when it seemed useful to have as many saints as possible. It's notable that Pius X was the 1st pope to be canonized since Pius V, who was Bishop of Rome from 1566 until 1572.

The element of atomic number 78 is platinum (Pt), an extremely inert metal which is probably the most expensive in the world (that anyone would want to buy, that is: some of the radioactives do come a little pricey, especially those with very short halflives, when a few atoms may cost millions . . .). Its uses are as a catalyst, in jewellery, in laboratory equipment, etc.

There are 78 cards in the Tarot pack: 4 suits of 14 cards each (cups, wands, swords and pentacles) plus *22 major trumps.

Seventy-Nine

Recent startling research carried out in the USA by Dr Joyce Brothers has shown that, on average, an American woman kisses (discounting familial and platonic pecks) 79 men before marriage. My visa application is in the post.

☆

The element of atomic number 79 is gold (Au), a rather pretty and very expensive metal whose most important uses are in electrical circuits and for filling teeth; it has uses also in decoration and as a monetary standard. Its purity is expressed in terms of carats (see *24).

Eighty

According to the temperature scale devised by René Antoine Ferchault de Réamur (1683–1757), the boiling point of water is 80°R, the freezing point of water 0°R. His scale fell out of use rather swiftly.

☆

The element of atomic number 80 is mercury (Hg), still often referred to as "quicksilver", a metal of peculiar popularity among schoolchildren of all ages because it is liquid at room temperature (its freezing point is −39°C). Its most everyday uses are in thermometers and barometers; in connection with the latter, it is still customary to express atmospheric pressure in terms of the height of the mercury column which the pressure will support (the standard is 760mm).

If this sounds opaque, think about making a simple barometer for yourself. Take a glass tube a bit longer than 760mm, sealed at one end, and fill it to the brim with mercury; put your thumb over the end. With your other hand, put some mercury in a bowl. Keeping your thumb over its end, invert the tube and place the thumbed end under the surface of your pool of mercury. Remove the thumb, and the level of mercury in the tube will drop to about 760mm. What's keeping the mercury to that height in the tube is the pressure of the air bearing down upon the surface of the pool of mercury.

Mercury is highly poisonous, as are most if not all of its compounds. Minute quantities may nevertheless be of medicinal use. Paracelsus (1493–1541) certainly believed so, continuing to place great faith in mercury compounds despite the fact that most of the patients he treated with them dropped dead.

The famous Baron von Richthofen, best known air ace of World War I, is officially credited with having downed 80 enemy 'planes.

Eighty-One

Because *9 is a sacred number, in some systems corresponding to the spirit, and because it is thought that critical periods in life recur every 9 years (but see *49), its square, 81, is regarded as a minor climacteric of the individual's life – assuming he or she lives that long, of course. It is nowhere near as important as the Grand Climacteric – see *63.

Johann Wolfgang von Goethe (1749–1832) finished his most famous work, *Faust*, when he was 81 years old.

The element of atomic number 81 is thallium (Tl), a soft blue-grey metal. It was discovered by use of spectroscopy in 1861 by the great British physicist Sir William Crookes, who is deservedly better known for other achievements. He was studying ores of selenium when he came across a pretty green line in their spectra which accorded with no known element. Thus he called his "new" element thallium from the Greek *thallos*, meaning a new, green shoot. The metal's compounds are extremely poisonous.

Between 1830 and 1838 *Fraser's Magazine* published 81 of the stars of the literary firmament, who thenceforth were known collectively as "The 81" or "the Fraserians". They include W. Harrison Ainsworth, Edward Bulwer-Lytton, Thomas Carlyle, William Cobbett, Samuel Taylor Coleridge, George Cruikshank,

Benjamin *and* Isaac Disraeli, Michael Faraday, James Hogg, Leigh Hunt, Washington Irving, Charles Lamb, Thomas Moore, Walter Scott, Sydney Smith, Talleyrand and William Wordsworth. There were some lesser lights, too. Dr Dionysius Lardner predicted both that steamships would never be able to cross the Atlantic because they would be unable to carry enough coal, an argument put forward in 1838, the year in which the 1st such crossing was made; and that, if high-speed rail travel were ever attempted, the passengers would suffocate to death. And the religious poet Robert Montgomery is today best known for the hilarious castigation of his work by Macaulay in the *Edinburgh Review* in 1830; Montgomery's contemporary success seems to have been little affected.

Eighty-Two

The element of atomic number 82 is lead (Pb), a metal with many uses (e.g., in radiation shielding), especially in alloys such as Babbitt metal, pewter, solder and type-metal. Traditionally, bullets are made of lead. Some 40% of the world's production of the metal is used in antimonial lead electrodes for automobile and other batteries; but a large proportion is used in the form of lead tetraethyl as an antiknock agent in petroleum, despite the fact that people exposed to large quantities of the resulting exhaust fumes are known to suffer brain damage. In the UK this problem particularly applies to children in the inner cities; successive governments have positively discouraged attempts to reduce lead levels in petroleum – presumably on the basis that kids don't vote while petroleum producers do. Kids can harm themselves, too, by eating lead-based paint, although the manufacturers are beginning to explore alternatives.

The "lead" in pencils is not lead at all (although lead can be used to write with); it is powdered graphite (carbon) mixed with clay. The higher the proportion of clay in the mixture, the higher the pencil is rated on the "H" scale; the higher the proportion of graphite, the higher the pencil is rated on the "B" scale.

Eighty-Three

Readers who have always believed that "supercalifragilisticexpialidocious" just *must* be the longest made-up word in popular song (see *34) should listen to the 1977 song, "The Lone Ranger" in which appears the 83-letter "taumatawhakatangihanakoauquotamateaturipukakpikimauncahoronukupokaiwhenuakitanatahu". And it is at this point that I would like to propose a vote of thanks to the typesetters of this book . . . or should I wait until the entry for *182?

The element of atomic number 83 is bismuth (Bi), a brittle metal with a predominantly silver-grey coloration noticeably tinged with red. It shares with water the unusual property of expanding on freezing (which it does at 271°C). Bismuth has the advantage, like barium, of having compounds which are both nontoxic and opaque to X-rays; these can therefore be used to examine the intestines without cutting you open.

Eighty-Four

If you happen to be pregnant, there is a 1 in 84 chance of your having twins.

The 84th pope was Sergius I, who reigned from 687 until 701.

His election is of some interest to students of the corrupt. Pascal, Archdeacon of Rome, offered the Emperor's representative in Italy, the Exarch of Ravenna, a bribe to ensure that he, Pascal, was elected pope; the bargain was struck between them even before the death of the 83rd pope, Conon. But a man called Theodore stood, for very honourable reasons, against Pascal; to cut a long story short, both of them regarded themselves as having been elected. Sergius was overwhelmingly put forward as a compromise candidate and solution to this dilemma; Theodore stood down willingly in his favour, Pascal "very unwillingly". The Exarch, annoyed by all this commotion and realizing that, because of Pascal's failure to capture the papal throne, he was out of pocket, accepted Sergius' pontificate only on payment of a sum of money equal to the bribe which Pascal had offered.

The element of atomic number 84 is polonium (Po), a metalloid, all of whose isotopes are radioactive. Its commonest isotope is polonium-210, with a halflife of 138.4 days. It was discovered in

1898 by Marie and Pierre Curie, following the recognition by Marie that there was more radioactivity coming out of uranium ores than could possibly be explained by the uranium content alone.

The mediaeval Arabic *Book of Ostanes* contains no less than 84 different names for the Philosophers' Stone. Also of note in its contents is an essay concerning the healing powers of the urine of white elephants. Something to remember at your next jumble sale.

Eighty-Five

They didn't bother with a trial in the case of the murderer Bruno Lüdke (1909–1944), who had confessed to killing 85 women in the period between 1928 and early 1943: they simply "put him to sleep", like the mad dog he was, by injection in a Vienna hospital.

The element of atomic number 85 is astatine (At), a radioactive metalloid whose most stable isotope, astatine-210, has a halflife of about 8 hours 20 minutes. It was discovered in 1940 by a team including Emilio Segrè, who was not unused to such excitements.

Astatine is the rarest of the naturally occurring elements. According to one estimate, there is a grand total of $\frac{1}{3}$ of a gram of it in the Earth's crust.

Eighty-Six

The element of atomic number 86 is radon (Rn), a radioactive gas whose most important and common isotope is radon-222, with a halflife of about 43 hours. It was discovered in 1900 by the German physicist Friedrich Dorn, who noticed that radium, in the process of decay, gave off a gas which was itself radioactive. This gas was, of course, radon.

The 86th pope was John VII, who reigned from 705 until 707. The year 705 saw the reinstatement on the Byzantine throne of the revolting Justinian II. John did not, as is popularly believed, merely kowtow to Justinian's whims – although it must have been tempting to do so, since Justinian gave him little "warnings" by having the eyes of both the Patriarch of Constantinople and the Archbishop of Ravenna plucked out. John dodged the various issues for long enough to be able to die before Justinian could turn even nastier.

Eighty-Seven

Many cricketers, especially Australian ones, dread the number 87: they believe that at this score, 13 short of the 100, something disastrous is almost bound to happen. Similarly loathed are 187, 287, etc.

The cricket team which John Grant plays for, Newtown St Matthews, is quite pleased to *reach* a score of 87.

The element of atomic number 87 is francium (Fr), a radioactive metal whose most stable isotope, francium-223, has a halflife of only about 21 minutes.

The 87th pope was Sisinnius, who reigned only from 15th January until 4th February, 780. On election he was apparently so crippled by gout that he couldn't feed himself, and his condition did not improve.

Cantharidin, the drug popularly known as "Spanish fly", is generally accepted as a powerful aphrodisiac – although even a small dose may cause internal haemorrhaging and death (it was only a decade or so ago that a New Zealand student was imprisoned for manslaughter for having tried it out on his girlfriend with fatal results). A 16th-century report from Provence tells of a woman who used the drug on her husband to such effect that, over the next couple of nights and days, he made love to her 87 times. Although by this time he was in poor health (to put it mildly), with his penis beginning to succumb to gangrene, he achieved orgasm 3 more times while being medically examined before death at last brought him peace.

I have my doubts about this story. Cantharidin irritates the genitals and may cause erection in males, but it certainly does not hasten orgasm – which it would have to do were someone to make love successfully every 33 minutes for 48 solid hours. I mean, I've tried, and . . .

Eighty-Eight

There are 88 keys on the standard piano keyboard, of which 52 are white and 36 are black.

☆

The element of atomic number 88 is radium (Ra), discovered in 1898 by Marie and Pierre Curie, who had earlier discovered the less important element polonium. The Curies' determination in the whole affair is worthy of awestruck admiration. Having discovered radium, they decided to process enough of it for proper chemical analysis – it's a very rare substance, although its longest-lived isotope, radium-226, has a halflife of a healthy 1622 years. They processed a full 8 tonnes of pitchblende in order to obtain a single gram of the element, a task which took them several years.

Pierre Curie died in 1906, being run over by a carriage. He and Marie had shared the 1903 Nobel Prize for Physics with Antoine Henri Becquerel; in 1911 Marie accepted the Nobel Prize for Chemistry for the Curies' discovery of 2 "new" elements. Despite being one of only 3 people ever to have won 2 Nobel science prizes (the others were John Bardeen, for Physics, 1956 and 1972, and Frederick Sanger, for Chemistry, 1958 and 1980; Linus Pauling won the 1954 Chemistry and 1962 Peace prizes), she was refused admission to the French Academy of Sciences on the grounds that she was only a woman!

Radium is the most toxic of all the elements, the naturally occurring radium-224 being quoted as 1700 times more toxic than plutonium–239.

☆

After years if not centuries of confusion, in 1930 the International Astronomical Union recognized and established a definitive list of 88 constellations: Andromeda, Antlia, Apus, Aquarius, Aquila, Ara, Aries, Auriga, Boötes, Caelum, Camelopardalis, Cancer, Canes Venatici, Canis Major, Canis Minor, Capricornus,

Carina, Cassiopeia, Centaurus, Cepheus, Cetus, Chamaeleon, Circinus, Columba, Coma Berenices, Corona Australis, Corona Borealis, Corvus, Crater, Crux, Cygnus, Delphinus, Dorado, Draco, Equuleus, Eridanus, Fornax, Gemini, Grus, Hercules, Horologium, Hydra, Hydrus, Indus, Lacertus, Leo, Leo Minor, Lepus, Libra, Lupus, Lynx, Lyra, Mensa, Microscopium, Monoceros, Musca, Norma, Octans, Ophiuchus, Orion, Pavo, Pegasus, Perseus, Phoenix, Pictor, Pisces, Piscis Austrinus, Puppis, Pyxis, Reticulum, Sagitta, Sagittarius, Scorpius, Sculptor, Scutum, Serpens, Sextans, Taurus, Telescopium, Triangulum, Triangulum Australe, Tucana, Ursa Major, Ursa Minor, Vela, Virgo, Volans and Vulpecula.

The 88th pope was Constantine, who reigned from 708 until 715. In 710 he had the courage to go to Constantinople to argue doctrinal matters with the repulsive Emperor Justinian II; surprisingly, he not only survived this encounter but actually won some concessions from the Emperor.

In 711, to general rejoicing and almost certainly to Constantine's considerable relief, Justinian was dethroned and beheaded. In fact, his head was sent by the usurper, Philippicus Bardanes, to Constantine as a grisly earnest of goodwill.

Hindu mystics maintain that there are approximately 88 thousand *chakras*, or points of connection between the astral and physical bodies.

Eighty-Nine

The element of atomic number 89 is actinium (Ac), the 1st and prototypical element of the group of elements called collectively the actinides. This radioactive metal was discovered in 1899 by the French chemist André Debierne, who was continuing the work on pitchblende in parallel with the Curies.

The 89th pope was Gregory II, who reigned from 715 until 731; like Gregory I he was one of the few really great and good popes. His main problem was that the new Byzantine Emperor, Leo III the Isaurian, who reigned from 717, was intent upon iconoclasm.

Perhaps influenced by the comparatively new cult of Islam, Leo abhorred the very thought of worshipping graven images, and therefore argued in favour of the destruction of all such *objets* – including icons. In 730 Leo issued an edict against icons; Gregory stood firm, but very soon died, leaving Gregory III to pick up the pieces.

Ninety

If you are a US male, you have 1 chance in only 90 of being murdered. If you're female, see *275!

In response to the criticism that 90% of science fiction is rubbish, the US science-fiction writer Theodore Sturgeon came out with his famous Law: 90% of *everything* is rubbish.

The element of atomic number 90 is thorium (Th), a silvery radioactive metal which used to be used in the making of the mantles for gas lamps, and which is still used as an additive to the tungsten in the filaments of electric lightbulbs. In nuclear reactors, it can be converted into the important fuel uranium-233. The element was discovered in 1829 by the great Swedish chemist Jöns Berzelius.

The unit of the folio, as used in reckoning the lengths of legal documents, is in the case of parliamentary documents equal to 90 words (but see also *72).

Ninety-One

The element of atomic number 91 is protactinium (Pa), a rare radioactive metal found in uranium ores. Its longest-lived isotope is protactinium-231, with a halflife of 34,000 years. The element was discovered in 1918 by Lise Meitner and Otto Hahn. In 1966 this remarkable pair became the 1st non-Americans, and Meitner the 1st woman, to be given the Fermi Award issued by the US Atomic Energy Commission.

Ninety-Two

Only 92 of CBS's 186 stations dared show a 1973 play called *Sticks and Bones,* which dealt with the return to his home of a US Vietnam veteran: the problem was, you see, that the play might upset the relatives of PoWs in Vietnam. Because of what can only be regarded as large-scale cowardice (on the basis that it would be folly to ban ghost-stories just because most of us have dead relatives), large areas of the USA were treated to what the British regard as everyday: nearly 2 hours without a single interruption for commercials.

The shortest-lived pope of all was the 92nd, Stephen II, who reigned for only 3 days (possibly 4) after his election on 23rd March, 752. Today he is often omitted from the records, because he failed to survive until his consecration; his successor adopted the title Stephen II, and ever since then there has been confusion. Perhaps to alleviate this, there has been no pope called Stephen since the reign of Stephen IX (or X), which lasted from 1057 until 1058.

The 1st artificial satellite was launched by the Soviet Union in October, 1957. Although the records are not exact (as is often the case with the Soviet space programme), it is believed that Sputnik 1, a mere 58cm in diameter, stayed in orbit for 92 days.

The US Government, which had persuaded itself to believe that the USSR was far behind in the race for space, was aghast; and instantly commissioned Wernher von Braun's team to match the achievement. The result was Explorer 1, launched in January, 1958.

On 12th April, 1961, Yuri Gagarin became the 1st man in space (the 1st man to *survive* in space, as persistent rumour has it), despite the fact that the US Government "knew" that its country was way ahead in the manned space race; on May 5th Alan Shepard was swiftly despatched skywards, although it was not to be until 20th February, 1962, that the US succeeded in sending an astronaut into orbit and thereby matching Gagarin's feat.

The US Government learnt its lesson, and within a few years (in July, 1969) organized a manned landing on the Moon – which the USSR has yet to achieve. Currently, the US government "knows" that it is way ahead in the space race . . .

☆

The element of atomic number 92 is uranium (U), the heaviest element to be found in nature and an important fuel; various politicians have discovered that it's useful, too, for killing people *en masse*. The 3 naturally occurring isotopes of uranium are, with their halflives: uranium-234, 250,000 years; uranium-235, 710,000,000 years; and uranium-238, 4,500,000,000 years – a figure more-or-less equal to the age of the Earth. As you might expect, more than 99% of natural uranium is U-238.

Discovered in 1789 by the great German chemist Martin Klaproth, uranium was named by him in honour of the discovery in 1781 by Sir William Herschel of the 7th planet, Uranus.

Ninety-Three

The city of Luxembourg has 93 bridges.

☆

The element of atomic number 93 is neptunium (Np), a radioactive metal produced in nuclear breeder-reactors.

The great Italian physicist Enrico Fermi thought in 1934 that he'd discovered element number 93 as a by-product of bombarding uranium with neutrons; in fact, he'd discovered nuclear fission, as the Japanese were to learn a decade later. Neptunium was actually 1st created in 1940 by the US physicists Edwin McMillan and Philip Abelson, who shared the 1951 Nobel Prize for Chemistry in honour of this and other work on the "transuranium elements".

Ninety-Four

About 94% of the Earth's crust, by volume, is oxygen. It's rather staggering to think that even Mount Everest is largely oxygen. (By weight the figure is about 50% – see *8.)

☆

The element of atomic number 94 is plutonium (Pu), the most important of the "transuranium elements", discovered in 1940 and put to use in 1945 in the bomb that was dropped on Nagasaki.

It was named in honour of the discovery, in 1930 by Clyde Tombaugh, of the 9th planet, Pluto.

Ninety-Five

We're all familiar with the dramatic scene in films, plays or broadcasts: in 1517 Martin Luther furiously nails his document concerning the abuses of the practice of selling indulgences to the door of the church in Wittenberg. It was, of course, the scene which sparked off the Reformation.

Well, that's the story: it's only since the latter part of the 17th century that the act has been seen as so important. Moreover, the nailing of Luther's "95 Theses" to the church door was not an act of wrath: it was merely the customary way in which the clergy brought forward matters for discussion. And, while Luther was indeed enraged about a particularly corrupt local sale of indulgences (the pardoning of sins in exchange for cash), he was more concerned, at this stage, over the abuse of the practice than over the practice itself – although he did jib at the way that money was being taken from the poor to help the rich. However, many of his "95 Theses" were points for discussion, the raising of theological problems, rather than the hard-and-fast declarations which popular mythology has made them out to be.

It was thanks to the colossal mishandling of the dispute in succeeding years by the Catholic Church, rather than to the "95 Theses" themselves, that the Reformation really got under way.

It may seem startling that, of all the stars in the sky, about 95% are smaller than the Sun. The reason for the startlement is that, when you look at the range of possible sizes stars can be, the Sun is rather smaller than average.

The 95th pope was Stephen III, elected in 768 only after the election of 2 antipopes since the death of his predecessor a year earlier. The 1st, Constantine, had actually been consecrated, in 767, through the use of force; he was merely a tool of some of the Roman patrician families. The 2nd, Philip, was similarly a tool of the Lombards.

Christopher, head of the priestly college of Rome, together with his son Sergius raised enough support for Stephen for him to be elected in place of these 2 rather craven fellows: they were to learn that Stephen was worse. Following the death of King Pepin the Short, the Franks were now ruled by Charlemagne and his brother Carloman, both of whom together confirmed Stephen's election; but they were siblings in dispute, and likely to have little time to come to the defence of the papacy. The Lombards therefore took the opportunity to march on Rome, and their King Desiderius persuaded the pope to allow them to execute, in vengeance for the antipope Philip, Christopher and Sergius – the very pair which had put Stephen on the papal throne in the first place!

Stephen's pontificate, indeed, was marked throughout by general barbarity. The antipopes and their supporters were treated with considerable cruelty at the hands of – depending upon their affiliation – the representatives of the Franks, those of the Lombards, or even those of the papacy; as Stephen lay dying in 772 his chamberlain, Paul Afiarta, in tandem with King Desiderius, was planning new atrocities. It is generally said that none of these crimes can be laid at Stephen's door, that he was merely a weak man unable to stop what was going on. This story rather rapidly wears a little thin.

Only 1 good thing came out of Stephen's pontificate. After his election it was decided, in April, 769, at a Lateran Council that, in view of the disarray following his predecessor Paul's death and the need for avoiding similar ructions in the future, from now on only the clergy could be involved in papal elections, only cardinals being eligible as candidates.

Astonishingly, in some martyrologies Stephen III is reckoned to be a saint!

Ninety-Six

In the state of South Carolina you can find the place called Ninety-Six.

Ninety-Seven

In $5\frac{1}{2}$ single-column inches, *The Times* for 22nd August, 1978, had 97 misprints. This is believed to be a record for all newspapers – including even *The Guardian*.

☆

The 97th pope was Leo III, who reigned from 795 until 816; from common stock, he was deeply disliked by some elements of the Roman aristocracy. In 799 he was almost deposed by a group of the latter: he was badly beaten about the face and eyes but escaped, to seek help from Charlemagne. Charlemagne took the opportunity to come to Rome, where he subjected Leo to a silly, humiliating show-trial, finding him innocent of charges of misconduct; but the act of trying a pope was, of course, something of an impertinence, with the state claiming to be competent to judge a clerical matter.

On Christmas Day, 800, Leo responded to Charlemagne's declaration of his innocence in an unusual way. At mass, to Charlemagne's professed annoyance, Leo unexpectedly crowned him Emperor. "Emperor of what?" is the obvious question – and one that has never really been answered. But here, of course, we have the origin of the theory of the Holy Roman Empire – a matter which was to be of some considerable importance a few centuries later.

Ninety-Eight

On average, by the time she is 16½, a girl has attained 98% of her final height – something which the average boy does not do until he is 17¾. However, some people do continue growing in stature long after this age: cases are known of people still growing in their 40s.

The 98th pope was Stephen IV, whose reign lasted only a few months, between 816 and 817. Although he did not seek imperial confirmation of his election (from Charlemagne's son and successor, Louis the "Pious"), he took the important step of travelling to Reims, France, to crown Louis and his consort Emperor and Empress; this happened on 18th October, 816. Stephen thereby established the precedent set by his predecessor, Leo III.

Ninety-Nine

According to Thornton Wilder, "99% of the people in the world are fools and the rest of us are in great danger of contagion."

The element of atomic number 99 is einsteinium (Es), a radioactive metal 1st discovered in 1952 in the debris from the 1st hydrogen bomb and named in honour of Albert Einstein. Since Einstein had devoted much of his energies from 1945 onwards to the fight against the proliferation of nuclear weapons, the tribute seems a curious one.

An old Ottoman proverb catches my eye: "The fox has 100 proverbs – and of these 99 are about poultry."

The 99th pope was Paschal I, who reigned from 817 until 824. He succeeded in formalizing the relationship between pope and emperor; however, as a commoner, he was deeply unpopular with the Roman aristocracy – and, like the *97th pope, Leo III, he was subjected by the Emperor, in this case Louis the "Pious", to a show-trial at which he was found innocent. The aristocracy, on Paschal's death, refused to permit his burial in St Peter's until they had ascertained the successful election of their own candidate to succeed him.

One Hundred

One Henry Harder managed to compose in Latin a 100-line poem about cats every word of which begins with the letter "c". The 1st line, for the benefit of those who enjoy nonchalantly dropping Latin tags into the conversation, runs: "*Cattorum canimus certamina clara canumque.*"

Barbers were notoriously underpaid in the ancient Near East, and so almost always added blood-letting to their services in a desperate attempt to earn a living wage. This is reflected in the Hebrew proverb: "100 bleedings for a zuz, 100 heads for a zuz, but 100 lips [i.e., moustache-trims] for nothing." A zuz was worth $\frac{1}{4}$ of a silver shekel, so plainly the barber's lot was not a wealthy one.

The element of atomic number 100 is fermium (Fm), 1st discovered in 1953 in the debris from the 1st hydrogen bomb (like the *99th element, einsteinium). It was named in honour of Enrico

Fermi, whose work was largely responsible for the dawn of the nuclear age.

☆

The 100 Years' War in fact lasted for *117 years.

☆

100 thousand German marks is the prize offered to anyone who can prove Fermat's Last Theorem before AD2007. Fermat wrote in the margin of a mathematics textbook: "Where n is a number larger than 2, there are no whole numbers a, b, c such that $a^n + b^n = c^n$, and of this I have found a most marvellous proof, but this margin is too small to contain it." Since Pierre de Fermat (1601–1665) was one of the finest mathematicians of all time, it is probable that he did indeed discover a proof of his assertion – but it doesn't survive, and no one's been able to rediscover it. Using iterative procedures, modern computers have been able to show that the statement is true for values of n up to several thousand.

Should you be hit by a flash of inspiration and scribble down the proof (in the margin of this book, perhaps), don't get too excited about the 100 thousand marks: they're old marks, and thus worth rather less than the area of paper you've just written on. But you'll make it into the history books . . .

☆

Very occasionally, members of the UK House of Commons will apply for the stewardship of the Chiltern 100s, which is tantamount to resignation. The reason for this is that, by law, MPs cannot resign; however, they can apply for a paid Crown Office, such as the stewardship of the Chiltern 100s. However, their occupation of it implies that they can no longer enjoy the privileges of being an MP – furthermore, they can then legitimately resign the stewardship.

Though a nominal office today, the stewardship of the Chiltern 100s had more meaning before about 1750: 3 areas of the Chiltern Hills in Bedfordshire were particularly troubled by bandits, and so the Steward of the 100s was appointed to quash these robbers and generally protect the neighbourhood.

The "100s" in the name of the Chiltern 100s refers to the old subdivision of a shire. The derivation of the name seems to be from the fact that, in theory at least, each 100 consisted of 100 "geld hides", a geld hide being the basic land unit, for purposes of taxation, of the Anglo-Saxons. (In various parts of the country, the 100s were known alternatively as wards and wapentakes.)

Each 100 held a monthly court at which, twice yearly, a sheriff would preside. In the Middle Ages, the interesting custom for a while held sway that the population of each 100 was collectively responsible for any crime committed within it – unless, of course, the guilty party were produced. A useful way to convict the innocent.

☆

In 1956 the Chinese communist government decided to permit criticism of its policies in the so-called 100 Flowers Campaign; the move was in imitation of Kruschev's similar short-lived policy in the USSR. As Mao put it, quoting from Chinese history, "Let 100 flowers bloom, and 100 schools of thought contend." As might be expected, by the summer of 1957 the Party had thought better of it all, so powerful were the criticisms directed against it, and repression returned.

Mao's quotation refers to the period between the 6th and 3rd centuries BC when the 100 Schools (as they were called; how many of them there were is a matter for debate) competed for supremacy; they were, of course, schools of philosophy. Among them were 2 which are still popular: Taoism and Confucianism.

☆

In French history the period of 100 Days was that between the return from exile on Elba of Napoleon to Paris, on 20th March, 1815, until the reaccession of Louis XVIII to the French throne, in the wake of Waterloo, on 28th June of the same year. Genuine purists will note that this period was actually 101 days long.

In Chilean history, the expression "the 100 Days" refers to the brief period of socialist government which the country enjoyed between June and September, 1932; because the government's period in office was so short before it was ousted by a military junta, it achieved little. Back to the traditional South American repression, folks, but this time apparently without the help of the CIA. At least the military didn't kill the deposed president, Marmaduque Grove, the way they were to kill President Salvador Allende, who tried to bring similar justice to Chilean society, in 1973.

In the USA the expression "the 100 Days" refers to the 1st 3 months or so of a new president's period of office. The expression dates from 1933 and the 1st 100 days of Franklin Roosevelt's New Deal administration.

☆

It seems strange that a hundredweight (cwt) is in fact 112 lbs; the reason for this curiosity is not known. It seems likely that originally 1 hundredweight was indeed 100 lbs but that, in the usual shuffling and adjustment that went on as badly defined units were brought into some kind of sensible, consistent relationship with each other, the hundredweight "accidentally" became 112 lbs. (As another example of this sort of thing, the number of pounds in a stone used to be anywhere between 8 and 24, as opposed to the currently acceptable 14.)

The US "short" hundredweight, on the other hand, is defined as 100 lbs.

Tsar Peter I, the Great (1672–1725), despite his various sterling characteristics, was a man of curious habits. Both he and his wife, Tsarina Catherine I, ordered the execution of 1 of the other's lovers; each member of this odd royal couple thereafter maintained the pickled head of his or her lover in the bedchamber, as a souvenir.

But the tsar's strangest, if less grisly, action was his imposition of a tax of 100 roubles on everyone (except members of the poorest classes) with a beard.

In the preface to *The Adventures of Gil Blas of Santillane* (1715–35), by Alain René Le Sage (1668–1747), the tale is told of 2 scholars making their way to Alamanca. They come across a gravestone on which is inscribed "Here Lies the Soul of Pedro Garcias". One scholar laughs at this and goes on his way, but the other looks under the stone and discovers a purse containing 100 ducats and the instruction to use this money better than "I did my money". The "soul of Pedro carcias" is thus now, by tradition, 100 ducats.

Mortally wounded when he was greedily laying siege to the Viscomte of Limoges' Castle of Châlus, demanding a hoard of gold which had been unearthed by a local peasant, Richard the Lion-Heart is alleged to have said to the archer who fired the fatal arrow "Youth, I forgive you", then to have instructed his attendants who were holding the man: "Take off his chains. Give him 100 shillings and let him go." Then Richard expired.

A decameron is a collection of tales supposed to have been told over a period of 10 days. The most famous is of course that of Giovanni Boccaccio (1313–1375), which appeared in about 1349–51. The 100 tales, some of which were to be adapted by Chaucer, had a particularly profound effect on English literature after William Painter translated many of them for his *Palace of Pleasure* (1566–67).

According to Greek mythology, the unburied were doomed to wander the banks of Cocytus, the River of Lamentation, one of the 5 rivers of Hell, for 100 years.

It was because of his 100 eyes that the giant Argus Panoptes was set to watch over a white heifer by Hera. Zeus, whose amorous attentions were ever wandering, had fallen in love with Io, the aunt of his former amour, Niobe. When Hera, his spouse, learnt of this Zeus responded duplicitously by transforming Io into a heifer – for the time being.

Hera was not deceived, and so appointed Argus Panoptes to keep watch upon the heifer. This giant was probably the best equipped guard of all time, for he needed to close only 50 eyes in sleep, the other 50 remaining open and alert until it was their turn to sleep. Nonetheless, the sly Hermes, at Zeus' behest, managed to chop Argus Panoptes' head off. As a posthumous reward for his faithful service, Hera had his eyes placed in the tail of the peacock – where we can, of course, still see them today.

Stung by a gadfly sent by Hera, the heifer rampaged over much of the ancient world, until reaching Egypt. There Io was transformed back into a woman by Zeus, whose son Epaphus she then bore.

Zeus next turned his attention to Danae.

Despite his historical importance as Elizabeth I's lord treasurer, William Cecil, Lord Burleigh, is probably best renowned for his indignant response when ordered by his sovereign to grant a pension of £100 to the poet Edmund Spenser: "What! All this for a song?"

In the UK, successive ministers of the arts have championed his attitude in their every deed.

PART TWO

One Hundred and One to Five Hundred

In which we learn the number of times Martin Luther thought married couples should make love each year, the number of oysters Balzac managed to down at a sitting, the IQ of Sir Isaac Newton, how the knights at the Round Table seated themselves, why 153 is interesting, the number of novels written by Edgar Wallace, the number of kisses in the most kissed-in movie of all time, how much Nancy Reagan spent on the White House crockery, the number of sensory cells in an Alsatian's nose, how the nose and the female genitalia are linked, the length of Noah's Ark, the number of diseases attributable to "invisibly small worms", the size of the jury at Socrates' trial, and much else besides.

Preamble

In the 1st part of this book we looked at each number in turn; in this, the 2nd part, we shall be rather less rigorous, alighting on numbers hither and thither at the dictation of fancy. Clearly, in this section, the selection of information to be included has been even more a matter of personal taste (i.e., arbitrary) than before. May I take this opportunity of apologizing if I have carefully missed out all your favourite numbers in the range 101–500.

One Hundred and One

At the time of writing (June, 1982), there have been 101 English football cup-final matches. The 101st such match was between 2nd Division Queens Park Rangers and 1st Division Tottenham Hotspur. The score was 1 all, both goals being scored in the last few minutes of extra time (Hoddle for Spurs, Fenwick for QPR).

Not bad for 2nd Division QPR! Unfortunately, in the replay a few days later, they lost 1–0.

The element of atomic number 101 is mendelevium (Md), an artificial element created by bombarding einsteinium-253 with helium nuclei. It was first prepared in 1955 and named in honour of the Russian chemist Dmitri Mendeléev (1834–1907), whose construction of the Periodic Table of the elements was largely responsible for the fact that so many of them have been discovered.

One Hundred and Two

The Empire State building is 102 stories high. Ardent fans of King Kong will know that it weighs about 330 thousand tonnes.

In Missouri there is a river called the 102 River, a name which may conjure up images of an explorer with a peculiar obsessional zeal for cataloguing his discoveries. Unfortunately, there are no traces of the 101 or 103 rivers, so putting that idea to a swift death. What seems to have happened is that French explorers rendered an Indian word meaning "high forest" as "*cent deux*", which was later simply translated into English.

The element of atomic number 102 is nobelium (No), a radioactive metal whose most stable isotope, nobelium-255, has a halflife of a mere 3 minutes or so. It was discovered in 1957 and named in honour not of the Swedish inventor Alfred Nobel, as you might expect, but of the Nobel Foundation, which he established. Before you leap to the conclusion that some chemists will try anything, even flattery, to get their fat little hands on a Nobel Prize, just remember that most of the work done in isolating nobelium was carried out at the Nobel Foundation.

One Hundred and Three

The French astronomer Charles Messier (1730–1817) was an enthusiastic comet-hunter; called by Louis XV "my little comet ferret", he was the 1st person in France to pick up Halley's Comet in 1758 (the year in which Halley had predicted, in 1682, that it would make its reappearance). Messier became so fed up with constantly mistaking permanent hazy patches in the sky for comets that he made a catalogue of 103 such objects *to be avoided*. Although he didn't realize it, the objects in his catalogue were exciting items like gaseous nebulae, star clusters and galaxies. These "fuzzy patches" in the sky are now often referred to in terms of Messier's listing: for example, M1 is the Crab Nebula, M31 the great galaxy in Andromeda, and M103 is an open star cluster in Cassiopeia.

There is some doubt as to what M102 was supposed to be. One suggestion is that Messier thought that M101 (galaxy in Ursa Major) was twins, but this seems a little unlikely: comet-hunters are, after all, by necessity among the most acute of observational astronomers.

The element of atomic number 103 is lawrencium (Lr), an artificial element 1st prepared in 1961. Its most stable isotope, lawrencium-256, has a halflife of a mere 35 seconds. It was named in honour of the US physicist who in 1929 invented the cyclotron, Ernest Lawrence.

One Hundred and Four

The average adult human being radiates about 104 calories per hour, which is equivalent to being a 120-watt lightbulb. This is why parties get hot.

The theoretical maximum duration of a total eclipse of the Moon is 104 minutes. This is substantially longer than the equivalent figure for an eclipse of the Sun – about $7\frac{1}{2}$ minutes – both because the geometry of the situation is different and because the Earth is, of course, substantially larger than the Moon.

The element of atomic number 104 is rutherfordium (Rf), named for the great physicist Sir Ernest Rutherford (1871–1937). According to Western orthodoxy, the element was 1st created in the US in 1969; however, Soviet scientists in 1964 claimed to have synthesized it, naming it kurchatovium, after the nuclear physicist largely responsible for the USSR being able to kill us all several times over with nuclear weapons, Igor Kurchatov (1903–   ).

Martin Luther advocated that young married couples should make love 104 times per year – in order to average a tidy twice a week. His recommended figure for unmarried couples was, of course, 0 times per year.

One Hundred and Five

There is a popular legend that the 105th pope was in fact a woman, "Pope Joan", who reigned under the pseudonym John VIII between 855 and 858. The legend emerged probably as an attempt to plug an apparent "gap" in the papal succession between the reigns of the 104th pope, Leo IV, and the real 105th, Benedict III. It is now known that no such gap existed.

Variant versions of the tale exist. One early one, by Stephen of Bourbon, dates "Joan's" reign to about 1100, and has her pregnant on election. During her procession to the Lateran she goes into labour and bears her child – only to be stoned to death. (Other versions have it that during the procession she dies in childbirth – a *little* more humane.)

It has been suggested that the confusion which sparked off the whole legend – widely regarded as fact during the Middle Ages, and still produced as such by the purveyors of "wonder tales" to hoodwink the credulous – was as a result of the abbreviation of "Joannes" (John) to "Joan.", which used to be common in manuscripts.

The real John VIII was the 108th pope, and reigned from 872 until 882.

☆

There are 105 certainly known elements, of which 88 are found in Nature, the remainder having been created in the laboratory. The 105th element is hahnium (Ha), named for Otto Hahn (1879–1968), the German physical chemist. In the USSR, which disputes the original synthesis, the element is called flerovium. Hahnium's most permanent isotope, hahnium-260, has a halflife of about 1.6 seconds.

One Hundred and Six

The "army" of Francisco Pizarro, the phenomenally successful conquistador, is said to have contained a mere 106 foot soldiers.

In 1974 a US team claimed to have isolated the element of atomic number 106. It was provisionally named unnilhexium (Unh).

One Hundred and Seven

The composer Franz Joseph Haydn (1732–1809) was probably the most prolific symphony writer of all time: he has a total of 107 to his credit, of which 1 has been lost.

It is sometimes claimed that there are 107 known elements – but see *105! Synthesis of the 107th, unnilseptium (Uns), was claimed in 1976 by a team of Soviet scientists.

One Hundred and Eight

In the UK there are 108 trades unions affiliated to the Trades Union Congress (TUC). Of these, the oldest is the National Society of Brushmakers and General Workers (established 1747), and the largest is the Transport and General Workers' Union (membership about 2 million).

108 guns were shifted around on board the *Royal George* in the Solent in 1782 during a refitting. The shifting of these guns caused the craft to capsize, with the loss of about 800 lives.

108 eager fishermen took part in an angling contest on 9th January, 1977, at Buckenham Ferry, Norfolk. This in itself is not, of course, exceptional. What is worthy of note is that the contest's winner, Peter Christian, achieved his success by having caught a single fish which weighed $1\frac{3}{4}$ grams – about $\frac{1}{16}$ of an ounce.

One Hundred and Ten

Honoré de Balzac (1799–1850), renowned not only for his literary skills but also for his gluttony, at one meal excelled himself by devouring 110 oysters – not to mention a duck, 2 partridges, 12 cutlets, 12 pears and several courses of dessert.

One Hundred and Eleven

The UN Charter, adopted in 1945, contained 111 articles, compared with the 26 articles of its predecessor, the League of Nations (see *63). The increase was largely as a result of the League's discovery that its terms of reference were neither broad nor precise enough.

Like *87, 111 is believed to be an unlucky score in cricket: it's called "the Nelson". "It's surprising how often," one television cricket commentator (Jim Laker) was recently heard to say, "something seems to happen when the score is 111."

One Hundred and Fourteen

World sales of the works of F. Scott Fitzgerald (1896–1940) in the year before his death totalled only 114 copies. (Perhaps, one is sneakily led to wonder, this is only what his publishers' royalty statements said . . .)

The 114th pope, Stephen VI, reigned for a short time during 896 (his predecessor, Boniface VI, had lasted an even shorter time – 15 days – before dying either of gout or at the hands of Stephen's supporters). Stephen is best known for putting to trial the corpse of the 112th pope, Formosus, who had reigned from 891 until

896. Formosus had incurred the wrath of the Spoletan Duke Lambert, who therefore forced Stephen to have the corpse pulled from its tomb, tried, condemned, stripped, and thrown into the Tiber. Stephen went further: he annulled all Formosus' acts, little realizing that one of them had been his own consecration as bishop – so that he was now ineligible for the papacy!

This clown of a pope was wisely thrown into gaol; shortly afterwards he was murdered there. His 2 successors, Romanus and Theodore II, each lasted only a few weeks in office; but the latter, during his 3-week reign, managed to find time to recover Formosus' body and reinter it, and to reverse Stephen's annullity of Formosus' acts.

One Hundred and Seventeen

The longest war on record – and hence almost certainly the longest war of all time (excluding those cases where a town or country is still theoretically at war because nobody's remembered to declare the peace) – was the Hundred Years' War, which in fact lasted 117 years, from 1337 until 1453, although there were a few relatively peaceful periods scattered within this timespan. The dispute was primarily between England and France, and centred on (a) English claims to the French throne and (b) English possessions within France. Curiously enough, had it not been for Joan of Arc (1412–1431) it is quite likely that France might have remained under English rule – perhaps even to this day. While Henry VI of England, also titular King of France, was of little importance (he was only 1 year old when he took the French throne in 1422), his Regent in France, John, Duke of Bedford, was an excellent ruler and much approved by the French people. His regime seemed set for establishment by popular consent until the revolt led by Joan in 1429. England held on to Calais until 1558, and still owns the largely French-speaking Channel Islands.

400 camels went everywhere that the Persian grand vizier Abdul Kassem Ismael (938–995) did: they bore his library of 117 thousand books. Moreover, they were trained to walk in a certain order, so that the books were arranged alphabetically from front to back of this literary caravan.

One Hundred and Twenty

Phyllostachys bambusoides, a species of bamboo, has the entrancing property that it flowers only once every 120 years – exactly. Moreover, all *P. bambusoides* plants flower at the same time, wherever they are. The last flowering of the world population of these plants was in 1959; it is unlikely, therefore that any of us will be around to see the next, in 2079.

One Hundred and Twenty-One

The biggest total ever achieved in the British Open Golf Championship was 121 for the 18-hole 1st round of the 1976 contest. This was achieved by Maurice Flitcroft who had, apparently, never before finished a full 18 holes.

One Hundred and Twenty-Two

The largest number of countries ever to be represented at an Olympic Games was 122 at the 1972 Games in Munich. 7147 competitors took part, accompanied by some 2000 officials. The Games is remembered more, sadly, for the murder at it of 11 Israeli athletes and officials by Palestinian terrorists.

At the other end of the scale, in 1896 only 12 nations were represented at the 1st Olympic Games of the modern revival, and only 9 at the 1904 Games in St Louis, where the vastly over-represented host country, the USA, more-or-less swept the board. This meeting is best remembered for the sudden discovery by the spectators that the apparent winner of the marathon had in fact ridden some 10 miles of the course on an automobile.

One Hundred and Twenty-Four

Emperor Hirohito (1901–   ), who has ruled Japan since 1926, is the 124th member of a single, uninterrupted imperial lineage. His family has been on the throne since the 6th century.

One Hundred and Twenty-Five

When auctioned in 1979 in Beverly Hills, a pair of Judy Garland's false eyelashes fetched $125.

One Hundred and Twenty-Six

The 126th pope, John XI, who reigned from 931 until 935, was the illegitimate son of the 120th pope, Sergius III, and one Marozia, a patrician woman who seems to have spread her sexual favours far and wide in her efforts to gain power, especially over the papacy. The appointment of her own son as pope was something of a triumph for her.

John XI was only too keen to play along, and did as mummy said in all things. But both had forgotten another son of hers, a legitimate one by her 1st marriage, Alberic II. Not long after John had conducted the theoretically incestuous marriage of Marozia to Hugh, King of Italy (her brother-in-law), Alberic II, whose political chances were likely to be wrecked by this union, found a good excuse to start a popular revolt against the couple. Marozia was thrown into gaol, where it is assumed she died at some point during the next few years, while Hugh was expelled from Rome. John was allowed to live out the rest of his pontificate, but under house arrest.

One Hundred and Twenty-Seven

Those who wish to kiss the Blarney Stone (in Blarney Castle, County Cork, Eire) must first climb a total of 127 steps – a laborious procedure but, by all accounts, well worth the effort.

The only woman whose lifespan is recorded in the Bible is Sarah, whose age at death was, according to *Genesis xxiii* 1, 127 years. She died in Canaan, having been the wife of Abraham and the mother of Isaac, both of whom, we are told, mourned her deeply.

One Hundred and Twenty-Nine

Some curious and sour-tasting facts emerged in the wake of the 1982 conflict between the UK and Argentina over the sovereignty of the Falkland Islands. Perhaps the most ironic, in light of the claims by the political Right and the gutter media that the war had shown Britain's greatness to the world, was the tale of the crewing of the *Canberra*, used as a troop-carrying ship in the Falklands.

When the ship returned to Britain, its passengers and crew were met by cheering crowds. But the crew were not all regular members of the *Canberra*'s complement: some of them had taken the place of non-British – mainly Asian – sailors who, it was felt, should not takc part in the dangerous venture (although they had volunteered to do so). These Asians had been sent back to their native lands.

129 of the returning heroes were, almost before the cheering died down, kicked out of their jobs: back on the dole for them. The reason? According to a P & O spokesman: "It is an unhappy situation that these seafarers now find themselves unemployed, but it is not something that we, as a company, can take responsibility for." It's curious how no one's ever responsible for irresponsible behaviour, isn't it? The real reason is that Asian seamen – being non-unionized – can be employed at remarkably low wages: £77–80 ($135–140) per month. A (unionized) sailor, on the other hand, has to be paid the hardly colossal sum of £320 ($560) per month; i.e., about £3850 ($6750) per year (although this sum can rise in some weeks, when a lot of overtime is worked, to as much as £150 ($265)).

Let's see now. There were the Asian sailors who lost their jobs and were shipped back to their homelands. There were the 129 returning heroes who lost their jobs and went back on the dole. There were the other Asian sailors taken on at exploitative wages. But "it is not something that we as a company can take responsibility for".

One Hundred and Thirty

According to a 1926 US series of estimates, Sir Isaac Newton, probably the greatest contributor to human knowledge and understanding in the history of our species, had an IQ of only

130. By way of comparison, the same survey reckoned that Byron had an IQ of 150 and Copernicus one of only 105.

I don't believe it!

One Hundred and Thirty-One

The practice of popes changing their names on elevation to the papacy was initiated by the 131st pope, John XII, who reigned from 955 until 964; his original name had been Octavian. (He was not in fact the 1st pope to change his name: that honour goes to John II, the 56th pope, who reigned some 4 centuries earlier.)

But John XII is remembered most for being one of the worst popes in history, promiscuous, totally hedonist, politically imbecile and laden with few shreds of honesty. His pontificate is noteworthy, though, for his coronation in 962 of the 1st Holy Roman Emperor, Otto I – whom John then promptly tried to betray! In 963 Otto deposed John in favour of Leo VIII (John's immorality had become too much for Church or state to tolerate further), but Leo was in turn deposed by John as soon as Otto's back was turned. John died before Otto could return to Rome to put a little more emphasis behind his decision.

One Hundred and Thirty-Three

No less than 133 claims were pressed during the 90-day hearing to determine the destiny of a quarter of a million dollars left by James Kidd in 1949 as a contribution to research into the survival of the human soul after death. At the end of the hearing, which took place in 1967, the money went to the Barrow Neurological Institute in Phoenix, Arizona.

Kidd's spirit, it is alleged, while less than thrilled about the result of the hearing, was nevertheless pleased to receive confirmation of the fact that he existed.

One Hundred and Forty

There is in Kent a place called Seven Score.

☆

The 70-page booklet *The History of Cornish Pubs* (1978) has an errata list 140 entries long. (The 1st edition of John Grant's 249-page classic, *A Directory of Discarded Ideas* (1981), has, for the sake of comparison, a mere 43 such little errors.)

One Hundred and Forty-Four

144 has on occasion been referred to as the "small gross", in contrast to the "great gross" of 12 gross ($12^3 = 1728$).

☆

In *Revelation* we learn (*vii* 4 and *xiv* 1) that 144 thousand out of all the people of Israel shall be saved, 12,000 from each of the 12 tribes (see *12 and *13). In addition, the City of God, which is 12,000 furlongs in length, breadth and depth, has walls which are 144 cubits high (*xxi* 17).

One Hundred and Forty-Five

The 145th pope, Benedict IX, was the worst of the lot – outstanding even in an age of obnoxious popes. To be fair, he was initially unwilling to accept the papacy, but was forced into it in 1032 by his family, the powerful Tusculani. For the next dozen years, until 1044, his conduct, which from the start had been bad, became steadily worse, until the clergy and people could no longer stand his whoring and his cruelty, and replaced him briefly with John, Bishop of Sabina (Sylvester III), who reigned from January, 1045, for only a few months until the Tusculani put Benedict back on the throne again.

But Benedict was fed up with the constraints of papacy (not that he paid much attention to them); he seems also to have wanted to get married. So he hit on the wheeze of *selling* the papal office. The buyer was his godfather, Giovanni Graziano, who in May, 1045, became Gregory VI; it seems that Gregory's motives were pure, that his purpose in accepting the offer was not so much to get himself onto the papal throne but to get Benedict off it.

In 1046 Sylvester III and Benedict IX both decided that they'd like to be popes again. Henry III of Germany held the Council of Sutri, and determined that none of the 3 were worthy of office. Benedict's dethronement was officially confirmed, Sylvester was imprisoned as a false pretender, and Gregory was removed from office on the grounds of simony – he seems to have been profoundly relieved. Suidger, Bishop of Bamberg, was declared Clement II, but died less than a year later – at which point Benedict returned to Rome and reinstated himself!

Finally, at the royal behest, in 1048 Boniface of Tuscany expelled Benedict from Rome, and Poppo, Bishop of Brixen, was installed as Damasus II (a pity that popes change their names, isn't it?). Benedict then dropped out of history . . . at last.

One Hundred and Forty-Seven

The highest-scoring single break in championship snooker is 147, a score achieved 3 times: by Joe Davis in 1955, by Rex Williams in 1965, and most recently by Steve Davis in 1982. One can make a higher "continuous score" than this; e.g., one's opponent might start, accidentally pot the black and thus forfeit 7 points.

One Hundred and Forty-Nine

It is estimated that the human population of Earth increases on average at the rate of 149 people every minute (the birth-rate is, of course, much higher). China alone may account for between 25 and 30 of these additional human beings, although recent birth-control drives there may have pulled this figure down considerably.

One Hundred and Fifty

There are 150 psalms in *The Book of Psalms.*

☆

The Round Table of King Arthur – at which, according to legend, sat 150 knights – was 1st mentioned in a verse saga by the Jersey poet and chronicler Wace in about 1155; it soon became an integral element of the Arthurian cycle. The principle behind its construction was that, with a rectangular table, the knights would inevitably quarrel over who had precedence – i.e., over who should sit nearer to the king's end – although a couple of moments' thought leads one to wonder just how the use of a circular table could be expected to solve this problem. Another difficulty is the size that the table would have had to be, a matter aired wittily in T. H. White's *The Once and Future King* (1938–58). Merlin points out that, by the simple application of the formula $2\pi r$, the table would need to be some 50 yards across.

Edward III (1312–1377) dallied with the notion of reviving the Round Table, but instead settled for the Order of the Garter, in 1348. The famous Round Table in the hall of Winchester Castle – which is designed to seat Arthur and 24 of his knights – despite occasional claims to the contrary certainly cannot be the "genuine" one. It may date back as far as the 13th century, with Tudor decorations added at some point during the 15th.

One Hundred and Fifty-One

There was a certain Russian called Vladimir Ilyich Ulyanov who during the course of an eventful life used many pseudonyms, of which 151 are on record. The best known of these is Vladimir Ilyich Lenin.

One Hundred and Fifty-Three

According to *John xxi* (a chapter which may have been added by one of the Apostle's disciples), on Christ's 3rd appearance to the Apostles after his death they were fishing. Christ told Peter to bring in the net, and they found there were 153 fish in it – but that, surprisingly, it had not broken under the strain.

It may seem odd that the number of fish is specified so precisely, 153 being apparently a rather undistinguished number. However, it is in fact the 17th "triangular" number (see page 11), which is to say that it is equal to 1 + 2 + 3 + 4 + 5 + 6 + 7 + 8 + 9 + 10 + 11 + 12 + 13 + 14 + 15 + 16 + 17. In his *City of God* St Augustine (354–430) makes much of this, suggesting that it indicates on the one hand the number of saints who will be resurrected, and on the other that its "17-ness" refers to the *10 Commandments together with the *7 Gifts of the Holy Spirit which make it possible for mortals to obey the Commandments and thereby become saints.

This is far from the only appearance of 153 in the Bible. In *I Maccabees ix* we are told that the villainous Alcimus, set on destroying some of Jerusalem's sacred buildings, suffered a stroke and died in the 2nd month of the year 153; his death brought temporary peace to the land of Judah. Elsewhere, various patriarchs are mentioned as having lived to the age of 153. We may, of course, be reading far too much into all this . . .

In the autumn of 1980 in Glasgow, Scotland, a 29-year-old woman was attacked by three or four youths who dragged her to a deserted hut where she was repeatedly raped and slashed across the face, buttocks, genitals and thighs with a razor. When they had finished, they jammed the door of the hut shut and left her to die. But she survived and escaped. She staggered to a nearby flat, from where she was rushed to hospital: 153 stitches were needed to sew up her wounds.

About 10 days later 4 youths were arrested. Shortly afterwards, Glasgow's procurator fiscal, James Tudhope (male), released the youths on bail. By May of the following year one of the youths had confessed to his part in the crime and agreed to appear for the prosecution; the other 3 had been more seriously involved, yet 1 of them had confessed, too.

In June, 1981, a psychiatrist, Raymond Antebi (male), interviewed the woman and reported that, should she be brought to court to give evidence in the case, there was a risk of suicide (which she had already attempted, in February). In September the lawyers representing the accused were informed by Tudhope, acting on the instructions of Alan Johnston QC (male), that the charges had been dropped. The reason was said to be that, without the victim's evidence, a prosecution would probably not have been successful.

The woman was not told of this decision: she learnt about it when she read an article on the case in the Scottish newspaper the *Daily Record*. In the heat of the publicity following the revelation of this noisome business, she announced that indeed she would be prepared to give evidence, in a closed court; moreover, it emerged that there were more than 40 witnesses prepared to give evidence, so that the prosecution's case didn't appear to be all that slender. (Consider the situation had the case been one of murder, which it almost was.)

The authorities' conduct was defended in January, 1982, in the House of Commons by the Solicitor General for Scotland, Nicholas Fairbairn (male; "Rape is a crime I have never been forced to commit"), who then promptly resigned, and in the Lords by the Advocate General, Lord Mackay of Clashfern (male), who did not.

In Spring, 1982, the woman succeeded in bringing a private prosecution against the 3 youths, who had been aged 16, 15 and 14 at the time of the crime. The judge, Lord Ross (male; "If a woman voluntarily consumes alcohol to such an extent as to be virtually insensible, it is not rape to have intercourse with such a woman, just as it is not rape to have intercourse with a sleeping woman. That is the situation with a woman who is virtually insensible with alcohol. I don't understand that to be the case here . . ."), dismissed the razor-attack charges against the 2 younger youths on the grounds of insufficient evidence; they received a 1-year deferred sentence for indecent assault. The 3rd youth was sentenced to 12 years' detention in a young offenders' institution.

153 stitches. Some justice.

One Hundred and Fifty-Seven

The doctrine of transubstantiation was 1st officially declared the faith of the Church in 1079 by a council of the 157th pope, Gregory VII (reigned 1073–85). In succeeding centuries the doctrine was modified to explain a very real criticism: the bread and wine just didn't *taste* like flesh and blood. The Aristotelian idea was invoked that the bread and wine had both "form" and "substance". Thus in the Eucharist, although the *form* of the bread and wine didn't change – physically and chemically they were the same after as before – their *substance* became Christ's flesh and blood.

One Hundred and Fifty-Nine

The most prolific writer in the history of science fiction is almost certainly the British author R. Lionel Fanthorpe (1935–   ). His vast *corpus* appeared between 1954 and 1966 under a bewildering variety of pseudonyms, and it will probably be impossible ever to produce a complete list of his works. His practice was, apparently, to hide under the bedclothes dictating his stories into tape-recorders, the tapes being typed up by friends and members of his family. Each book took a weekend, and for this he was generally paid a flat fee of £25 (worth up to £250 today).

According to the lists produced by Malcolm Edwards in *The Encyclopedia of Science Fiction* (ed. Peter Nicholls, 1979), of the 159 books which Fanthorpe is known to have produced during this 13-year period, 110 were novels and 49 either short-story collections or issues of book-size magazines to which Fanthorpe, in various guises, had contributed all the stories. His pseudonyms included Lee Barton, Thornton Bell, Leo Brett, Bron Fane, Victor La Salle (a name used also by other writers), John E. Muller (a name used also by other writers), Lionel Roberts, Neil Thanet, Trebor Thorpe, Pel Torro and Karl Zeigfreid (a name used also by other writers).

After a 15-year retirement from the sf scene, he has recently founded a new publishing house, Greystoke Mowbray, and more Fanthorpe works must be expected.

(On the subject of sf pseudonyms, it's worth noting that George Alec Effinger has written as Susan Doenim – known to friends as Sue – and a group of writers known to John Grant is currently working on a spoof disaster novel under the pseudonym Catherine A. Strophe.)

One Hundred and Sixty-One

The great showman P. T. Barnum (1810–1891) started his long career as an exhibitor of freaks by purchasing an elderly female slave, Joice Heath, who claimed to have been the property of George Washington's father and to be 161 years old. Although probably only in her 80s, she earned Barnum a tidy income during the few months in which she entertained the credulous . . . until she died of old age.

One Hundred and Sixty-Three

The eruption on 27th August, 1883, of the volcanic island of Krakatoa wiped 163 villages off the map. Nearly 37,000 people were killed by the tsunamis generated by the explosion, which was estimated to be equivalent to some 1000 million tonnes of TNT.

One Hundred and Sixty-Six

In 1912 in Pennsylvania, in the qualifying round of the Shawnee Invitational for ladies, one competitor achieved what is given by

The Guinness Book of Records (1982 edn.) as the record for the most strokes in a single hole of golf. After slicing her drive into a nearby river, she persuaded her husband to row after the ball while she attempted to swat it from the rowing-boat. A couple of hours and 166 strokes later she completed the hole.

One Hundred and Sixty-Seven

After a raid in 1906 on Brownsville, Texas, Theodore Roosevelt (see *26) ordered 167 black soldiers – the "Brownsville Raiders" – alleged to have been involved to be cashiered out of the army, although he delayed his decision until after his campaign for reelection as president in 1908 – for political reasons. It was only in 1972 that his decision – based as it was on dubious evidence – was reversed by the Army, although their vindication can have come as little consolation to the disgraced soldiers, who by this time were all dead.

One Hundred and Sixty-Eight

An 88-year-old Iranian, questioned recently as to the secret of his success on the occasion of his 168th marriage, replied that it was a result of the health-giving and aphrodisiac effects of consuming 2 pounds of raw onions each day. (Presumably about a dozen tubes of toothpaste are required daily, too.)

At the time of writing, there are 168 independent countries in the world, the most recent to attain its independent status being Antigua, on 1st November, 1981; it had formerly been one of Britain's West Indies Associated States. The smallest is the Vatican, with an area of about 110 acres and a population of perhaps 750. A further 56 dependencies bring the total number of countries in the world to 224, of which the smallest is the UK colony of Gibraltar, with an area of about 2.5 square miles and a population of about 28,000.

168 people died in the worst disaster in circus history when fire ravaged the Ringling Brothers' big top in Hartford, Connecticut, on 6th July, 1944. Among the lucky survivors were the "Great

Wallendas", an aerial troupe who had been performing, without a safety net, on the high wire when the fire broke out.

There are 168 hours to the week – as Bianca mourns to her distracted lover Cassio in *Othello*:

> *What, keep a week away? seven days and nights?*
> *Eight score eight hours, and lovers' absent hours,*
> *More tedious than the dial, eight score times?*
> *O weary reckoning!*

Of course, if Bianca's estimate of the lovers' clock be correct, then she had genuine grounds for complaint: her lover had not visited her for 26,880 subjective hours – or 3 years and a month.

One Hundred and Sixty-Nine

The 169th pope, Adrian IV, who reigned from 1154 until 1159, was the only British pope. Born in about 1100 near St Albans, Hertfordshire, as Nicholas Breakspear, Adrian was a rather undistinguished pope: his pontificate was marked by steadily deteriorating relations between himself and the Holy Roman Emperor Frederick Barbarossa (whom he had crowned in 1155), as well as by other political gaffes and near-gaffes on Adrian's part.

One Hundred and Seventy-Three

One of the most prolific writers of the 20th century has been (but see *500) Edgar Wallace, who between 1905 and his death in 1932 wrote 173 novels. One of the reasons for the rapidity of his output was the publication of his 1st, and probably still most famous, novel *The Four Just Men* (1905). Wallace paid for the publication of this book and for a massive advertising campaign offering a prize of £500 to anyone who could come up with the correct solution to the book's "impossible" crime. Unfortunately, sales nowhere near repaid his expenditure on production and publicity; to make matters worse, *several* people sent in the correct solution. The early part of his career was therefore spent in a frenzied effort to write enough books to be able to pay off his debts.

One Hundred and Seventy-Six

In general terms, the human ear can detect sounds of pitches between 16 cycles per second (Hz) and 20 thousand Hz: we even have a branch of science, ultrasonics, concerned with sounds of pitch higher than 20 thousand Hz. However, experimental results published in 1950 by Claus Timm show that, if the crude mechanism of the eardrum vibrating in air is circumvented by the simple expedient of holding the source of the note tightly against the skull, human beings can hear sounds of pitch up to a staggering 176 thousand Hz (I make this about the 9th E above middle E), which, if translated into radio terms, would be equivalent to the frequency of a long-wave broadcast. Unfortunately, despite its astonishing sensitivity to pitch in the "audible frequencies", the human organism cannot tell the difference in pitch between notes of 20 thousand Hz and those of 176 thousand Hz.

If you'd like to play a note of this pitch on your guitar, simply "stop" the top E string about 1 mm from the bridge and use a needle as a plectrum. Can't hear anything but a click? I couldn't, either.

One Hundred and Eighty

The most infamous pope of all time must be the 180th, Innocent IV, who reigned from 1243 until 1254. He it was who, in 1252, authorized the use of torture in the Inquisition.

The Inquisition's roots can be traced back to the reign of the 170th pope, Alexander III, who encouraged the lay princes to punish as they wished heretics discovered by his clergy. In general, this wheeze of encouraging others to shed the blood of those who disagreed with the Church was extended by his several successors. In 1231, a few years after it had become standard practice, the 178th pope, Gregory IX, adopted burning at the stake as the mandatory punishment for heresy as official Church policy – be damned to the 6th Commandment.

Victims of the Inquisition were not allowed any defending counsel – on the basis that if they were innocent they had nothing to fear – and were not told who their accusers were (in case a victim were somehow declared innocent, and then decided to take revenge upon those who had landed him in this hell . . .

the Church didn't want to discourage the high-minded accusers, in case all those heretics got away).

The Spanish Inquisition, mounted in 1478 by that revolting pair Ferdinand and Isabella (well worth sailing across oceans to get away from), was a separate institution. Under the insane Tomás de Torquemada (himself responsible for the burning of over 2000 heretics), it swiftly became a means for political repression by the rule of terror. It is astonishing, and depressing, to realize that it was not dissolved until 1820 – at a time when Britain was enjoying the novels of Jane Austen.

A great deal of human misery, then, must be placed at the feet of the 180th pope, Innocent IV. It is pleasing to note that, unlike so many popes, in no calendar has he ever been accounted a saint.

One Hundred and Eighty-Two

The longest nonscientific word is the English transliteration of one which appears in a play by Aristophanes (*c*450–385BC) called *The Ecclesiazusae*: the word contains 182 letters (although in the original Greek it has only 170) and describes a sweet-and-sour fricassee of 17 specific ingredients. Hats off to any actor who can get through "lopadotemachoselachogaleokranioleipsanodrim-hypotrimmatosilphioparaomelitokatatkechtmenokichlepikossy-phophattoperisteralektryonoptekephalliokigklopeleiolagoiosir-aiobaphetraganopterygon".

Other enormous words lie well beyond the scope of this book. The full name of the protein $C_{1289}H_{2051}N_{343}O_{375}S_8$ contains over 1900 letters, and other scientific words stretch even further! *The Guinness Book of Records* (1982 edn.) tells us of a protein whose full name has over 8000 letters; fortunately, though, there is a handy abbreviation of it, containing only 4059 letters – a mere couple of pages of this book.

One Hundred and Eighty-Four

One of the most remarkable bestsellers of recent times was *The Country Diary of an Edwardian Lady* (1977), which appeared on the *Sunday Times'* bestseller list 184 times between June, 1977, and April, 1981; the achievement is all the more remarkable in that the *Sunday Times* did not appear for 10 months of this period, so that the book might have appeared on the list a further 40 or so times. on 64 occasions it was No. 1 on the list.

One Hundred and Eighty-Six

The velocity of light in free space is about 186 thousand miles per second. In 1956 Frank Ross, in *Space Ships and Space Travel*, noted that this is "twice as fast as the speed of a bullet leaving the muzzle of a United States Army rifle".

One Hundred and Ninety-One

Don Juan, made in 1926 and starring John Barrymore, is reputed to be the film with the most kisses ever made. In it, Barrymore kisses 191 separate times: since the film is 2 hours and 47 minutes long, this means that he gets to kiss someone every 52.46 seconds of camera time.

One Hundred and Ninety-Two

The tale of the 192nd pope, Celestine V, is a touching one.

Over 2 years had passed since the death of the 191st pope, Nicholas IV, and the cardinals still had not elected a successor. The tale is that they received a letter from a hermit called Peter [of] Morrone saying that to fail to elect a new pope was to offend God. "Aha!" they cried. "Let's make this Peter Morrone pope. He's supposed to be jolly pious." Whether or not the tale is true, genuinely pious men were in short supply at the time, and Morrone had the useful advantage, for a stop-gap pope, of being about 80 years old.

His papacy was disastrous. The crunch came just a few months after his election when he announced that, as always, he intended to spend Advent in retreat, leaving the governance of the Church in the hands of a committee of cardinals the while. It took little to persuade the modest Celestine that perhaps it would be better if he resigned, which he did in December, 1294, before a consistory of cardinals at Naples.

His successor, Boniface VIII, was concerned lest this abdication might not be completely legal, and so had Peter Morrone locked up in a cell in the castle of Fumone. Peter was not upset: as a hermit, he liked cells. However, less than a year later he died.

When he was canonized in 1313, only a couple of decades after his death, he was named St Peter Morrone, rather than St Celestine.

One Hundred and Ninety-Four

The longest accredited sneezing fit on record was suffered by a 12-year-old English girl, Patricia Ray, who had been sneezing for 194 days by the time treatment in a French clinic brought her relief in April, 1980. By this time she was something of a media celebrity: fame can come in curious ways.

Two Hundred

In some Islamic sources we find that, after his expulsion from Eden, Adam was compelled to stand on one foot for 200 years. Too tall a tale for you? Well, bear in mind that on Mount Serendip, Sri Lanka, there is a foot-shaped depression in the rocks which bears mute testimony to Adam's ordeal.

In 1878 Ruskin remarked of Whistler's "Nocturne in Black and Gold": "I have seen, and heard, much of Cockney impudence before now; but never expected to hear a coxcomb ask two hundred guineas for flinging a pot of paint in the public's face."

Although the exact number of his victims will probably never be known, Herman Webster Mudgett (*alias* H. H. Holmes and H. M. Howard) was one of the worst mass murderers of all time – outside the military and political spheres and ignoring public executioners, of course. He is known to have murdered *at least* 200 people, generally under conditions of extreme sadism, the vast majority of them young women lured during the Chicago Exposition of 1893 to his "Torture Castle", seduced, drugged, suffocated and later dissected. He confessed in detail to *27 of the murders before execution cut short his account.

Although this figure may seem high, it is by no means a record. The so-called "Colombian Monster", Pedro López, on his capture in 1980 confessed that he had killed over 300 prepubescent girls in Ecuador, Peru and Colombia. Also in Colombia, the *smallest* number of murders officially believed to have been committed by a bandit called Teófilo Rojas is 592; he was under 30 when he died. The lesbian Countess Elizabeth de Báthory (d. 1614) is believed to have tortured 600–650 girls to death for sexual pleasure, bathing in their blood in the search for rejuvenation. In 1978 in Guyana the People's Temple leader, Jim Jones, induced 913 people (including himself) to kill themselves by swallowing cyanide. The Indian Thug Buhram is believed to have murdered up to 1000 people between 1790 and 1840.

Military and political figures have been left out of the reckoning, as noted. If they were to be included, they would dwarf these amateurs. For example, Sergeant-Major Mold at Auschwitz once gassed over 6000 people in a single day. In countries such as Iran, El Salvador, Argentina and Kampuchea there must be people alive today whose tolls more than rival those of all the others mentioned here except, perhaps, Mold. In the case of Argentina, the UK public heard little about such atrocities until the Falklands Crisis of Spring, 1982, Argentina having been up until then a useful trading-partner.

☆

According to *The Life of Mahomet* by Washington Irving (1783–1859), 200 virgins broke their hearts for the love of Abdallah, the Prophet's father. Mind you, Abdallah had an advantage: there were more virgins around in those days.

☆

At the end of the 19th century Cyrus Reed Teed ("Koresh"), the originator of the theory that we live *inside* a hollow Earth, founded in Florida the community of Estero, in the confident expectation that he would attract about 8 million followers. As it turned out, the figure was about 200.

Two Hundred and Five

In 1950 Senator Joseph McCarthy inaugurated his reign of terror with the announcement that he had "here in my hand a list of 205 – a list of names that were known to the secretary of state as being members of the Communist Party and who nevertheless are still working and shaping the policy in the State Department". Ignoring for the moment McCarthy's rotten grammar, it's pleasing to note that, after he had brought to trial most Americans of any moral stature, he himself fell from grace rather swiftly – thanks in part to Lyndon Johnson (see *36).

Two Hundred and Six

In theory the skeleton of an adult human being has a total of 206 bones (not counting the clusters of minute "sesamoid bones" in the tendons of the thumb, etc.), but some individuals have more than this. This is because the skeleton of a new-born baby may have 300 or more bones, many of which fuse during the process of growing-up. Quite often the fusion fails to take place in all cases – about 5% of people have an extra rib, for example.

I told our 4-year-old that she had more bones than I did, and she looked at me as if I were some kind of a maniac . . .

Two Hundred and Seven

According to Rabelais's *Gargantua and Pantagruel* (1532–52), the giant Gargantua – who was so huge that he borrowed the bells of Notre Dame to put around his horse's neck as jingle-bells! – was a giant in intellect as much as in physique. Not only was he learned in *every* field of study, he knew how to play 207 games.

Two Hundred and Nine

In her refurbishing of the White House on arrival in 1981, First Lady Nancy Reagan spent $209 thousand on crockery alone.

The 209th pope was Calixtus III, who reigned from 1455 until 1458; he suddenly becomes more interesting when you learn that his original name was Alfonso Borgia. The 2 main hallmarks of his reign were: (1) the mounting of a foolhardy crusade against the Turks, which had minimal effect because it was boycotted by all the European sovereigns; and (2) his breathtakingly corrupt nepotism, which substantially enriched the Borgia family, especially his nephews Roderigo Borgia (to become the *214th pope), Pedro Borgia (whom Calixtus attempted to put on the throne of Naples), and Luis de Mila.

Two Hundred and Ten

The loudest deliberately created noise to be measured under laboratory conditions is reported to have been a din made in 1965 in Huntsville, Arizona, using a horn nearly 50 ft long: the recorded noise-level was 210 decibels. Since doubling the amount of noise produced by anything increases the decibel rating by a mere 3, 210 decibels is about 3,500,000,000 times louder than the noise you would hear if you stood on the runway at Heathrow directly under a landing jet (115 dB).

Two Hundred and Twelve

After the socialist government of Salvador Allende had been overthrown in 1973 (Allende being murdered) by the military under General Augusto Pinochet Ugarte – a coup inspired by the economic difficulties (such as inflation) brought to Chile by Allende's radical programme of economic reform – inflation increased by a staggering amount. In a single month during the first 2 years of Pinochet's rule, the cost of living rose by 212%.

Two Hundred and Fourteen

It is hard to do justice to the 214th pope, Alexander VI, within the confines of a single volume. Originally named Roderigo Borgia, he reigned from 1492 until 1503. His election was a result of his bribing the cardinals by promises of lucrative posts should he become pope. He had at least 6 children, and maintained a live-in mistress throughout his pontificate; she persuaded him to make her brother (later to become the 220th pope, Paul III) a cardinal. Alexander made his son Cesare a cardinal at the age of 18. When the Dominican monk Girolamo Savonarola spoke out against his immorality, he arranged for Savonarola's trial as a heretic and subsequent execution.

Cesare Borgia, having given up his post as cardinal, in 1500 arranged for the murder of his sister Lucrezia's 2nd husband, Alfonso, Duke of Biseglia. Alexander seems to have been at least a passive participator in this plot – the successful outcome of which enabled him to make the politically useful move of marrying off Lucrezia to the Duke of Ferrara. And so it went on –

although it seems unlikely that there is much truth in the popular legends about him poisoning those who disagreed with him.

In 1493 he issued a bull granting Africa and India to Portugal and the New World to Spain. By the Treaty of Tordesillas (1494), the 2 countries shifted the demarcation westwards, so that Portugal was able to claim eastern Brazil.

Two Hundred and Seventeen

The siege of Mafeking, during which a garrison under Baden-Powell held out against the Boers, lasted for 217 days, ending on 17th May, 1900. When news of the siege's raise reached Britain the public jubilation was so great that a new word was admitted to the language: to "maffick", meaning to overreact, *en masse*, to good tidings.

The 217th pope was Leo X, born Giovanni de' Medici, who reigned from 1513 until 1521; he was a son of Lorenzo the Magnificent. It is largely as a result of his activities that the Reformation came about. Not only was he corruptly nepotistic, he was also keen on Church building, which cost money – and so he encouraged the practice of selling indulgences (the forgiveness of sin in response to a financial contribution to the Church). It was local abuse of this sale which prompted Luther in 1517 to post his *95 Theses.

In 1518 Leo proclaimed Luther a heretic – a description which Luther at that stage vehemently disliked, considering himself a faithful servant of the pope, and especially since his position had already gained considerable support, even at high level, within the Church Establishment. The row between the 2 men became more and more acrimonious, with each becoming more and more intransigent, until by 1520 Luther had rejected almost every teaching of the Catholic Church – in retaliation for which Leo excommunicated him. Had either been a more temperate or sensible man, the Reformation might never have happened.

Leo is noted also for having given Henry VIII of England the title *Defensor Fidei* (Defender of the Faith) in 1521 as a reward for Henry's anti-Luther writings. Henry retained the title – as does to this day the British monarchy – even after his excommunication in 1533 and his establishment of himself as Supreme Head of the Anglican Church the following year.

Two Hundred and Eighteen

In February, 1982, Sri Lanka played its 1st ever cricket Test Match, at Colombo, against England. In its 1st innings this new addition to the Test-playing "family" chalked up 218 runs against an attack including such bowlers as Bob Willis, Ian Botham, Derek Underwood and John Emburey. 54 of those runs were scored by an 18-year-old schoolboy called Arjuna Ranatunge, whose achievement was applauded not only by the crowd but also by the English team.

Two Hundred and Twenty

An Alsatian (German shepherd-dog) has 220 million olfactory sensory cells in its nose, compared with the mere 5 million in the nose of an adult human being. While this might suggest that the dog's sense of smell is a staggering 44 times more sensitive than ours, in fact the true figure is that it is *over 1 million* times more sensitive.

Two Hundred and Twenty-Nine

The 229th pope, Gregory XIV (reigned 1590–91), made one reform of considerable note. He ruled that it was an excommunicable offence to bet on the results of papal elections!

Two Hundred and Thirty-One

It was reported in February, 1982, that in the 1st year after alcohol had been banned from Scottish football matches – because drunk fans had been injuring and maiming people – 231 resolute devotees of the bottle had been discovered attempting to get round the ban by the cunning ruse of going to matches with the alcohol *already inside them.*

Two Hundred and Thirty-Five

Approximately every 235 lunations, the Moon returns to its original position with respect to the Sun. This means that every 19

Julian years (see *365) the dates of full Moon, new Moon, etc., concur. This Metonic cycle, named for the Greek astronomer Meton (born *c*440BC) whose realization that the cycle existed (although he was far from the 1st to notice it) meant that it was incorporated fundamentally into the Greek calendar, is still of importance in the Jewish calendar – and to the Christian Church, since it is used in the calculation of the date of Easter. Easter is the Sunday after the 1st full Moon following the vernal (Spring) equinox. In 1981, for example, the vernal equinox coincided with the full Moon on 20th March. Fortunately, the day of the next full Moon, 19th April, was a Sunday, so that Easter was not quite as late as it might have been.

The reign of the 235th pope, Urban VIII, which lasted from 1623 until 1644, is most notable for the famous trial and condemnation of Galileo, in 1633, for his espousal and promotion of the Copernican hypothesis (that the heavenly bodies do not revolve about the Earth, but that the Earth and the other planets travel around the Sun). It should be noted that, contrary to popular legend, this crisis was very much more of Galileo's than of the Church's making: had he merely published his results in the normal way, all would probably have been well, but, like a sort of 17th-century John Allegro, he went out of his way to be offensive to established Churchianity. That said, Galileo was in many ways quite right to take this line: there is nothing more depressing than the widespread publication of, and consequent popular belief in, false knowledge. Galileo's condemnation did more than anything else to hasten the general acceptance of the Copernican system.

There is, by the way, good reason to believe that, at his trial, Galileo *did* come out with "*E pur si muove*" ("Still, it *does* move" – referring of course to the Earth). A portrait of him painted during his last years bears this sentence as an inscription.

Two Hundred and Forty

At the moment of writing, 240 new human beings are born each minute. (Compare *149.) If no one died, the world's population would double every 30 years or so. However, people die . . . and because there are ever more people in the world the birth-rate per minute increases. These 2 effects to a great extent cancel each other out, with the net result that the population can be expected to double every 35 years or so. Iain Nicolson has pointed out that, at this rate, should the Galaxy contain 100 thousand million habitable planets (an overoptimistic figure), in order to maintain our current standards of living over the next 1300 years we must colonize and *fill* every one of them. Since the Galaxy is more than 1300 light-years across, this chore is impossible.

There seems to be a certain sort of Malthusian inevitability, then, about the nuclear holocaust . . .

☆

Until decimalization, the UK pound sterling contained 240 pennies – that is, 20 shillings each of 12 pennies. It has frequently been pointed out that this was actually a much more efficient number of pennies to have to the pound than is the current 100: indeed, 240 has more whole-number divisors than any number smaller than it. (See also *12.)

240's whole-number divisors are 2, 3, 4, 5, 6, 8, 10, 12, 15, 16, 20, 24, 30, 40, 48, 60, 80, 120, while those of 100 are 2, 4, 5, 10, 20, 25, 50.

Two Hundred and Forty-Nine

On being requested to send a simple explanation of Einstein's Theory of Special Relativity by telegram, the US polymath Buckminster Fuller managed to cram the pertinent ideas into a mere 249 words. To reduce the opacity of the explanation somewhat, I have inserted punctuation and rendered the telegram in upper- and lower-case letters rather than in the traditional capitals. The telegram reads:

> Einstein's formula [for the] determination [of] individual specifics Relativity reads: "Energy equals mass times the speed of light squared." Speed of light identical speed [of] all radiation – cosmic, gamma, X, ultraviolet, infrared rays, etc. – one hundred eighty thousand miles per second[1] which squared is top or perfect speed giving science a finite value for basic factor in motion [in the] Universe. Speed of radiant energy being directional outward [in] all directions [on the] expanding wave surface, [the] diametric polar

[1]A poor approximation. 186,000 miles per second is a better one (see *186).

> speed away from self is twice speed in one direction, and speed of volume increase is square to speed in one direction[2] – approximately 35 billion volumetric miles per second. Formula is written letter "*E*" followed by equation mark followed by letter "*m*" followed by letter "*c*" followed closely by elevated small figure two, symbol of squaring. Only variable in formula is specific mass. Speed is unit of rate, which is an integrated ratio of both time and space, and no greater rate of speed than that provided by its cause – which is pure energy, latent or radiant – is attainable. The formula therefore provides a unit and a rate of perfection to which the relative imperfection or inefficiency of energy release in radiant or confined direction of all temporal space phenomena may be compared by actual calculation. Significance: specific quality of animates is control, willful or otherwise, of rate and direction [of] energy release, and application not only to self-mechanism but of from-self-machine divided mechanisms. Relativity of all animates and inanimates is potential of establishment [i.e., can in theory be established] through Einstein formula.

While I have added a few explanatory words in [square brackets] and would not 100% agree with Fuller's explanation (and see the footnotes), I'd draw your attention to the fact that 27 words of the 249 are "wasted" in describing how to write $E = mc^2$, and a further 16 (the 1st sentence) could be regarded as redundant, since everybody knows the formula. To compress a theory so at odds with that most unreliable of our intellectual tools, common sense, into 206 words is indeed no mean feat!

Two Hundred and Fifty-Five

Astonishing as it might seem (well, it surprised me), the doctrine of papal infallibility is little over a century old – it dates from the 1st Vatican Council (1869–70), in the reign of the 255th pope, Pius IX) reigned 1846–78). Before that, while the Church's infallibility was more-or-less taken for granted unless the pope in question

[2] This is more than a little obscure. Does he mean that the rate of increase of the surface area of the expanding wavefront is proportional to the square of the "velocity in one direction"? No, no – he talks of volumetric miles, while $180{,}000^2$ *is* about 35 billion. ($186{,}000^3$, the genuine volumetric increase, is about 2.695×10^{16} miles^3.) Oh dear . . .

was manifestly a clown or a crook (which many of them were), it had never been an official dogma.

Popes are infallible only when speaking *ex cathedra* – which is rarely – on matters of morals and/or faith, and when ratifying the pronouncements of an oecumenical council.

Two Hundred and Fifty-Seven

The 257th pope, Pius X, who reigned from 1903 until 1914, is the most recent to have been declared a saint. He was canonized in 1954 by the 250th pope, Pius XII (reigned 1939–58).

Two Hundred and Fifty-Eight

A Dominican called Placentius (d. 1548) is known for only 1 of his poetic endeavours, *Pugna Porcorum*: in its 258 Latin hexameters, every word begins with the letter "p".

According to one astonishingly accurate reckoning, about which, it must be said, I have my doubts, by the beginning of the 1st century BC there were exactly 258 bakeries in Rome.

Two Hundred and Sixty-Three

The 263rd pope was the 1st to take a double name: born Albino Luciani, he became Pope John Paul I on 26th August, 1978, and died during the night of 28th/29th September in the same year, of a heart attack.

Two Hundred and Sixty-Four

The current pope, John Paul II, is the 264th. He was elected on 16th October, 1978, at the age of only 59. He was the 1st non-Italian pope – he's Polish – for 455 years and the youngest for over a century. His pontificate so far has been marked, on the one hand, by a tremendous relationship with the common people encouraged by frequent pastoral visits to various countries, and, on the other, by a stance on contraception which could hardly be calculated better to increase the misery of the common people concerned.

Our descendants, if any (see *240), therefore may not much revere the name of John Paul II.

Two Hundred and Sixty-Six

At his infamous Last Stand in 1876, General George Armstrong Custer is said to have had under his command 266 men. Unfortunately his opponent, the Sioux chief Crazy Horse, had some 3500 warriors.

Do not waste tears on Custer. Not long before he had ordered his troops to massacre a peaceful Indian settlement, despite the fact that the Red Indians had already shown the flag of truce.

Two Hundred and Sixty-Seven

The average human pregnancy lasts for 267 days (just under 9 months). By way of comparison, the giraffe's gestation period is about 450 days and that of the porpoise 360 days. Since it is often said that there is a correlation between mankind's long gestation period and the species' intelligence, we have in these statistics food for thought.

Two Hundred and Seventy-Three

Probably the most all-embracing piece of legislation in human history is Article 273 of the penal code of Bulgaria, which bans you from disseminating "false remarks which could incite mistrust of the state power or cause confusion in society". Come back, Catch-22: all is forgiven.

Two Hundred and Seventy-Five

If you're a US female, you have 1 chance in 275 of being murdered. If this depresses you – the odds against aren't *that* great – just remember that US males have a 1 in *90 chance of being murdered.

Two Hundred and Eighty

According to ancient tradition, the duration of human pregnancy is 280 days. This notion probably arose because of the health-giving properties assumed to be possessed by the number *40 – 280 is, after all, 40 times magic *7. In fact, today the more generally accepted figure is *267 days.

Two Hundred and Eighty-Two

Hammurapi, the 6th King of the 1st Dynasty of Babylon, who died in either 1750BC or 1686BC, is best remembered as the compiler of the great Code of Hammurapi (or Hammurabi), the best source for which is a stele found in 1901 in Iran. The Code consists of a total of 282 laws, either expansions of earlier ones or new pronouncements.

Two Hundred and Eighty-Four

Between 1887 and 1902 Sigmund Freud was intellectually infatuated by an eccentric psychologist called Wilhelm Fliess (see *23). Fliess proposed, for example, the theory that the interior of the nose contains "genital spots", the application of cocaine to which can be used to treat neuroses. His mightiest work was indubitably *Die Beziehungen zwischen Nase und Weibliche Geschlechtsorganen in Ihrer Biologischen Bedeutungen Dargestellt* (1897) – a title which can be roughly translated as "The Relationship Between the Nose and the Female Genitalia Viewed from the Biological Standpoint" before being burnt by the nearest feminist.

Alas, Freud destroyed all the letters sent to him by Fliess, thereby robbing the world of hours of innocent mirth. However, Fliess's widow was able to get a good price for the 284 surviving letters written by Freud to Fliess.

Two Hundred and Eighty-Six

Old Moore's Almanack, the famous predictive guide to the year to come, has been appearing without a break since 1697. Ignoring jokes about unforeseen circumstances, this means that the edition published at about the same time as this book, in Autumn 1982, should be its 286th. *Old Moore's Almanack* sells roughly a million copies a year.

Two Hundred and Ninety-Four

The shortest book in the Bible is *The Third Epistle of St John*, which has 14 verses containing, in the Authorized Version, 294 words. (*2 John* has fewer verses, 13, but more words, 298.)

Three Hundred

While it is generally realized that in Roman numerals C stands for 100, M for 1000, etc., it is less well known that B stands for 300. This is because the convention was little used, although it's nice to think that 1982 could be represented as MDBCLXXXII rather than MDCCCCLXXXII, thereby saving a couple of letters.

According to *Genesis vi* 15, Noah's Ark was 300 cubits in length, 50 in breadth and 30 in height. According to St Augustine (in *City of God*) and to many other writers at least up until the Renaissance, these dimensions in fact showed that the Ark represented the human body, for they claimed that the height, breadth and thickness of the body go in the ratio 300:50:30.

I am 5 ft 8 in tall. Dividing this by 300 we get the unit for the ratio: 0.226666 . . . inches. Multiplying this by 50 we get 11.333333 . . . inches and by 30 we get 6.8 inches. In fact, these figures aren't all that inaccurate (or, at least, they wouldn't be if it weren't for the beer), so one is tempted to believe Augustine's interpretation.

Mind you, you do get some odd looks at parties when you come out with: "I say! Do you realize that I'm approximately the same shape as Noah's Ark?"

Three Hundred and Seven

In a mere two days, in 1974, 307 people died in the US Mid-West when the region was struck by a phenomenal 148 tornadoes. The casualty list could certainly have been longer: in March, 1925, a single tornado killed 689 people in the US.

Three Hundred and Seventeen

The 317ct Cullinan II diamond, as well as the 530ct "Star of Africa", is cut from the world's largest known rough diamond, the Cullinan, which weighed, when discovered in 1905, a grand total of 3106ct (about 1lb 6oz).

Three Hundred and Eighteen

The mass of the giant planet Jupiter is greater than those of all the other planets in the Solar System added together: it is 318 times that of our Earth. Since Jupiter is a lot less dense than the Earth, you could drop about 1400 Earth-sized planets into it before it was "full".

Jupiter not big enough for you? Well, the Sun's only a medium-sized star, but you'd still need about 1,300,000 Earths to "fill" it up!

Three Hundred and Nineteen

There are approximately 319 billion different ways in which the first 8 moves of a game of chess can be played. (The exact figure, for what it's worth, is 318,979,564,000.)

Three Hundred and Twenty-Six

The highest-numbered street-name in the USA is 326th Street in – no, no, not New York (264) or Chicago (146) as you might expect – but in Toledo, Ohio.

Three Hundred and Twenty-Seven

During a speech made in December, 1961, President John Kennedy managed to utter 327 words during one particular minute, while remaining perfectly intelligible throughout. This may have been a result of his having developed his talents as a speed-reader in order to absorb the maximum amount of documentation in the minimum amount of time. Some reports say that he could read about 5000 words – about 16–18 pages of this book – per minute and still understand and remember what he was reading about (he may have been helped by being a skilled "skipper").

With his ability to chalk up rates like 327 words per minute, spirit mediums must dread clients who say: "I'd like to speak to President Kennedy . . ."

Three Hundred and Thirty-Four

Books with purely number-titles are rare – although algebraists might pedantically campaign for the inclusion in the list of Charles Fort's unpublished books *X* and *Y*. There are, in addition, a few books whose titles are merely dates, like Jack Lindsay's *1764* and Arthur C. Clarke's *2001* (usually accompanied by its subtitle, *A Space Odyssey*).

However, Thomas M. Disch's *334* (1972) seems a genuine candidate for a book with a purely number-title. Centred on a Manhattan apartment building at 334, East 11th Street, the book can be read either as a novel or as a collection of linked stories of what life may be like in an authoritarian New York in the not-so-distant future.

Three Hundred and Thirty-Six

Humphrey Bogart, who died on 14th January, 1957, was 336 days older than you always thought. Warner Brothers felt that, somehow, it would have been more romantic had he been born on Christmas Day, 1899, instead of on 23rd January of that year, and so they just lied about his date of birth.

Three Hundred and Forty-Six

Fredrick Augustus (died 1699), Elector of Saxony and then King of Poland, fathered a grand total of 346 known children. Of these, 1 was legitimate.

Three Hundred and Fifty

The 1st edition (1555) of *Les Prophéties de M. Michel Nostradamus* contained 350 prophetic verses, or quatrains. The edition of 1568 (Nostradamus died in 1566) was the 1st to contain his full 10 "centuries" – i.e., 1000 quatrains all told.

Three Hundred and Fifty-Two

In Pacific Grove, California, it is against the law to kill – or even to threaten – a butterfly, thanks to City Ordinance number 352.

Strange that there should have to be a law against it . . .

Three Hundred and Fifty-Four

The lunar year of 12 months (where the word "month" refers to the period between successive full Moons, rather than to the period of the Moon's revolution about the Earth) is quite substantially shorter than the solar year of 12 calendar months: it is a little over 354 days long. The 10–11 day difference between the 2 sorts of years is called the "epact". The word "epact" can, confusingly, be used also to denote the age of the Moon (i.e., the number of days since the last new Moon) on the 1st day of the calendar year.

Three Hundred and Sixty

The practice of counting 360° to a full circle seems to date back to perhaps as early as 2500BC, when some anonymous Babylonian genius devised it. The reason for his selecting 360 can be found in the fact that the Babylonians counted to the base *60. Why 360 rather than 300 or 420? Possibly because 360 is divisible by 8, which the other 2 numbers aren't (240 and 480 share this advantage, but perhaps gave too coarse and too fine a measurement, respectively). Possibly because if you arbitrarily allocate to the important angle of the equilateral triangle a value of 60° you find that there are 360° to the circle. Most likely because, to the Babylonians, the number of days in the year was extremely close to what they regarded as a good, round number (certainly the earliest Egyptian calendars had 12 months of 30 days each, adding the extra 5 days later). The Babylonians, keen astronomers, would note that the Sun appeared to pass through 1 degree each day of the year.

Three Hundred and Sixty-Four

According to Bergen Evans, in his delightful *The Natural History of Nonsense* (1947), the sea lion would seem to be the most fecund creature in the animal kingdom: "The female sea lion is pregnant three hundred and sixty-four days a year, sometimes a little more . . ." One assumes that the figure of 364 days is a norm rather than an average!

Three Hundred and Sixty-Five

The tale is told that in 1276 the Countess of Henneberg gave birth to 365 very small children, all in one go, as the result of a beggar's curse. The Countess, subscribing to an ancient popular fallacy, accused the beggarwoman of having committed adultery because she had borne twins . . . to which the woman retorted – and quite right, too – that she (expletive deleted) hoped the Countess would give birth to as many children as there are days in the year. Sure enough, this came to pass: the Countess bore 182 boys and 182 girls, together with a 365th child they were a wee bit uncertain about.

One curious flaw in the legend is that 1276 was a leap year.

Ask any child how many days there are in the year and you'll get the answer "365" (some smart-aleck kids may say "365 and a quarter"). This is of course wrong, but by just how much it is wrong is hard to say. The trouble is that the correct answer depends upon the type of year you're talking about. The tropical year, the interval between successive passages of the Sun through the 1st Point of Aries (see *12), is of length 365.24 2 19 days; the anomalistic year, the time between successive passages of the Earth close to the Sun, is of length 365.25964 days; the sidereal year, the true year as measured against the fixed stars, is of length 365.25636 days; the Gaussian year, calculated from Kepler's Laws, is of length 365.25690 days. Other types of years could be added to the list (see *354, for example).

If you really want to impress your nearest schoolchild with your arcane accuracy, you might mention that the officially defined tropical year is that of 1900: it was 31,556,925·947 seconds long. (See also *366.)

The year AD365 was not surprisingly known as the "Year of Days". It was confidently expected that the world would come to an end in this year.

According to those strangely dotty natural historians of the Ancient World, the crocodile had the same number of teeth, 365, as there are days in the year. Yes, I know what you're saying, but surely they could have counted the teeth on a *dead* one.

The Irish sect the Culdees had a harsh regimen for those who sought to save a soul from Hell: "A commutation for rescuing a soul out of hell: 365 paters, 365 genuflexions, 365 blows of the scourge every day of the year and a fast every month rescues 1 soul from hell." Ignoring the rest of it, that meant hitting yourself 133,225 times!

As the Pythagoreans moved from being a scientific/philosophical school more and more towards being a secret mystical society, new initiates swore an oath of silence, which they maintained for the first 3 years. In numerological terms, therefore, the number $3 \times 365 = 1095$ came to be seen as the number of silence; that is, it was decided that the essential nature of silence was its "1095-ness".

In Casco Bay, Maine, there are 365 islands – known, of course, as the Calendar Islands.

The most recent experiment with the calendar in Western Europe seems to have been that between 1795 and 1805, when the French National Convention divided the year into 12 months each of 30 days, each month being divided into 3 10-day weeks, with an extra 5 days being added on at the end of the year. If this system were still in use, the French would be getting about 30% less weekends than everybody else! No wonder the scheme was shelved.

Three Hundred and Sixty-Six

There are of course 366 days in a leap year – a matter so elementary that few of us bother to think about how this came to be.

In constructing calendars, the problem is that the year (see *365) cannot be expressed in terms of a whole number of days: it is approximately 365.25 days long. The earliest calendars known to us are Egyptian: they have 12 30-day months, although not long afterwards 5 extra days were added to give the more accurate value 365. The Greeks operated the system of adding 3 extra months every 8 years – a rather unsatisfactory arrangement, as can be imagined. In 46BC the Roman calendar was reformed under Julius Caesar: the year was of 365 days for 3 out of 4 years, with the 4th being 366 days long.

This system was regarded as fine until 1582, by which time the calendar had become about 10 days out of step with the seasons. The 226th pope, Gregory XIII, therefore decreed that 10 days should be omitted from that year, and that thereafter "century years" (e.g., 1600, 1700 would be counted as leap only if divisible by 400. Thus 1900 was not a leap year but 2000 will be. It took a while for the Gregorian Calendar to catch on – it didn't do so until 1752 in Britain, where there was rioting and protest about the "loss" of 11 days from the year. Nonetheless, it is today in use throughout much of the world.

People who believe that every 4th year the Earth takes a day longer to go around the Sun are surprisingly many.

Three Hundred and Sixty-Eight

The famous Long March of the Chinese Communists in 1934–35 lasted 368 days. Surrounded by Kuomintang forces, the Red Army, at a strength of about 90–100,000, broke through the ring and set off on what was to prove a 6000-mile hike which saved the Chinese Communist movement from extermination. Led by Mao Tse-tung, Lin Piao and Chou En-lai, during their heroic trek they crossed 24 rivers and 18 mountain ranges, under Kuomintang attack the whole while, and lost upwards of 70,000 people.

Three Hundred and Seventy-Five

Statistics show that women have a 1 in 375 chance of living to be 100 or over; men have only a 1 in 1400 chance of doing the same.

Three Hundred and Seventy-Eight

The adult flea can jump about 12 inches, or 200 times its own body-length. This is equivalent to John Grant (height 5ft 8in – or "just under 6ft", as friends put it) performing a leap of 378 yards.

Three Hundred and Eighty

Some 380kg of lunar rock and soil were brought back to Earth by the US Apollo astronauts between 1969 and 1972, when the programme was halted in an act of repulsive obeisance to public stupidity. Surprisingly, owing to the inability of certain US senators – notably William Proxmire – to comprehend that the examination of such material might have a certain scientific value, some 85% of it remains unexamined. The reasoning is that it costs money to examine Moonrock, and this is a time of governmental spending cuts (except on "defence"). You know, like buying a car and refusing to put petrol in it.

Proxmire is a man of interest in many fields. In 1975 he came out with: "Two million Americans want to leave some things a mystery, and right at the top of those things that we don't want to know is why a man falls in love with a woman and *vice versa*."

And a few years ago in a fury the US radioastronomer Frank Drake blurted out that Proxmire ought to be awarded an Honorary Membership of the Flat Earth Society. A few days later, Drake was startled to receive a 'phonecall from Proxmire's secretary, asking Drake what the Flat Earth Society stood for and describing the Senator's delight on hearing that he might be awarded an Honorary Membership of this doubtless august body . . .

The next thing you know, the man'll be President.

Four Hundred

In the early 6th century BC the great Solon (*c*639–*c*559BC) set up in Athens the Council of 400 as a part of the important social reforms he was carrying out. In essence, while his reforms were aimed at giving a fair deal to the peasants, the Council was created to represent the propertied classes and to pave the way for a popular assembly.

The French Utopian philosopher François Marie Charles Fourier (1772–1837) advocated an early form of communism. Society was to be divided into farming cooperatives, phalansteries, each containing 400 families, the produce from which would be commonly shared. Other activities and industries would play a part in the running of the phalansteries. Merit and industry would receive their just rewards, and no one would be allowed to laze – all would be guaranteed a high standard of living.

In 1841 George Ripley (1802–1880) founded Brook Farm in Massachusetts along these lines, but the experiment lasted only until 1847.

Each year about 400 people in the US are killed by being struck by lightning: this makes lightning the USA's most dangerous natural mishap of all.

Four Hundred and Twenty-Two

422 people lost their lives on 20th August, 1977, in Abadan, Iran, when the cinema in which they were watching a movie was fired by arsonists. While this ghastly crime was blamed on anti-Shah, pro-Khomeini terrorists, eyewitnesses claim that police were seen barricading the cinema and battling off would-be helpers – while the crews from the nearby fire-station didn't arrive until the fire had burnt out. The Iranian people, not long afterwards, decided that they would rather be tortured, shot and hanged by the authorities than burnt alive.

Four Hundred and Twenty-Three

The Nebuchadnezzar of *Daniel* was in fact King Antiochus IV Epiphanes. The pseudonym involves a sort of numerological pun: in the gematric system, the Hebrew letters of both names add up to 423.

Four Hundred and Twenty-Four

According to Michel Peissel's *Mustang* (trans., 1968), in Lo Mantang, the capital city of Mustang, a tiny and forgotten kingdom on the Nepal/Tibet border, medicine has recognized 424 diseases which can be attributed to invisibly small worms (it sounds as if Western ideas of germs have been incorporated into local shamanism). These worms are the tools of 1080 malicious demons, who use them to harass mankind. To add to the doctors' dilemma, there are 360 "calamities" (such as falling over) caused by one's karma, and 15 ghosts with special responsibility for children's diseases.

Four Hundred and Thirty-Two

Inspired by his accession to the throne of the united nation of Scotland and England, James VI & I in July, 1603, at Whitehall raised no fewer than 432 people to the knighthood.

Four Hundred and Thirty-Eight

Between 1903 and 1911, when it was shot by the hunter and best-selling author Jim Corbett, a tigress called the Champawat Man-Eater killed an accredited 438 men, women and children in Nepal.

Four Hundred and Thirty-Nine

The 57th Foot earned their nickname "the Die-Hards" in 1811 at the Battle of Albuera. Before the fighting started, the 57th's Colonel Inglis exhorted the men to "Die hard, my lads, die hard!"

– which they duly did. 439 out of an original 608 officers and men were killed, including 23 out of 24 of the officers.

To the end of 1980, there were in London 439 of the famous "blue plaques" which commemorate the birth-places, dwellings, etc., of the famous. Of these, 179 are in the City of Westminster, 84 in the borough of Kensington and Chelsea, 71 in Camden, 18 in Wandsworth, 13 in Hammersmith, 11 in Tower Hamlets and 10 in Lambeth, the rest being scattered in smaller numbers among the other boroughs.

A few of the famous are commemorated with more than 1 plaque, although none have more than 3 – a figure shared by Henry Fielding (1707–1754), W. E. Gladstone (1809–1898), Lord Palmerston (1748–1865), Dante Gabriel Rossetti (1828–1882) and William Makepeace Thackeray (1811–1863).

Four Hundred and Fifty-Eight

In 1961, Hugh Nicholson held 458 company directorships simultaneously. A liquidating chartered accountant, he already held 7 directorships before becoming a director of all the 451 different companies of the Jasper Group. This, according to *The Guinness Book of Records* (1982 edn.), is a world record.

Four Hundred and Ninety-Six

496 is the 3rd smallest of the *26 known perfect numbers (1 + 2 + 4 + 8 + 16 + 31 + 62 + 124 + 248 = 496).

Five Hundred

"Cinque Canto" (literally, 500) is – or was – a derogatory tag applied to the artists of the century 1501–1600. That the term is derogatory is a source of mystery, since of course it is synonymous with "late-Renaissance".

The British crime novelist John Creasey (1908–1973) was so prolific that the exact number of books he wrote, under various names, will probably never be known: all that we can be certain about is that he wrote at least 500. A persistent man – his collection of rejection slips before 1st achieving publication numbered 743.

Enthusiasts of legal history will be intrigued to learn that at Socrates' trial the jury was 500 strong. 280 said that he was guilty, as against 220 who said that he was innocent.

Five Hundred and One

Ah, but we're only going as far as 500. If you really *must* feast your eyes on some larger numbers, turn to Appendix I.

APPENDIX I

666 and ∞

Six Hundred and Sixty-Six

Thanks to recent spates of movies about the Devil and his works, 666 has become an extremely popular number. It is, of course, the famous Number of the Beast, or Apocalyptic Number. *Revelation xiii* 16–18 has:

> And he causeth all, both small and great, rich and poor, free and bond, to receive a mark in their right hand, or in their foreheads:
>
> And that no man might buy or sell, save he that had the mark, or the name of the beast, or the number of his name.
>
> Here is wisdom. Let him that hath understanding count the number of the beast: for it is the number of a man; and his number *is* Six hundred threescore *and* six.

It is virtually certain that the author(s) of *Revelation*, scared of the consequences of naming a name, used the gematrian system of numerology. The most likely candidate is Nero, whose name Neron Kesar (the Hebrew version of Nero Caesar) or NRON KSR can be calculated as 50 + 200 + 6 + 50 + 100 + 60 + 200 = 666. His candidature is supported by the fact that variant versions of *Revelation* give the Number of the Beast as 616, which is the result you would get from Nero Kesar.

Other possibilities are Lateinos (Greek), meaning the Roman Empire, and the Hebrew word meaning "leader of blasphemy". Neither is very convincing.

Returning to Nero, a certain confusion arises because of the identification of the Beast's 7 heads with 7 Roman Emperors – as well as an 8th: ". . . the same also is the eighth, and is of the seven . . ." The confusion is generated because, at the time of *Revelation*'s writing, Nero was already dead. However, it seems likely that the writer(s) did not know this: certainly there was for some years after Nero's death a popular belief that he had not died but had fled into hiding – possibly to join the Parthians in order to form an army with which to avenge his dethronement.

All that said, there is the very strong possibility that invocation of the gematrian system is misleading: perhaps the significance of the number 666 is more strictly numerological. If 6 falls short of the ideal, 7, then 666 must trebly so; interestingly in this context, the number of Christ is 888, which is trebly one better than the ideal. Alternatively, perhaps both this and the gematrian approach are too simplistic: it has been suggested that the Beast is simply the Chaos Monster of Hebrew Myth, identified perhaps with Nero and perhaps with the Roman Empire. This idea is supported by the fact that "primal chaos" in Hebrew is equal, according to the gematria, to 666 (although this doesn't help to explain the variant reading, 616). In other words, the author(s) of *Revelation* might simply have been using an already well established synonym for the Chaos Monster.

None of these considerations have had much effect on later numerologists. The Jesuit Father P. Bongus, of the 16th century, was able to show that the Beast was in fact Martin Luther while, more or less at the same time but on the other side of the fence, John Napier (1550–1617), the Scots inventor of logarithms, proved conclusively that the Beast was the pope – *any* pope. A little earlier the German mathematician Michael Stifel (1487–1567) showed, with a certain justification, that the Beast was the *217th pope, Leo X. (Leo Decimus gave LDCIMU, because "e" and "o" have no numerical value. Stifel added "X", because the pope was Leo X, and removed "M", for "mystery", to end up with LDCIUX. "U" becomes "V", clearly. Shuffling the letters around, Stifel produced DCLXVI, which is 666 in Roman numerals! No, I don't believe him, either.) During World War I it was conclusively proved, several times over, that Kaiser Wilhelm was the Beast; a later generation discovered that it was Hitler, or Stalin, or . . . At the moment it's popular to notice that the *40th US President has 6 letters in each of the names Ronald Wilson Reagan; however, numerology of either the gematrian or the everyday school does not bear out what would otherwise be an attractive hypothesis.

While it has been virtually commonplace to describe your enemies as being the Beast 666, it's unusual to find a mother using the description of her child. But this is what happened in the case of a certain Mrs Crowley. She and her husband were staunch Plymouth Brethren, a fact which led her son Aleister

(1875–1947) to adolescent rebellion of an extreme form – clearly, she thought, he was the Beast. Crowley's adolescent rebellion did not end with his adolescence, however, and in later life he was to adopt the title of "The Great Beast 666" with pride . . . and not just the title: he claimed to *be* the Beast. He therefore practised sexual magick (his spelling) with many candidates for the office of Whore of Babylon, or "Scarlet Woman", as he tactfully re-named her. Curiously, one of his books is called *777*.

It is very likely that we shall never know for certain quite what the author(s) of *Revelation* intended the Beast 666 to represent, and the possibility must always lurk at the back of our minds that the riddle is truly indecipherable – that the Beast was called 666 purely on whim, in much the same way that a novelist might pick the names of his characters. However, if this unlikely possibility is ever shown to be in fact the case, it will be a sad day for numerology.

Infinity

It may seem curious to include in a book about *numbers* a section on ∞: ∞ is, after all, by definition innumerable. However, ∞ is clearly of considerable numerical interest, especially in that it can be used in conjunction with other, more familiar, numbers; e.g., $1/\infty = 0$. To this one must immediately add that there is no *proof* that ∞ is not a number. To be sure, it is hard to conceive of the sequence 1, 2, 3, 4 . . . ever coming to an end, but there is no proof that it does not. And, if it does come to an end, its final term, ∞, will have a definite numerical value.

The problem with such a speculation is that there seem to be several "values" of infinity. If we denote the theoretical "final term" of 1, 2, 3, 4 . . . by ∞_1, then we have to think of the result of adding $1 + 2 + 3 + 4 + \ldots + \infty_1 = \infty_2$. Then there are $1 \times 2 \times 3 \times 4 \ldots \times \infty_1 = \infty_3$, and such niceties as $\infty_1 \times \infty_2 \times \infty_3$! One could go on in this vein endlessly – to reach something approaching an infinitude of "values" for ∞. (It's tempting to suggest that, if $1/\infty = 0$, and there are a plurality of values for ∞, then presumably there ought to be a plurality of values for 0. Tempting, but . . .)

∞ has some curious properties, if that can be the correct term. For example, it seems clear that there are infinitely many positive integers, and that there are infinitely many *even* positive integers. Moreover, though, it seems clear that there *must* be more positive integers than even positive integers – roughly twice as many. But consider the set of positive integers, which we shall call A, and that of even positive integers, B. A is 1, 2, 3, 4, 5, . . . and B is 2, 4, 6, 8, 10 . . . – from the writing out of which it is clear that each member of A can be paired with a member of B by the simple expedient of multiplying it by 2. And if you remove all the elements from A which appear also in B, you are left with the set 1, 3, 5, 7, 9 . . . which has an infinite number of members. In other words, you can subtract from ∞ without changing its numerical value, and similarly divide, multiply and add to it.

Considered as a number, then, ∞ has such curious properties that it is tempting to think of it as in some way indefinite, a useful artifice but without real meaning. This is irritating and possibly merely a result of our way of looking at things, in much the same way that for a while the gorilla was dismissed as a figment of travellers' imaginations. In the physical Universe ∞ has a very real meaning: there is, for example, almost certainly a (theoretically measurable) ∞ of time, from the Big Bang to the Universe's death, there being no such thing as time "before" the former event or "after" the latter; and similarly there are infinite values in terms of distance and volume . . . while c, the velocity of light, may well be the infinite velocity.

Perhaps our very distant descendants may learn to appreciate the numerical meaning, if it has one, of ∞. The thought is rather awe-inspiring.

APPENDIX II

Number Fun

Please sit back, now, and allow me to indulge myself. It's been a well kept secret throughout this book, but I am an appallingly poor mathematician. Nevertheless, I can't help myself from trying to solve number puzzles and play number games whenever I come across them. I can remember at least two advertising campaigns in recent years – I've forgotten what they were advertising, I'm afraid – which involved presenting the "mark" with a series of mathematical puzzles which, if he or she could solve, showed that he or she was suitably qualified to . . . well, as I say, I can't remember what the products or services were. One of these campaigns involved cards in the London subway trains, and I can remember as a student, whenever I had to use the subway, trying to spot which carriage had the number puzzles so that I could ride in that one.

At least several – if not lots of – books of mathematical puzzles and diversions are published each year: the best known are those by Martin Gardner, an excellent writer whose books of mathematical diversions seem to get more interesting each time. If you don't have a mathematical background but are interested in plunging into the world of number fun, then your best plan, after you've read this appendix, is probably to get hold of a copy of Eugene P. Northrop's *Riddles in Mathematics* (about paradoxes – in print in Pelican) to arm yourself with the right spirit and the necessary background knowledge to tackle the Gardner books.

So far as I know, none of the following diversions have appeared in the Gardner books (which I deliberately haven't checked in case I found something irresistible). Most are reasonably well known on mathematicians although at least one doesn't seem to have been in print since the 1920s.

From time to time throughout this book I've referred to the gematric numerological system, in which, working in either

Greek or Hebrew, in which languages the letters can be used also to represent numbers, one can add up the name of something to draw some obscure numerological conclusion. For the sake of the typesetters, we'll work in Greek.

The most interesting system, from our point of view, is the Ionic one. This took 3 extra symbols to add to the 24 of the Greek alphabet, to give 27 whose values were as follows:

Α	1	Ι	10	Ρ	100
Β	2	Κ	20	Σ	200
Γ	3	Λ	30	Τ	300
Δ	4	Μ	40	Υ	400
Σ	5	Ν	50	Φ	500
F	6	Ξ	60	Χ	600
Ζ	7	Ο	70	Ψ	700
Η	8	Π	80	Ω	800
Θ	9	9	90	Π	900

(Numbers higher than 900, up to 9000, were designated by the addition of a slash to the 1st 9: /A meant 1000, /B 2000, etc.)

Using this system, and fudging slightly (w, for example, was originally uu; u represented the Greek upsilon, Y, and so if you've got a w in your name you can either take the value of upsilon or take twice that value, 800), we can set to work. Here's an example:

J	I	10
O	O	70
H	H	8
N	N	50
G	Z	3
R	P	100
A	A	1
N	N	50
T	T	300
		592

The exact numerological significance of 592 momentarily escapes me, but should you come across a collection of 592 things or people anywhere you'll know, in future, that they're subtly imbued with general John-Grantishness. The point, you see, is that names which add up to certain numbers represent similarities in quality of the things which possess those names, and this quality is in turn shared by (in this example) collections of 592 things or the 592nd in any particular list.

If you find that your name comes out as 666, please do not write to me.

Children of all ages find a tremendous fascination in playing the kind of "conjuring tricks" in which they ask you to think of a number, then to add to and subtract from it, multiply and divide it, etc., and then to tell them the result of these various manipulations. From this result they "magically" tell you the number you first thought of.

Most of such tricks, on analysis, break down in fairly uninteresting fashion – usually the complicated manipulations you were asked to carry out were simply a blind. Take this trick, for example:

(*a*) pick a number, N;

(*b*) multiply it by 3;

(*c*) if the product is even, divide it by 2; if it's odd, add 1 to it and then divide by 2;

(*d*) multiply the resulting number by 3;

(*e*) state the number of times 9 can be divided into this new number (i.e., if the number is 56 the answer here is 6, since $6 \times 9 = 54$).

From this answer to (*e*) the original number can be calculated quite simply. If the answer to (*e*) is n then the original number was either $2n$ or $2n + 1$, depending upon whether the number was even or odd.

This may seem quite impressive until one realizes that the mathematical operations are merely a smokescreen. All even numbers have the form $2n$, all odd ones $2n + 1$ (obviously). To take the case of an even number, what we are doing is:

(*a*) picking a number $N = 2n$;

(*b*) multiplying by 3 to get $6n$;

(*c*) dividing by 2 to get $3n$;

(*d*) multiplying by 3 to get $9n$;

(*e*) dividing by 9 to get n.

Thus, whatever value N has, one is simply telling the "magician" what half of it is: this becomes even clearer if you consider the operations in the order (*a*), (*c*), (*b*), (*d*), (*e*)! The argument in the case of an odd number is very similar – and left to the reader.

But not all of these "conjuring tricks" collapse quite so readily in the face of examination. For example:

(*a*) pick a number N between 0 and 59;

(*b*) divide by 3 and note the remainder, x;
(*c*) divide by 4 and note the remainder, y;
(*d*) divide by 5 and note the remainder, z.

When playing this game it is best to have pen and paper handy, since the value of N is given by the *remainder* when the sum $40x + 45y + 36z$ is divided by 60. Why? Well, in case you'd like to have the pleasure of working it out for yourself, I've put the explanation on page 238.

A similar trick is to ask someone to think of a number, perform various arithmetical operations on it, and then tell them the result of the operations. The classic example is:

(*a*) pick a 3-digit number, N, the difference between whose 1st and 3rd digits is greater than 1 (i.e., 321 is OK but 221 isn't);

(*b*) form a 2nd number from this by reversing the order of the digits (so that from 321 you get 123);

(*c*) subtract the smaller from the larger of these 2 numbers ($321 - 123 = 198$);

(*d*) take your new number and add to it the number formed by reversing the order of *its* digits . . .

And the answer is always 1089! Once again, if you'd like to know why, look at page 238.

"Cryptarithmetic" is the name given to the type of puzzle in which a mathematical operation is set out on the paper, but with the integers replaced by letters. Clearly this is very different from straightforward algebra: in algebra, if $a = 3$ and $b = 6$ then $ab = 18$, but in cryptarithmetic ab would mean 36. Thus, while in the puzzle worked out below, it might *look* as if we were solving an equation in 8 unknowns, in fact there are fairly strict restraints on the values which those unknowns might have – most importantly the fact that there are only 10 possible values for each – 0, 1, 2, 3, 4, 5, 6, 7, 8, and 9.

This puzzle is a cryptarithmetical problem belonging to the subsection of the field known as "alphametics" – that is, the letters involved spell out a message. It is the most famous example of the genre (and frequently sent by me to my publisher):

```
   s e n d
 + m o r e
 ---------
 m o n e y
```

The solution is easier than it looks.

(*i*) Clearly m must equal 1, since the largest 5-digit number resulting from the addition of 2 4-digit ones is $9999 + 9999 = 19{,}998$.

(*ii*) Since s cannot be greater than 9, and $m = 1$, the maximum value of $s + m = 10$. In the column where this addition is carried out, there might also be a 1 carried over from the column to the right, so that we have a maximum for the sum of $s + m + 1 = 11$. o is therefore either 0 or 1; but it is one of the rules of this game that no 2 letters can represent the same integer. Thus, since $m = 1$, we find that rather pleasingly $o = 0$.

(*iii*) This means in fact there *wasn't* a 1 carried over, as we suggested in (*ii*), implying that $s + m = 10$ and hence that $s = 9$.

(*iv*) Looking at the column involving the addition of e and o, and remembering that $e + 0 = e$, we must deduce that there is a 1 carried over from the next column to the right; thus $e + 1 = n$. Moreover, looking at that next right-hand column, we see that either $n + r$ or $n + r + 1$ gives us a number ending in e. Thus we know that either $r + 1 = 10$ or $r + 1 + 1 = 10$; i.e., that r equals 8 or 9. But $s = 9$, and so r must equal 8.

(*v*) Of the 4 letters left to solve (e,n,d,y), none can be greater than 7. But, looking at the addition in the rightmost column, we see that $d + e$ yields a number larger than 10 – a number ending in y. Moreover, this number cannot be 11, because y cannot equal 1; and it cannot be 14, because this would mean that $d = e = 7$. It must, therefore, be either 12 or 13. In either case, either d or e must equal 7, the other of the pair being 6 or 5. But we remember that $e + 1 = n$, so that e cannot be either 7 or 6 – thus $e = 5$ and $d = 7$.

(*vi*) Since $d + e = 12$, and since $e + 1 = n$, we have values for y and n of 2 and 6, respectively.

The problem, in more orthodox form, thus reads:

$$\begin{array}{r} 9567 \\ +\ 1085 \\ \hline 10652 \end{array}$$

which is approximately the sum I'd like my publisher to send.

The 1st cryptarithmetical puzzle of the modern school appeared in the Belgian journal *Sphinx* in 1931; it, like the one above, has been reprinted many times and is something of a classic. If you've been able to work your way through the last few paragraphs of explanation, you might like to try this puzzle on your own (answer on page 239). The challenge is the solution of this long-multiplication problem:

```
 abc
  de
 ---
 fec
dec
----
hgbc
```

Of course, in some areas the strict use of numbers creates apparent paradoxes. Two such problems are the best known of the 4 paradoxes put forward by the Greek philosopher Zeno of Elea (*fl* 450BC). One concerns the race between Achilles and the tortoise.

If Achilles gives the tortoise a 10m start, and can run 10 times as fast as the tortoise (I'm choosing the numbers for convenience of working, of course: Achilles should do better than this), when will he overtake it? The answer is, apparently: never. If you think about it, by the time Achilles reaches the place where the tortoise started, that plucky animal has advanced 1 metre; by the time Achilles reaches this new position, the tortoise has travelled a further 0.1 m . . . and so on.

In the real world, of course, you don't win much if you back the tortoise on this basis: Achilles passes it pretty damn' quickly. This is because most athletes are unaware of the existence of convergent series. The series involved are

Tortoise	1 + 0.1 + 0.01 + 0.001 + . . .
Achilles	0 + 1 + 0.1 + 0.01 + . . .

I've set them out that way to show why it is "obvious" that the tortoise will always be slightly ahead of Achilles – and equally "obvious" that neither athlete can ever get any further than 1.1111111111111 . . . metres past the tortoise's starting-point!

Another problem of Zeno's was the flight of an arrow. At any one instant an arrow is motionless: how then can it *ever* move? The idea of time being made up of discrete instants, a very numerical idea since it implies that you can number the instants 1, 2, 3, 4 . . . , seems to be at fault. Time moves in a continuous flow and so, as with the race between Achilles and the tortoise, the numerical approach breaks down.*

*I have an unpopular suspicion that the idea of the "flow" of time taking place as a series of discrete "instants" does *not* break down, though. If, as quantum theory seems to imply, there is a smallest possible distance, then a photon travelling across this smallest distance can't, as it were, "stop in the middle": it has to "jump". The time taken for this "jump" would seem to me to be 1 instant, the "quantum of time", the shortest

With any luck, you're in a suitably confused state of mind to be deceived by a very popular problem which has caught out cleverer people than me and thee. Bearing in mind that the numerical approach is notoriously useless in problems of this type, consider:

Two trains are standing in stations exactly 100 km apart; they are facing each other and are on the same line. Each cruises at 50 km per hour (slow, but there's a work to rule), and for the sake of simplicity we'll assume that they have such fantastic accelerations that they can reach this velocity less than an instant after starting. We'll assume, too, that the line is a straight one (it makes life easier if we do).

On the front of one of the trains sits a singularly stupid bee, which can cruise at 100km per hour. The two trains start simultaneously, and the bee, startled into activity by the realization that it has been selected to play the star role in a silly problem, leaps up and flies down the line. After a while, it spots the other train: it lands on the train's front and instantly sets off in the direction from which it came. In due course it meets the first train, and performs the same manoeuvre – and so on, and on, and on.

The question is: when the bee is crushed in the train-crash, how far has if flown? If you really don't know, turn to page 239; but don't tell anyone else that you've had to . . .

Not strictly in the field of number games are pocket-calculator games, but they can be fun too. The most popular one is making your calculator tell you what it thinks. Here's a typical example:

If John Grant wrote 22 books a year, each of 100,000 words, this would imply an output of 2,200,000 words. Although the average working year is of only 250 days, John Grant would be working so rapidly that his energies would be the square of anbody else's, and $250^2 = 62{,}500$. However, working so swiftly, he would make a lot more mistakes than usual – say, 165 per book: $22 \times 165 = 3630$. Matters might not be helped by the proximity of his 4-year-old, so subtract 4. He reckons that he's twice as nice as anybody else (so multiply by 2) except, of course, his wife and daughter (add 2). We can thus reduce the operation of writing all those books to simple mathematics (although you

---

possible time in which change may occur in the Universe, with no 2 events being able to be closer together in time than this. As I say, this is merely an intuitive suspicion . . . and I'll come quietly, doctor.

will appreciate the sophistication of the thought processes required to make the reduction, I trust);

$$
\begin{array}{rr}
 & 2{,}200{,}000 \\
+ & 62{,}500 \\
- & 3{,}630 \\
- & 4 \\
\times & 2 \\
+ & 2
\end{array}
$$

The question is, what would the resulting books be like? Well, read the number your calculator shows upside-down to find out – and to find out why I don't write 22 books a year!

There are a lot of other examples of such "spelling games" – you might like to devise a few. Remember that there's a certain fuel company interested in the number 77,345 . . .

Another useless occupation, tiresome with pen and paper but fun with a calculator, is the "palindrome game". Take a number at random – 13521, say – and enter it onto the display. Add its "reverse", 12531: answer, 26052, so add 25062. Keep doing this a couple more times and you end up with 92229, which is a palindrome.

The curious thing is that *whatever* the number you choose to start off with you'll end up after only a few such additions with a number which is a palindrome. The reasons aren't too hard to deduce, so I guess this is really a calculator-game for the simple-minded, but it amuses me (from which fact you may draw your own conclusions). If you'd like to start with one of the difficult ones, try 99.

If you're interested in becoming a "calculating prodigy" – one of those people who can be given a complicated problem which they solve in no time flat – then there is little direct help I can offer you, not being such a prodigy myself. However, if you have a good memory for numbers and the "feel" for mathematics which enables you to swiftly break down complicated operations into a series of simple ones, it's possible you'll be able to train yourself. (Bear in mind that, despite the claims of the credulous, there are no "occult" powers involved.)

Here is a little help. One such prodigy, George Parker Bidder (1806–1878), gave some of his calculating methods in a lecture delivered in 1856. Using the mental qualities mentioned above, he might tackle the problem of calculating 999 × 373 as follows:

	cumulative total
900 × 300 = 270,000	270,000
+ 900 × 70 = 63,000	333,000
+ 900 × 3 = 2,700	335,700
+ 90 × 300 = 27,000	362,700
+ 90 × 70 = 6,300	369,000
+ 90 × 3 = 270	369,270
+ 9 × 300 = 2,700	371,970
+ 9 × 70 = 630	372,600
+ 9 × 3 = 27	372,627

And 372,627 is of course the right answer. What the prodigy has done is break the problem down in such a way that at any moment he or she has only a simple multiplication to do, plus the addition of only 2 numbers. In fact, in this example, the calculator would have been better off noticing that 1000 × 373 = 373,000, and 373,000 − 373 = 372,627!

Square roots are more difficult. There are two approaches: one is to memorize logarithm tables, which probably doesn't appeal to you; the other is to use an algorithm. (No, that's not a misprint for logarithm. It's the technical term for a series of simple operations which together constitute a complicated one – like the series we used for the multiplication problem.)

Should you wish to find the square root of 999, you have to start off with a guess at its value. I'll guess 25, and then go:

999/25 = 39.6
Average of 25 and 39.96 = 32.48
999/32.48 = 30.757389
Average of 32.48 and 30.757389 = 31.618695
999/31.618695 = 31.595232

and so on. As you can see, we're already very close to the accurate value of $\sqrt{999}$, which is 31.606961. The interesting thing is that it doesn't matter much how bad your initial guess is. Just for fun, I tried 500 (500^2 = 250,000), and found that it added only 3 or 4 stages to the computation. (All right, I confess I was cheating: I was using a pocket calculator.)

In a short appendix, clearly one can do little more than skim the very surface of the sea of mathematical recreations and number-games. I hope, however, that I've conveyed to you some of the reasons why I – along with so many other people – waste so much time on them. Or is it wasted time? Probably, like crosswords and mystery novels, number-games do serve a useful purpose in stimulating the intellect – waking up the brain.

So, why not do a couple of number-puzzles over the cornflakes tomorrow morning?

Solutions

You know, you really shouldn't need this section, but . . .

(a) Deducing the value of a number less than 60.
The first thing to notice here is that if you divide the statement $40x + 45y + 36z$ by 60 you get $2/3x + 3/4y + 3/5z$, the divisors thus being 3, 4 and 5. These numbers are prime to each other, and their product $3 \times 4 \times 5 = 60$.

Now, 40 is divisible by (4×5) but is 1 greater than a multiple of 3, 45 is divisible by (3×5) but is 1 greater than a multiple of 4, and 36 is divisible by (3×4) but is greater than a multiple of 5. If we designate the statement $40x + 45y + 36z$ by the letter N and the number which you selected as your "mystery" number by n, we can see that the only term in N which will give a remainder when divided by 3 is $40x$; similarly, on division by 4 only $45y$ will yield a remainder, and on division by 5 only $36z$ will give a remainder.

Let's look at the case of dividing $40x$ by 3. We can restate $40x$ as $(39 + 1)x$. $39x$ is clearly divisible by 3, so if we divide 3 into $(39 + 1)x$ we'll be left with the remainder x. The same applies, of course, to our "mystery" number n, so we can say that:

$N - n$ is a multiple of 3.

We can use exactly the same argument to show that:

$N - n$ is a multiple of 4; and

$N - n$ is a multiple of 5.

But if $N - n$ is a multiple of 3 and of 4 and of 5 then, as we have seen, it is necessarily a multiple of 60! Thus the difference between N, the result of our calculation, and the highest multiple of 60 less than N is n.

If you find this proof as difficult to follow as I did when working it out, try reading it through again with your eyes screwed up.

(b) The sum which always gives you 1089.
The easiest way of showing how this "trick" works is to take the example given, 321, and work it out in the left-hand column, while showing the general working on the right.

$$
\begin{array}{rr}
 & 321 \\
- & 123 \\
\hline
= & 198 \\
+ & 891 \\
\hline
= & 1089
\end{array}
\qquad
\begin{array}{l}
100x + 10y + z \\
100z + 10y + x \\
\hline
100(x - z - 1) + 90 + (10 + z - x) \\
100(10 + z - x) + 90 + (x - z - 1) \\
\hline
(1000 - 100) + 180 + (10 - 1)
\end{array}
$$

In fact, the result is based on the fact that we are working to the base 10; in general, the formula is that the last line of the calculation, where z is the base, is $z^2(z - 1) + 2z(z - 1) + (z - 1)$. Working to the base 8 we'd have the automatic answer 1067, which in common or garden decimal notation would be 567.

(c) Cryptarithmetic.
The problem is the long-multiplication

$$
\begin{array}{r}
abc \\
de \\
\hline
fec \\
dec \\
\hline
hgbc
\end{array}
$$

(*i*) As both $e \times c$ and $d \times c$ produce a number ending in c, c must be either 0 or 5. But $c + e$ gives c, not e, so c cannot be 0. Therefore $c = 5$.
(*ii*) $d \times a = d$, and so $a = 1$.
(*iii*) Since $e \times c$ produces a number ending in c (5), e must be an odd number – and the same applies to d. But the two partial products involved in the multiplication are 3-digit numbers (*fec* and *dec*), and so we know that neither d nor e can be 9 (and we already know they can't be 1 or 5). Since $d \times b$ is less than 10, we know that d can't equal 7: thus $d = 3$, $e = 7$ and $b = 2$ (since b can't be 0, 1 or 3, and since if it were 4 $d \times b$ would be greater than 10).
(*iv*) Now that we know that *abc* is 125, and that *de* is 37, all we have to do is complete the multiplication in the ordinary way!

(d) The bee and the trains.
The line is 100 km long, and the trains each travel at 50 km per hour. They thus crash an hour after starting. The bee travels at 100 km per hour. It has thus flown 100 km.

Don't kick yourself too hard.

APPENDIX III

Prime Numbers

Here are the prime numbers up to 5000 (well, up to 4999). I hope I've remembered to include all your favourites.

1	2	3	5	7	11	13	17	19	23	29	31
37	41	43	47	53	59	61	67	71	73	79	83
89	97	101	103	107	109	113	127	131	137	139	149
151	157	163	167	173	179	181	191	193	197	199	211
223	227	229	233	239	241	251	257	263	269	271	277
281	283	293	307	311	313	317	331	337	347	349	353
359	367	373	379	383	389	397	401	409	419	421	431
433	439	443	449	457	461	463	467	479	487	491	499
503	509	521	523	541	547	557	563	569	571	577	587
593	599	601	607	613	617	619	631	641	643	647	653
659	661	673	677	683	691	701	709	719	727	733	739
743	751	757	761	769	773	787	797	809	811	821	823
827	829	839	853	857	859	863	877	881	883	887	907
911	919	929	937	941	947	953	967	971	977	983	991
997	1009	1013	1019	1021	1031	1033	1039	1049	1051	1061	1063
1069	1087	1091	1093	1097	1103	1109	1117	1123	1129	1151	1153
1163	1171	1181	1187	1193	1201	1213	1217	1223	1229	1231	1237
1249	1259	1277	1279	1283	1289	1291	1297	1301	1303	1307	1319
1321	1327	1361	1367	1373	1381	1399	1409	1423	1427	1429	1433
1439	1447	1451	1453	1459	1471	1481	1483	1487	1489	1493	1499
1511	1523	1531	1543	1549	1553	1559	1567	1571	1579	1583	1597
1601	1607	1609	1613	1619	1621	1627	1637	1657	1663	1667	1669
1693	1697	1699	1709	1721	1723	1733	1741	1747	1753	1759	1777
1783	1787	1789	1801	1811	1823	1831	1847	1861	1867	1871	1873
1877	1879	1889	1901	1907	1913	1931	1933	1949	1959	1973	1979
1987	1993	1997	1999	2003	2011	2017	2027	2029	2039	2053	2063
2069	2081	2083	2087	2089	2099	2111	2113	2129	2131	2137	2141
2143	2153	2161	2179	2203	2207	2213	2221	2237	2239	2243	2251
2267	2269	2273	2281	2287	2293	2297	2309	2311	2333	2339	2341
2347	2351	2357	2371	2377	2381	2383	2389	2393	2399	2411	2417
2423	2437	2441	2447	2459	2467	2473	2477	2503	2521	2531	2539
2543	2549	2551	2557	2579	2591	2593	2609	2617	2621	2633	2647
2657	2659	2663	2671	2677	2683	2687	2689	2693	2699	2707	2711

2713 2719 2729 2731 2741 2749 2753 2767 2777 2789 2791 2797
2801 2803 2819 2833 2837 2843 2851 2857 2861 2879 2887 2897
2903 2909 2917 2927 2939 2953 2957 2963 2969 2971 2999 3001
3011 3019 3023 3037 3041 3049 3061 3067 3079 3083 3089 3109
3119 3121 3137 3163 3167 3169 3181 3187 3191 3203 3209 3217
3221 3229 3251 3253 3257 3259 3271 3299 3301 3307 3313 3319
3323 3329 3331 3343 3347 3359 3361 3371 3373 3389 3391 3407
3413 3433 3449 3457 3461 3463 3467 3469 3491 3499 3511 3517
3527 3529 3533 3539 3541 3547 3557 3559 3571 3581 3583 3593
3607 3613 3617 3623 3631 3637 3643 3659 3671 3673 3677 3691
3697 3701 3709 3719 3727 3733 3739 3761 3767 3769 3779 3793
3797 3803 3821 3823 3833 3847 3851 3853 3863 3877 3881 3889
3907 3911 3917 3919 3923 3929 3931 3943 3947 3967 3989 4001
4003 4007 4013 4019 4021 4027 4049 4051 4057 4073 4079 4091
4093 4099 4111 4127 4129 4133 4139 4153 4157 4159 4177 4201
4211 4217 4219 4229 4231 4241 4243 4253 4259 4261 4271 4273
4283 4289 4297 4327 4337 4339 4349 4357 4363 4373 4391 4397
4409 4421 4423 4441 4447 4451 4457 4463 4481 4483 4493 4507
4513 4517 4519 4523 4547 4549 4561 4567 4583 4591 4597 4603
4621 4637 4639 4643 4649 4651 4657 4663 4673 4679 4691 4703
4721 4723 4729 4733 4751 4759 4783 4787 4789 4793 4799 4801
4813 4817 4831 4861 4871 4877 4889 4903 4909 4919 4931 4933
4937 4943 4951 4957 4967 4969 4973 4987 4993 4999

An interesting point is that no one has yet devised a formula for generating prime numbers. Possibly the best attempt was that made by Eratosthenes (*c*276–*c*196BC), the so called "sieve": here you simply write down all the odd numbers (even numbers are obviously out of contention) and then delete all the 3rd ones after 3, all the 5th ones after 5, all the 7th ones after 7, all the 11th ones after 11, and on, and on, and on. Many but not all prime numbers can be expressed in the form $2^n - 1$, where n is itself a prime (11 is an early example of a prime which can't be expressed this way, and most succeeding primes are likewise); moreover, the formula can be used to generate non-primes (e.g., $2^{11} - 1 = 2047$, which is 23×89).

So, if you want to achieve fame in the mathematical world, why not try to seek out a formula for generating prime numbers? There are worse ways of wasting your time.

Reference Sources

The production of a complete list of sources consulted during the compilation of this book would be a pointless and lengthy procedure: most of the sources from which information has been culled contain each only one relevant datum – and in some cases that datum has had to be checked and cross-checked in yet further sources. (For example, the information on Dylan Thomas' whiskies – see *18 – was discovered in one source and checked in two others (whereupon it was found that the original source had it wrong): it would be a waste of space to list here three separate biographies of Thomas.)

I decided, therefore, to list only those reference books which I had found most useful. While I cite these as my authorities, it is of course understood that any errors of fact, judgement or interpretation which you may find in *A Book of Numbers* are my responsibility, and mine alone.

Ackerman, A. S. E., *Popular Fallacies* (4th edn.), London, Old Westminster Press, 1950

Adams, James Truslow; and Coleman, R. V. (eds.), *Dictionary of American History*, New York, Scribner's, 1940

Arlott, John (ed.), *The Oxford Companion to Sports and Games*, London, OUP, 1975

Asimov, Isaac, *Asimov's Biographical Encyclopedia of Science and Technology* (2nd edn.), Garden City (NY), Doubleday, 1972

Asimov, Isaac, *Isaac Asimov's Book of Facts*, London, Hodder, 1980

Attwater, Donald, *The Penguin Dictionary of Saints*, Harmondsworth, Penguin, 1965

Ball, W. W. Rouse, *Mathematical Recreations and Essays* (revised edn.), London, Macmillan, 1939

Benét, William Rose, *The Reader's Encyclopedia*, London, A. & C. Black, 1965

Bibles: Authorized Version, Oxford, British and Foreign Bible Society, 1901

Jerusalem Bible, London, Darton, Longman & Todd, 1968

Black, Matthew (ed.), *Peake's Commentary on the Bible*, London, Nelson, 1962

Blom, Eric, *Everyman's Dictionary of Music* (5th edn., revised), London, Dent, 1974

Blundell, Nigel, *The World's Greatest Mistakes*, London, Octopus, 1980
Book of Saints (5th edn.), compiled by the Benedictine Monks of St Augustine's Abbey (Ramsgate), London, A. & C. Black, 1966
Brewer, E. Cobham, *The Dictionary of Phrase and Fable* (2nd edn.) London, Chatto and Windus, 1894
Brewer, E. Cobham, *The Reader's Handbook of Famous Names in Fiction, Allusions, References, Proverbs, Plots, Stories and Poems* (2nd edn.), London, Chatto and Windus, 1898
Bullock, Alan; and Stallybrass, Oliver, *The Fontana Dictionary of Modern Thought*, London, Collins, 1977
Cavendish, Richard (ed.), *Encyclopedia of the Unexplained*, London, Routledge and Kegan Paul, 1974
Chambers's Encyclopaedia, London, International Learning Systems, 1973
Cohen, J. M. and M. J., *A Dictionary of Modern Quotations*, Harmondsworth, Penguin, 1961
Considine, Douglas M. (ed.), *Van Nostrand's Scientific Encyclopedia* (5th edn.), New York, Van Nostrand, 1976
Cross, F. L. (ed.), *The Oxford Dictionary of the Christian Church*, London, OUP, 1974
Dale, Rodney, *The Tumour in the Whale*, London, Universal, 1978
de Bono, Edward (ed.), *Eureka!*, London, Thames and Hudson, 1974
Delaney, John J.; and Tobin, James Edward, *Dictionary of Catholic Biography*, London, Hale, 1962
Dictionary of National Biography
Douglas, J. D. (ed.), *The New International Dictionary of the Christian Church*, Exeter, Paternoster Press, 1974
Dröscher, Vitus B., *The Magic of the Senses*, London, W. H. Allen, 1969 (trans.)
Edwards, Paul (ed.), *The Encyclopedia of Philosophy*, New York, Macmillan and The Free Press, 1967
Ekwall, Eilert, *The Concise Oxford Dictionary of English Place-Names* (4th edn.), Oxford, OUP, 1960
Encyclopaedia Britannica (14th edn.), Chicago, Encyclopaedia Britannica Inc., 1973; (15th edn.), Chicago, Encyclopaedia Britannica Inc., 1980; yearbooks, 1976, 1977, 1978, 1979, 1980, 1981
Encyclopedia Americana, Danbury (Conn.), Americana Corporation, 1978
English Place-Name Society, *Survey of English Place-Names*, Cambridge, CUP (various volumes with different dates)
Evans, Bergen, *The Natural History of Nonsense*, London, Michael Joseph, 1947
Everyman's Encyclopaedia (6th edn.), London, Dent, 1978
Franklin, Charles, *The World's Greatest Mistakes*, London, Odhams, 1969
Gaute, J. H. H.; and Odell, Robin, *The Murderer's Who's Who*, London, Harrap, 1979
Gibb, H. A. R.; and Kramers, J. H. (eds.), *Shorter Encyclopaedia of Islam*, Leiden, Brill, 1953
Gibson, Walter B. and Litzka R., *The Encyclopaedia of Prophecy*, London, Souvenir, 1974 (elsewhere published as *The Complete Illustrated Book of Divination and Prophecy*)

Gillispie, Charles Coulston (ed.), *Dictionary of Scientific Biography*, New York, Scribner's, 1970

Golesworthy, Maurice, *The Encyclopaedia of Cricket* (5th edn.), London, Hale, 1974

Grant, Sir Francis J. (ed.), *A Manual of Heraldry*, Edinburgh, John Grant, 1962

Grant, John (ed.), *The Book of Time*, Newton Abbot, Westbridge, 1980

Grant, John, *A Directory of Discarded Ideas*, Sevenoaks, Ashgrove Press, 1981

Green, Jonathon, *The Directory of Infamy*, London, Mills and Boon, 1980

Grimley, Gordon, *The Origins of Everything*, St Albans, Mayflower, 1973

Guthrie, D.; and Motyer, J. A. (eds.), *The New Bible Commentary Revised*, London, Inter-Varsity Press, 1970

Hallam, A.; Hutchinson, P.; and Barnett, P. (eds.), *Planet Earth: An Encyclopedia of Geology*, Oxford, Elsevier-Phaidon, 1977

Halliwell, Leslie, *Halliwell's Film Guide* (3rd edn.), London, Granada, 1981

Harvey, Sir Paul, *The Oxford Companion to English Literature* (4th edn., revised), Oxford, OUP, 1969

Hastings, James (ed.), *A Dictionary of the Bible*, Edinburgh, T. & T. Clark, 1900

Herbermann, Charles G., *et al.* (eds.), *The Catholic Encyclopedia*, New York, Encyclopedia Press, 1913

Howard, A. V., *Chambers's Dictionary of Scientists*, London, Chambers, 1964

Jacobs, Arthur, *A New Dictionary of Music* (revised edn.), Harmondsworth, Penguin, 1961

John, Eric (ed.), *The Popes: A Concise Biographical History*, London, Burns and Oates, 1964

Jones, Robert M., *Can Elephants Swim?*, New York, Time-Life, 1969

Katz, Ephraim, *The International Film Encyclopedia*, London, Macmillan, 1979

Lapedes, Daniel N. (ed.), *McGraw-Hill Encyclopedia of the Geological Sciences*, New York, McGraw-Hill, 1977

Little, William, *et al.* (eds.), *The Shorter Oxford English Dictionary* (3rd edn., revised), Oxford, OUP, 1965

McGraw-Hill Encyclopedia of Science and Technology, New York, McGraw-Hill, 1977

McWhirter, Norris (ed.), *The Guinness Book of Records* (1982 edn.), Enfield, Guinness Superlatives, 1981

Marvin, Dwight Edwards, *Curiosities in Proverbs*, New York, Putnam, 1916

May, John; Brittain, David; Chesterman, John; Marten, Michael; and Torrey, Lee, *Curious Facts*, London, Secker and Warburg, 1981

Mitton, Simon (ed.), *The Cambridge Encyclopaedia of Astronomy*, London, Cape, 1977

Morgan, Chris; and Langford, David, *Facts and Fallacies: A Book of Definitive Mistakes and Misguided Predictions*, Exeter, Webb and Bower, 1981

Morris, Richard B. (ed.), *Encyclopedia of American History* (Bicentennial Edition), New York, Harper and Row, 1976

New Columbia Encyclopedia, New York, Columbia University Press, 1975

New Larousse Encyclopedia of Mythology (2nd edn., 10th printing), London, Hamlyn, 1974

Newman, James R. (ed.), *The International Encyclopedia of Science*, London, Nelson, 1965 (elsewhere published as *The Harper Encyclopedia of Science*)

Nicholls, Peter (ed.), *The Encyclopedia of Science Fiction*, St Albans, Granada, 1979

O'Connell, J. B. (ed.), *The Roman Martyrology* (4th edn.), London, Burns and Oates, 1962 (trans.)

Oxford Dictionary of Quotations (2nd edn., revised), London, OUP, 1970

Palmer, Scott, *A Who's Who of British Film Actors*, Metuchen (NJ), Scarecrow Press, 1981

Pile, Stephen, *The Book of Heroic Failures*, London, Routledge and Kegan Paul, 1979

Radford, E. and M. A., *Encyclopaedia of Superstitions* (revised edn.), London, Hutchinson, 1961

Reilly, John M. (ed.), *Twentieth-Century Crime and Mystery Writers*, London, Macmillan, 1980

Robinson, J. Hedley; and Muirden, James, *Astronomy Data Book* (2nd edn.), Newton Abbot, David and Charles, 1979

Room, Adrian, *Place-Names of the World*, Newton Abbot, David and Charles, 1974

Sanford, Vera, *A Short History of Mathematics*, Boston, Houghton Mifflin, 1930

Sladek, John, *The New Apocrypha*, St Albans, Hart-Davis MacGibbon, 1974

Stewart, George R., *American Place-Names*, New York, OUP, 1970

Stewart, George R., *Names on the Globe*, New York, OUP, 1975

Swanton, E. W. (ed.), *The World of Cricket*, London, Michael Joseph, 1966

Symons, Julian, *Bloody Murder* (revised edn.), Harmondsworth, Penguin, 1974

Thomson, David, *A Biographical Dictionary of the Cinema*, London, Secker and Warburg, 1975

von Matt, Leonard; and Kühner, Hans, *The Popes*, London, Muller, 1966 (trans.)

Wallechinsky, David; Wallace, Amy; and Wallace, Irving (eds.), *The Book of Lists*, London, Cassell, 1977

Wallechinsky, David; Wallace, Amy; Wallace, Irving; and Wallace, Sylvia, *The Book of Lists 2*, London, Elm Tree, 1980

Ward, A. C., *Longman Companion to Twentieth-Century Literature*, London, Longman, 1970

Ward, Philip, *A Dictionary of Common Fallacies* (2nd edn.), Cambridge, Oleander, 1980

Waring, Philippa, *A Dictionary of Omens and Superstitions*, London, Souvenir, 1978

Webb, James, *The Occult Establishment*, Glasgow, Richard Drew Publishing, 1981

Webster's Biographical Dictionary, Springfield (Mass.), Merriam, 1974

Webster's New Geographical Dictionary, Springfield (Mass.), Merriam, 1972

Webster's Sports Dictionary, Springfield (Mass.), Merriam, 1976

Williams, Trevor I. (ed.), *A Biographical Dictionary of Scientists*, London, A. & C. Black, 1969

Wilson, Colin; and Grant, John (eds.), *The Directory of Possibilities*, Exeter, Webb and Bower, 1981

Yule, John-David (ed.), *Phaidon Concise Encyclopedia of Science and Technology*, Oxford, Phaidon, 1978

Periodicals: *Ansible, Common Ground, Guardian* (London), *New Scientist, New Statesman, Private Eye, Spaceflight*, etc., etc.

Classificatory Index

To have a full alphabetical index to this book would obviously be to defeat the object of the exercise: my case is, after all, that knowledge can be presented in numerical order to interesting and perhaps revealing effect. However, I did feel that it might be useful to have this brief "classificatory index", so that the reader might follow up, should he or she wish, the various themes explored in the preceding pages. Throughout, "*p*" stands for "*passim*". Numbers are page references.